THE FEW

THE FEW

SUMMER 1940, THE BATTLE OF BRITAIN

PHILIP KAPLAN
AND RICHARD COLLIER

INTRODUCTION BY PETER TOWNSEND

GREENWICH EDITIONS
NEW ORCHARD

FOR TOMMY SOPWITH, SYDNEY CAMM AND R.J. MITCHELL

This edition specially published in 1996 for Greenwich Editions,
Bibliophile House, 10 Blenheim Court, Brewery Road, London N7 9NT.

First published in the UK in 1989 by Blandford Press (A Cassell imprint)
Reprinted in 1990

ISBN 0 86288 083 1

Printed and bound in Italy by Manfrini S.p.a. Calliano (TN)

CONTENTS

INTRODUCTION
BY PETER TOWNSEND

The Sun is sweet on rose
and wheat/And on the
eyes of children;/Quiet
the street for old men's
feet/And gardens for the
children.
The soil is safe, for widow
and waif,/And for the
soul of England,/Because
their bodies men
vouchsafe/To save the
soul of England.
Fair days are yet left for
the old,/And children's
cheeks are ruddy,
Because the good lads'
limbs lie cold/And their
brave cheeks are bloody.

(from *Storm* by
Wilfrid Owen)

When, in 1933, aged eighteen, I entered the R.A.F. as a flight cadet it was not, frankly, through sheer patriotism nor in the hope of winning glory in some future conflict. No; I was driven only by a longing to fly. Luftwaffe pilots, long after the war was over, told me it was the same with them – the sound, the sight, the touch and the smell of an aeroplane had an irresistible appeal to all senses. More is the pity that it led us to kill each other.

After two years at the R.A.F. College learning to be an officer and a gentleman and, of course, a pilot, my first posting in 1935 was to No. 1 Fighter Squadron at Tangmere, in Sussex. The airfield was in truth a huge hayfield where, after the crop, sheep did softly graze – except when our biplane Hawker Furies took off and landed. The hangers were built by German prisoners in World War I; the next generation of Germans, in their bombers, would demolish them in World War II. Not far away, near the coast, tall lattice masts were being erected. Occasionally someone might indiscreetly mention RDF (radio direction finding, later Radar) but the inventor, Dr Watson-Watt, was unknown to us, the subject taboo and the masts themselves in a no-go area. We fighter pilots enjoyed our pastoral life, conscious of belonging to the best flying club in the world.

At the time Fighting Area (as it was called) was but thirteen fighter squadrons strong. In 1936, faced with the menace of Hitler's Germany, the tiny R.A.F. began to muscle up. Yet at the Munich crisis of September 1938, Fighter Command (as it was now called) was utterly incapable of repulsing the threatening Luftwaffe bombers. At Tangmere our station commander was Group Captain Keith Park, tall, lean, good-looking, but severe. We called him "The Saint." I was now with 43 Squadron; our Furies, with their twin Vickers guns mounted in the cockpit, were slower than the enemy bombers. We all, pilots included, spent a night daubing our silver aircraft with drab camouflage war-paint. Supposedly, Britain's first line of defence, yet conscious of our shortcomings, I must admit we felt rather silly.

Then came the Prime Minister, Neville Chamberlain, back from Munich waving a little white paper, signed by Hitler and guaranteeing "Peace in Our Time." Not everybody was taken in: R.A.F. expansion and re-equipment continued apace. By December our first Hurricanes arrived – swift, sturdy fighters with a terrible fire-power. Spitfires were coming in too, though more slowly. Anti-aircraft, radar and civil defence were being organised; workmen were digging trenches in the London parks and children, their baby faces made grotesque by hideous-looking gas-masks, were being told what to do – in case. As for us, the fighter boys, once we had mastered our new aircraft, our morale soared until we felt 'let them come, we will bust them.'

Soon after the 3rd September 1939, when Britain and France declared war, our commander-in chief, Sir Hugh Dowding, paid us a visit. Solemn and unsmiling, "Stuffy" Dowding's genius lay in faultless generalship and his concern for us so-called 'chicks'. Shortly afterwards No. 1 squadron flew to France and we ourselves steered north to protect the coast-bound convoys and the naval base at Scapa Flow. There, above the tumultuous winter seas, we fought our first combats. In May 1940, shortly after the German offensive in Europe began, I travelled south by train to take over command of 85 (Hurricane) Squadron just back from France. During the journey I fell in with some Luftwaffe prisoners. One of them jibed "Your navy O.K., but where is your airforce?" Another assured me with a smile that he expected to be back home in Hamburg for Christmas. Both were in for a surprise.

In the Battle of France R.A.F squadrons (including 85), fighting alongside their French allies of the Armee de l'Air, had inflicted serious losses on the Luftwaffe, but at grievous cost. At this point Dowding recalled his Hurricane squadrons—there were no Spitfires in France. While 85 was reforming at the end of May, other squadrons were fighting fiercely and at extreme range, to protect the evacuation of the British army from Dunkirk. Combats were often fought out of sight of the soldiers on the beaches below so, not unnaturally, the army cursed the air force for failing them; "Woody," one of our bravest pilots, was booed in an Aldershot cinema. But Winston Churchill, Prime Minister since 10 May, addressed the Commons on a different note. Wars are not won by evacuations, he said, but

the Air Force had gained a signal victory and so "we got the Army away." He went on: "May it not be that the cause of civilisation itself will be defended by the skill and devotion of a few thousand airmen?" And his bold, defiant peroration set our hearts on fire: "We shall defend our island whatever the cost may be . . . we shall never surrender." The hour, the finest hour, of the whole British people had struck. It had struck too, more urgently, for their first-line of defence, Fighter Command as yet untried in the role. With the King and Queen in their midst and the Prime Minister and Cabinet entrenched in Whitehall, Britain stood ready for the onslaught.

When in July the battle began, 85 squadron were in 12 Group, north of London, commanded by Trafford Leigh Mallory. I had reported to him in May, the first time I had met him since as a 14-year-old schoolboy I had made my first flight at Old Sarum (Salisbury) where "L-M" was commanding an army-cooperation squadron—he was not bred as a fighter pilot. Short and solid of build, his alert mind could cope with issues both great and small. As I left his office he called after me, "By the way, young Townsend, it's time you had a haircut." In the midst of a life and death struggle!

Later in the battle 85 moved to 11 Group, south of London, commanded by Keith Park. New Zealander, tall, lean, icy calm, he was a fighter pilot to the manner born. During the battle, clad in a white helmet, he regularly flew his Hurricane to visit his squadrons. He was a brilliant tactician, employing his squadrons (twelve aircraft) indi-

Much that is untrue and misleading has been written on the pilot in this war. Within one short year he has become the nation's hero, and the attempt to live up to this false conception bores him. For, as he would be the first to admit, on the ground the pilot is a very ordinary fellow. Songs such as 'Silver Wings'—They say he's just a crazy sort of guy, But to me he means a million other things, make him writhe with very genuine embarrassment.

The pilot is of a race of men who since time immemorial have been inarticulate; who, through their daily contact with death, have realized, often enough unconsciously, certain fundamental things. It is only in the air that the pilot can grasp that feeling, that flash of knowledge, of insight, that matures him beyond his years; only in the air that he knows suddenly he is a man in a world of men. 'Coming back to earth' has for him a double significance. He finds it difficult to orientate himself in a world that is so worldly, amongst a people whose conversation seems to him brilliant, minds agile, and knowledge complete—yet a people somehow blind. It is very strange.

In his village before the war the comfortably-off stockbrokers, the retired officers and business men, thought of the pilot, if they thought of him at all, as rather raffish, not a

Cᵈ PETER TOWNSEND. D.S.O: D.F.C.   85 SQUADRON

vidually while skillfully concentrating them all on incoming raids. Leigh Mallory, incited by the most remarkable of the fighter pilots, Douglas Bader, favoured the use of 'wings' of three or more squadrons.

Douglas had no legs; both had been amputated after a crash some years earlier. He would lead his squadron daily to Martlesham Heath, where we became friends. Some time later we were convened before the King who was visiting the station. Douglas said to me "the only thing I can't do is to stand to attention, so if I look like falling over, please come to the rescue."

Another visitor was Lord Trenchard, fondly known as the father of the R.A.F. Our most brilliant pilot, Dickey Lee, was his godson. He had disappeared before my eyes into the sea. "Is there anything you can tell me of that great boy?" asked Trenchard. I could only tell him the worst. I was at nursery school when Trenchard began his lonely battle to save the R.A.F, created in 1918 as the first ever independent air force, from extinction. Because of him we were there with the fate of Britain in our hands.

The Battle of Britain was a victory for the whole British people — the man and woman and child, in the street, the civil defence units, the Navy, the Army and the Bomber and Coastal Commands of the R.A.F. We "few" happened to possess the necessary weapons to fight the enemy hand to hand. Those weapons were the Spitfire and the Hurricane — thirty-three Hurricane squadrons and nineteen squadrons of Spitfires. Machine for machine, the faster Spit had a very slight edge on the Hurricane but in the aggregate the Hurricane squadrons did far greater execution on the enemy and consequently suffered, in all, heavier losses of young lives. So all honour, hitherto lacking, to the Hurricane. We of Fighter Command were joined by pilots who came from near and far — volunteer pilots from other R.A.F. commands and from the Royal Navy; pilots from Canada, South Africa, Australia and New Zealand, from European countries whence they had escaped the Nazis and, notably, from Poland and Czechoslovakia; as well as illegally, from the neutral United States. Living — and dying — in that exuberant, varied company, that band of brothers, has marked me for life.

Bill Millington, a young Australian, and I, both wounded, lay in adjacent beds in hospital. He wrote to his parents "I go forth into battle light of heart . . . I regard it as a privilege to fight for all those things that make life worth living — freedom, honour and fair play . . . Flying has meant the companionship of men . . . the intoxication of speed, the rush of air and the pulsating beat of the motor awaken some answering chord deep down which is indescribable . . ." He spoke for us all.

Peter Townsend (signature)

ORIGINS: THE UNEASE

German Foreign Minister and former Ambassador to Great Britain Joachim von Ribbontrop and his wife boarding a Crilly Airways Fokker FXII at Croydon airfield following talks in London with British Foreign Minister Lord Halifax, March 13, 1938.

Instructors and students of the University of London Air Squadron prepare for an afternoon's flying in their Avro Tutors.

THE KEY WORD of the age was 'appeasement'. It was whispered through the chancelleries and conference chambers of the nineteen-thirties as insidiously as the pop tunes of the day permeated the lives of the people: 'Top Hat', 'Smoke Gets In Your Eyes', 'Love in Bloom'. It signified, in essence, a tacit acceptance of naked aggression: that Adolf Hitler, Führer and Chancellor of the Third Reich, should, at noon on March 7, 1936, send a handful of battalions to occupy the 9,000 square miles of the demilitarised Rhineland in

defiance of the 1919 Treaty of Versailles. This was a treaty, which was designed to curb the militarism of Kaiser Wilhelm's time, that still, after seventeen years, rankled in so many German breasts.

Appeasement meant that Benito Mussolini, Italy's *Il Duce* of Fascism, whose goal was a new and glorious Roman Empire, could, with impunity, on October 3, 1935, launch an unprovoked seven month conquest of the ancient kingdom of Ethiopia. Since the sanctions invoked by the 50-strong League of Nations—another creation of Versailles—stopped short of oil, the Duce's brigandage went unopposed.

Never openly voiced, although silently acknowledged, was the realisation that World War II would involve whoever opposed the dictators in a rain of devastation from the

Child of Delight! with sunbright hair,/And seablue, seadeep eyes:/Spirit of Bliss, what brings thee here,/Beneath these sullen skies?

(from *The Two Children* by Emily Bronte)

air—and that the air forces of the uneasy allies, Britain and France, were in no shape to counter that threat.

The much-vaunted Royal Air Force, formed on April 1, 1918, had soon stood revealed as the nine-day wonder that it was. A total of 184 squadrons operational on Armistice Day had, by early 1920, whittled down to 18—of which only three were based in England. Although 1925 saw the creation of an Auxiliary Air Force, an officers-only Territorial Association of wealthy amateurs, who made up 'the finest flying club in the world,' a Royal Air Force Volunteer Reserve, aimed at raising R.A.F. strength from 29,000 to 90,000 in three years, had barely reached the drawing-board stage by June, 1935.

Behind this compound of stupidity, cowardice and petty self-interest lay a genuine belief that Hitler and Mussolini, initially seen as bastions of order and stability against the extreme left, were essentially responsible statesmen. And, given enough territory they would, ultimately, prove quite amenable to reason. ("Hitler," Lord Lothian, a prominent appeaser among the Liberal Party's ranks, rationalised the Rhineland seizure, "is doing nothing more than taking over his own back garden.") Conveniently ignored were the truths that the National Socialists had for three years worked as silently as termites in timber, in flagrant defiance of Versailles, to create a standing army of 500,000 men, a Luftwaffe of almost 2,000 aircraft. For Hitler's freely-avowed aim was *Lebensraum* (living space), a Reich whose frontiers would soon extend beyond all normally accepted frontiers, and ultimately *Lebensraum* would mean war.

All through the late nineteen-thirties, when the pipe of Stanley Baldwin and the umbrella of his successor, Neville Chamberlain, symbolised security for so many of the British, the R.A.F. were striving to keep pace. On November 6, 1935, five weeks after Mussolini's Ethiopian incursion, the first of designer Sydney Camm's Hawker Hurricane Mark Is, was airborne from Brooklands airfield, in Surrey; climbing to 15,000 feet with a top speed of 330 m.p.h. Although 1,000 would be ordered, the first would not reach their destined squadron, No. 111, until well into January, 1938.

On March 5, 1936, two days before the Rhineland débâcle, Reginald Joseph Mitchell's little blue monoplane fighter, already known as the Spitfire, soared triumphantly on its own test flight, above the blue waters of the Solent at Eastleigh, Hampshire. An initial 450 would be bespoken from Vickers-Supermarine; it would be August, 1938, before 19 Squadron, at Duxford, traded in their Gloster Gauntlets for the first of these new machines.

Throughout 1936, the landmarks charting the way to the greatest air war in history became increasingly apparent. On July 14, Air Marshal Sir Hugh Caswall Tremenheere Dowding arrived at 'the most singular place on earth', the 166-year-old Bentley Priory, perched on a hilltop at Stanmore, Middlesex, to form the headquarters of the newly-created Fighter Command. A remote and glacial widower, then aged 54, Air Marshal Dowding, invariably known as "Stuffy," faced a task more

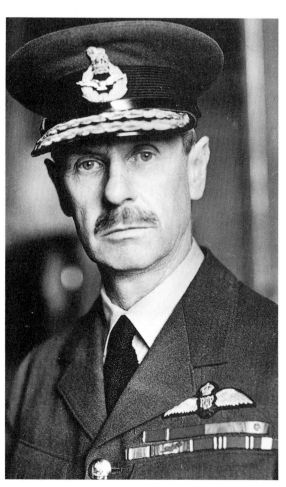

formidable than any air commander had ever known.

Four months later, the Condor Legion, 370 handpicked fliers, assembled in Seville, bent on abetting General Francisco Franco's Nationalist Armed Forces in their struggle against the Republicans that marked the Spanish Civil War. As Hitler saw it, this was an invaluable proving ground for his new Luftwaffe, and the Führer was right; one up-and-coming ace, *Leutnant* Adolf Galland, was to fly 280 missions over the hotly-contested Ebro River. Above all, the campaign was an unparalleled boost to Luftwaffe morale; the tactical successes of the Junkers 87 dive-bombers, the Stukas, conjured up a chilling, if ultimately misleading, picture of twentieth century air power. "The Stukas in Spain," one historian noted, "spread fear far beyond it."

As far, indeed, as Austria, where no voices were raised in protest between February 12 and March 11, 1938, as Adolf Hitler achieved a bloodless *Anschluss* (union) of that country with his Third Reich. As far, on the

top left: Air Officer Commanding, No.11 Group, Air Vice Marshal Keith R. Park; *top right*: Air Officer Commanding, No.12 Group, Air Vice Marshal Trafford Leigh-Mallory; *left*: Air Officer Commanding-in-Chief, Fighter Command, Air Chief Marshal Sir Hugh C.T. Dowding.

dark, rainy Friday afternoon of August 5, as Czechoslovakia, when the code word 'Diabolo' brought Fighter Command, for the first time, to a state of war readiness. At Biggin Hill, in Kent, pilots like Pete Brothers and Michael Crossley and others of No. 32 Squadron, sadly set to work with pots and brushes, disfiguring their gleaming Gloster Gauntlets with drab green and brown camouflage. Out went 32 Squadron's crest, emblazoned on every rudder, a "Hunting Horn stringed in a broad white arrow." Alongside them worked the pilots of Squadron Leader Paddy Pritchett's 79 Squadron, silently obliterating their "Salamander salient in flames."

In truth, the alarm was premature. Czechoslovakia's western province, the Sudetenland, with its large German-speaking minority, would, through the complicity of Neville Chamberlain and France's Edouard Daladier, be "given" to Hitler through the mechanism of the September 29 Munich conference, a last-ditch attempt to forestall the Führer marching in on October 1. It was a conference from which the Czechs, from first to last, were ostentatiously excluded. "It is peace in our time," Chamberlain told the cheering crowds at London's Heston airport.

"This is my last territorial demand in Europe," Hitler was to assure Chamberlain and the world, a promise which at least one sceptic begged leave to doubt. "This time it is different," Chamberlain contradicted him, baring his teeth in a complacent smile, "This time he has made his promises to me."

On March 15, 1939, when the German forces poured unopposed across the borders to occupy all Czechoslovakia, Chamberlain was unrepentant "We will continue to pursue our policy of appeasement" he said to the House of Commons.

Most verdicts on Munich were searing in their contempt. "If you have sacrificed my nation to preserve the peace of the world, I will be the first to applaud you," Jan Masaryk, the Czech Minister in London told the Foreign Secretary Lord Halifax, "But if not, gentlemen, God help your souls!" "The government had to choose between shame and war," charged the Right Honourable Member for Epping, Winston Churchill, "They chose shame and they will get war." It was Hitler, not surprisingly, who spoke as the supreme realist of the Age of Appeasement. "What does it matter how strong the concrete is," he mused, surveying the formidable might of the Czech bunkers, "so long as the will is weak?"

The one dissentient voice, ironically, was that of "Stuffy" Dowding. "It was a very good thing that he (Chamberlain) did act in that way," was his heartfelt verdict, for in the autumn of 1938, the R.A.F.'s 600 fighter aircraft—of which only 360 were then available operationally, only one in five of them modern—were as yet no match for the ascendant Luftwaffe.

The position was marginally better by the summer of 1939, when the war drums were sounding yet again; by now Dowding could look to fully 29 squadrons, manning 406 fighters, more than a quarter of them monoplanes, with 200 modern aircraft in reserve. This time the bone of contention was the Danzig Corridor, incorporated into Poland

14

by the Treaty of Versailles to give the Poles access to the sea. Since this effectively sealed off East Prussia from the rest of Germany, Hitler had demanded its cession as far back as the time of Munich. Determined to resist, the Poles, as early as April 6, had agreed a temporary mutual assistance pact with Britain and France, and this became a fully-fledged treaty on August 25.

The stage was now set for war; two days earlier, Hitler's Foreign Minister, Joachim von Ribbentrop, had signed a German-Soviet Non-Aggression Pact in Moscow. At 4.45 a.m. on Friday, September 1, German troops were streaming across the Polish frontier.

"The Germans are today crushing Poland like a soft-boiled egg," reported Otto Tolischus, foreign correspondent of *The New York Times*, with truth. By October, ninety per cent of the Poles' operational aircraft, seventy per cent of their air-crews, had been virtually wiped out.

At 11.15 a.m. on September 3, on a dozen south-coast airfields like Tangmere and Hawkinge, Dowding's pilots, basking in the warm sunshine at dispersal, heard through loudspeakers the voice of an old tired man, his voice cracking with strain: "This morning the British Ambassador in Berlin handed the German Government a final Note stating that, unless we heard from them by eleven o'clock that they were prepared at once to withdraw their troops from Poland, a state of war would exist between us . . ."

". . . I have to tell you now that no such undertaking has been received and that consequently this country is at war with Germany."

Now the world waited: for the dams to burst, for the waters to rise.

Why art thou patient, man? thou shouldst be mad;/And I, to make thee mad, do mock thee thus./Stamp, rave, and fret, that I may sing and dance.

(from *Henry VI, part 3*, by William Shakespeare)

"OOO! SEE WHAT THAT WICKED CHAMBERLAIN MAKES ME DO!"

Don't let's be beastly to the Germans When our victory is ultimately won,/It was just those nasty Nazis who presuaded them to fight And their Beethoven and Bach are really far worse than their bite,/Let's be meek to them—/And turn the other cheek to them/and try to bring out their latent sense of fun. Let's give them full air parity—/And treat the rats with charity,/But don't let's be beastly to the Hun.

(from *Don't Lets Be Beastly To The Germans* by Noel Coward)

A STATE OF WAR
EXISTS

THE R.A.F. WAS always rich in slang. Some of its idiom was both technical and necessary: 'angels' always signified height, so that 'bandits seventy-plus at Angels one-five' signified 'more than seventy German raiders approaching at 15,000 feet'. To 'scramble' was to take-off; to 'pancake' was to land. But many other phrases marked the idiosyncracies of a highly individualistic emergent service. And no pilot ever crashed a plane, he 'pranged' it. If events went awry, they had 'gone for a Burton', in which case the pilot was never put out or fed up; he was 'browned off' or 'cheesed off', and this mental malaise likewise prevailed if he was called upon to 'stooge' (fly uneventfully).

If his performance was erratic, too slow, or ill-conceived, he was admonished to 'take your finger out'.

In the last resort, no man among them ever died in action; he 'bought it'.

Thus, for all Dowding's pilots, September 3, 1939, was always 'the day the balloon went up', as indeed they did: 400 barrage balloons over London alone and at least fifty over coastal ports like Dover, grey, motionless, sixty-five feet wide by twenty-five deep, linked by a perilous mesh of steel cable. There they would remain moored for the nine long months of the Phoney War or Sitzkrieg, while the pilots endured twenty-five degrees of frost in one of the coldest winters of that century.

On September 2, squadron after squadron had recorded in its diary, 'We are ready for anything', yet uneventful week succeeded uneventful week.

Despite this aerial stalemate, Air Chief Marshal Sir Hugh Dowding faced a critical dilemma. By late September, when Lord Gort's British Expeditionary Force moved across the English Channel to France, four Hurricane squadrons—Nos. 1, 73, 85 and 87—moved with them. By mid-November, when a German invasion of the Low Countries was rumoured, two more squadrons, the Gladiators of Nos. 607 and 615, were sent as back-up.

THE English love their country with a love Steady, and simple, wordless, dignified;/I think it sets their patriotism above/All others. We Americans have pride/We glory in our country's short romance./We boast of it and love it. Frenchmen when/The ultimate menace comes, will die for France/Logically as they lived. But Englishmen/Will serve day after day, obey the law,/And do dull tasks that keep a nation strong./Once I remember in London how I saw Pale shabby people standing in a long/Line in the twilight and the misty rain/To pay their tax. I then saw England plain.

(from *The White Cliffs* by Alice Duer Miller)

Against a planned minimum of forty-six squadrons, Dowding was left with no more than thirty-five for home defence.

For the pilots, these, as yet, were high-level concerns. In this long spell of enforced idleness, their preoccupations were as varied as the men themselves. Acting Pilot Officer Richard Hillary, soon to join No. 603 (City of Edinburgh) Squadron, arguably the most famous of all R.A.F. 'guinea pigs', was reflecting that the fighter plane pointed a return "to war as it ought to be, war which is individual combat between two people . . . I shan't get maimed: either I shall get killed or I shall get a few pleasant putty medals and enjoy being stared at in a night club."

At Hedon Aero Club, outside Hull, Sergeant James 'Ginger' Lacey had no such consoling convictions. Within weeks, he was slated to join No. 501 (County of Gloucester)

Squadron at Filton, near Bristol, yet, as he recorded in his diary, 'The prospect of fighting in a war scared me stiff'. The irony was palpable. In the battle to come, Lacey was to destroy more German aircraft—eighteen, including the Heinkel that bombed Buckingham Palace on September 13, 1940—than any other pilot.

Many still lamented the vanished grace-notes of peacetime. For Flying Officer Al Deere, a phlegmatic New Zealander, life with No. 54 Squadron at Hornchurch now added up to long hours at readiness, camping out in tents, humping sand bags to build dispersal pens and blast protection bays alongside civilians paid an hourly rate for the same job. At North Weald, 20-year-old Pilot Officer Barry Sutton, of No. 56 Squadron, thought wistfully of the daily working parades, the leisurely leaves, the guest nights and the civilian clothes that had gone. Now, as a combatant-to-be, Sutton promptly sought out the Adjutant to make his will: £30 worth of belongings to his fiancée, Sylvia, his leaky two-seater Austin Seven to his cousin John.

As 1939 yielded to 1940, Dowding's was still a strangely disparate Command, a bewildering mix of confident professionals and wet-behind-the-ears novices. Pilot Officer 'Johnnie' Johnson, with No. 616 (South Yorkshire) Squadron at Coltishall, Norfolk, would ultimately enter the battle with no more than twenty-three flying hours on Spitfires in his log book. It was the same for Flying Officer David Crook, later a notable flight commander with No. 609 (West Riding) Squadron. Until December, 1939, Crook and his

fellow cadets passed each evening in the bar of The New Inn, Gloucester, sweltering in their greatcoats. Their wingless tunics would have betrayed their fledgling status to the world.

At all levels, the thirst for action fought with soul-searching doubts. At Acklington, on the north-east coast, the night of January 30, 1940, saw three Flight Lieutenants of No. 43 Squadron, Peter Townsend, Caesar Hull, a chunky South African, and John Simpson launch into a wild near-hysterical jig, *La Cachita*, a cross between a rumba and an apache dance, which sent chairs and tables flying. Their manic elation was understandable: each man had that day shot down the first three Heinkel bombers to crash on English soil. They had killed and they had lived to tell the tale.

A privileged few—all of them triumphant survivors of the battle to come—had early on fallen heavily for Reginald Mitchell's Spitfire Mark I. For the South African Flight Lieutenant Adolph 'Sailor' Malan, of 74 Squadron, Hornchurch, exchanging their Hawker Furies for the Spitfire at the time of Munich was "like changing over from Noah's Ark to the *Queen Mary*." Two months later, at Duxford, 65 Squadron's Pilot Officer Roland Robert Stanford Tuck, a slim dandy given to monogrammed silk handkerchiefs, was equally entranced. For Tuck, the Spitfire was "thirty feet of wicked beauty . . . with practically no relation to any of the aircraft I'd flown previously." So eager was he to master this answer to a fighter pilot's prayer that he patented a private mnemonic—BTFCPUR (brakes, trim, flaps, contacts, petrol, under-

Sunday 12 May

I did two patrols today and on the first I got lost and almost toured France trying to find the aerodrome, but having landed at a French aerodrome I eventually got back. We didn't see anything on either patrol but we thought we had on the latter and I got so excited. I now have had 6 hours sleep in 48 hours and haven't washed for over 36 hours. My God am I tired . . . and I am up again at 3am tomorrow.

(from the diary of Pilot Officer Denis H. Wissler No. 17 Squadron)

The poignant misery of dawn begins to grow . . . We only know war lasts, rain soaks, and clouds sag stormy./Dawn massing in the east her melancholy army/Attacks once more in ranks on shivering ranks of gray,/But nothing happens.

(from *Exposure* by Wilfrid Owen)

preceding spread: Spitfire Mk.1s in 1939.
top left: Balcony leading to the office of Air Chief Marshal Dowding at HQ Fighter Command, Bentley Priory, Stanmore;
left: Dowding's office as it appears in 1988.

Sad girls in gym-slips and crepe de Chine blouses;/Shy boys in jerseys and grey flannel trousers;/Cardboard-boxed gas-masks and tag-label strings;/Porters and teachers who planned journeyings/To Highlands of Scotland, or Canada-far;/To Monmouth, Tredegar or Leamington Spa.,/This how I remember our school refugees/Who then I much envied as 'evacuees.'
They later related adventures abroad;/Of living in homes few could ever afford;/Of life in the country with horses and cattle.,/Remote from the dangers and din of the Battle/That we who remained had observed every day—/Had ever been part of, we proudly could say!/A messenger boy in our grand Fire Brigade.

(from *A Boy At War* by Barry Winchester)

No..7.7.3.......

BOROUGH OF BROMLEY, KENT
AIR RAID PRECAUTIONS

This is to certify that the bearer

IVY RAPLEY

25, Lovelace Avenue, Bromley.

is a duly qualified
AIR RAID WARDEN

in the Air Raid Precautions organization of this Borough.

Date 25th Oct. 1939.   Town Clerk

If found kindly drop in nearest pillar box.

carriage, radiator)—which enabled him to start up a Spitfire blindfolded.

Another convert was the legendary Flying Officer Douglas Bader, who eight years earlier, after stunting in a Bulldog over Woodley airfield, near Reading, had had both legs amputated below the knee. Incredibly, in October, 1939, the 29-year-old Bader became the first man with artificial legs ever to pass a medical for General Duties, as flying was known. Posted to No. 19 Squadron, at Duxford, in February, 1940, Bader, too, was soon enthralled by the way the Spitfire handled, "like a highly-strung thoroughbred."

Significantly, long before battle was joined, all three men, so at ease in their Spitfires, were more and more coming to question the Fighter Command Number 1 Attack, where fighters swung into line behind their leader, queuing to deliver a three-second attack before swinging away, their underbellies a sure target for a German rear gunner. For Malan, it was "pretty to watch and excellent for drill purposes" but totally unsuited to a Spitfire's maximum speed of 355 m.p.h. Tuck saw what he called the tight 'guardsman' formations as counter-productive; pilots were too busy watching each other's wing-tips to keep their eyes peeled for enemy aircraft.

Bader, the most explosively outspoken of the three, presciently saw the battles to come as they would eventuate, a whirling pattern of individual dog fights with every man for himself. "The chap who'll control the battle will still be the chap who's got the height and sun, same as the last war," he dogmatised, "That old slogan of Ball, Bishop and McCudden

20

(Three Royal Flying Corps veterans, all of whom were awarded the V.C: Albert Ball, William Avery Bishop, and James Byford Mc-Cudden), 'Beware of the Hun in the sun' wasn't just a funny rhyme. Those boys learned from experience.''

These tactics would ultimately be proven right, although for months to come many squadrons would continue to fly in the strange

Life is just one damned thing after another.

(—authorship disputed)

Few examples of the WWII tank barriers known as 'dragon's teeth' remain today in England. These are at Cripp's Corner, Sussex. *right:* One of the many funds set up at the local level to finance fighter planes; *above:* a favourite Hornchurch haunt.

tight formation that the Luftwaffe called "the bunch of bananas." Yet what all three men failed to ask themselves was one salient question: would the planes in which to pursue those tactics be forthcoming from the assembly lines? In the four months from January to April, 1940, the Air Ministry was to produce 2,729 aircraft—but only 638 of them were the desperately needed fighters.

On May 10, 1940, Fighter Command's salvation was at hand. At 5 a.m. on that day, the sirens screamed from Lyons to Newcastle upon Tyne; the code-word 'René, René, René' passed from army post to army post along the Belgian frontier. Hitler had struck in the west against Belgium, France, Holland and tiny Luxembourg simultaneously. Two days earlier, a damning House of Commons debate on

22

Britain's failure to wrest Norway—which Hitler had attacked on April 9—from Germany's grasp had toppled the Chamberlain Government. On May 10, Winston Churchill, that longtime prophet of aerial doom, became the new Premier.

It was now, to put an end to what he called "the muddle and scandal of the (Air Ministry's) aircraft production branch," that Churchill appointed the 61-year-old Canadian newspaper tycoon, bustling ruthless little William Maxwell Aitken, first Baron Beaverbrook, to the newly-created position, Minister of Aircraft Production.

From the first, "The Beaver" seemed to vie with Churchill as to how many toes he could trample on; to him, the entire Air Staff were, to the bitter end, "the bloody Air Marshals." If Beaverbrook sought storage space he snatched it from the Air Ministry without prior consultation, then padlocked it. To make aircraft factory workers feel "important" he flashed messages onto cinema screens recalling them to duty. To instil the same sense of belonging into the nation's housewives, he launched a personal campaign of "Saucepans Into Spitfires," beseeching them: "Send me your pots and pans, send me your aluminium." Whether a single Spitfire was created from the resultant cornucopia remains dubious, but in those anxious days the housewives, knew a true sense of purpose.

Working from Stornoway House, St James's Park, his London home, rather than from the M.A.P. building on Millbank, Beaverbrook soon refused to adhere to any appointments schedule; all took potluck, first

MOTHERS
Send them out
of London

left: Citizens of Portsmouth filling sandbags at Southsea beach in 1939, to protect local buildings and construct make-shift shelters; below: English children awaiting evacuation.

W.A.A.F.s at the launch of a Portsmouth barrage balloon near Garrison church; *right:* a child's 'Mickey Mouse' type gas mask.

come, first served. Papers were piled on spare beds, typewriters were glimpsed in bathrooms, and meals, at irregular intervals during a 16-hour day, were delivered on trays. Often, in an office plastered with slogans—"Organisation is the Enemy of Improvisation"—"It Is A Long Way from Knowing To Doing"—six officials were lined up before Beaverbrook's desk at one time with memos to present.

When he decided to merge the industrial complex of Lord Nuffield, the "British Ford," with the old-guard firm of Vickers-Armstrong, Beaverbrook despatched a secretary to haul Nuffield out of bed at midnight and break the news. Nuffield's subsequent impassioned plea to Churchill fell on deaf ears. "I cannot interfere with the manufacture of aircraft," was Churchill's firm rejoinder.

Beaverbrook's credo was aptly expressed in a letter to Sir Samuel Hoare, soon en route as ambassador-extraordinary to Franco's Spain: "I don't care if the middle classes lie sleepless in their beds, so long as the workers stay active at their benches." For what Beaverbrook sought to do, fearing the massed might of Luftwaffe bombers, was to disrupt bomber production deliberately for the sake of stockpiling fighters.

"I saw my reserves slipping away like sand in an hour glass," Dowding was to report later, ". . . without his (Beaverbrook's) drive behind me I could not have carried on in the battle." And Beaverbrook's figures spoke for themselves. The 638 fighter output of the Phoney War was eclipsed almost overnight. From May to August, the height of "The Beaver's" war effort, M.A.P., produced 1,875

We used to say 'if pigs could fly!'/And now they do./I saw one sailing in the sky/Some thousand feet above his sty,/A fat one too!/I scarcely could believe my eyes,/So just imagine my surprise/To see so corpulent a pig Inconsequently dance a jig/Upon a cloud./And, when elated by the show I clapped my hands and called 'Bravo!'/He turned and bowed./Then, all at once, he seemed to flop And dived behind a chimmey-top/Out of my sight./'He's down' thought I; but not at all, 'Twas only pride that had the fall:/To my delight He rose, quite gay and debonair,/Resolved to go on dancing there/Both day and nights.
So pigs can fly,/They really do,/This chap, though anchored in the slime,/Could reach an altitude sublime—/A pig, 'tis true!/I wish I knew Just how not only pigs but men/Might rise to nobler heights again/Right in the blue/And start anew!

(from *To A Barrage Balloon* by May Morton)

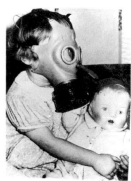

fighters, and, thanks to the truculent persistence of one chief, Trevor Westbrook, repaired 1,872. A pastmaster of cannibalisation, Westbrook saw to it that three damaged aircraft could ensure one fit for service; if instruments were lacking, Westbrook's solution was to unabashedly pillage R.A.F. depots.

It was not a programme achieved without the 'blood, toil, tears and sweat' which were all that Churchill had offered the British. Robert Bruce Lockhart, who looked in on one midnight meeting of Beaverbrook and his department chiefs at Stornoway House never forgot it. The exchanges were as staccato as Browning machine gun fire.

"How many planes are you producing this week? Double it."

Any protest produced a fearsome, "Why not?"

"Because I am short of mechanics."

"How many do you need?"

"Thirty or forty."

"Which figure do you mean?"

"Thirty."

"You'll have them on Monday. Double your figure."

The urgency was appropriate. Across the Channel, within two weeks of Hitler's headlong blitzkrieg, a vast military disaster was in the making.

IF THE GAS RATTLES SOUND

29

If I were asked . . . to what the singular prosperity and growing strength of that people ought mainly to be attributed, I should reply: To the superiority of their women.

(—Alexis de Tocqueville)

Sunday 9 June

The W/Commander woke me up at 3:30 with some Alka Seltzer, brought me his bath robe and had already run my bath. I was still drunk but after a cold bath felt better. We took off for France, Count Czernin and I. Got lost. Force landed 4 times, 3 in fields and got to the aerodrome at Le Mans at about 5 o'clock, having taken over 12 hours to do a 1 hour journey. The place here is all upside down and I am sleeping in a tent.

(from the diary of Pilot Officer Denis H. Wissler No. 17 Squadron)

left: Volunteer ambulance crews at Portsmouth, with anti-gas steel helmets.

THE FALL OF FRANCE

ON THE LATE AFTERNOON of Wednesday May 15, Air Marshal Sir Hugh Dowding was a man with a mission. At this hour, the War Cabinet was once again in full session, some thirty men flanking the green baize table on the first floor of No. 10, Downing Street—among them, Dowding noted gratefully, such committed allies as Lord Beaverbrook, "the little nut-brown man," and the ruddy-faced mild-eyed Air Chief Marshal Sir Cyril Newall, Chief of the Air Staff.

Presiding over this meeting, Winston Churchill was scowling balefully—for Dowding's presence, at his own urgent request, was until now unprecedented.

At issue were the ten fighter squadrons which Churchill, on an impulse, had that very morning promised France's Premier, Paul Reynaud, since the entire French front was crumbling under the onslaught of German armour. It was now, for five or ten minutes, "as elegantly as possible," that Dowding would put his case for the squadrons' retention in England—finally flinging down his pencil so forcefully that Beaverbrook was convinced he was about to resign. Then, rising from his seat, Dowding advanced deliberately on Churchill, a hastily-sketched graph in red ink clutched in his hand.

"This red line shows the wastage of Hurricanes in the last ten days," he told the Premier flatly, "If the line goes on at the same rate for the next ten days there won't be a single Hurricane left, either in France or in England."

For Dowding it seemed then that his cogent argument had won the day—as indeed, for a little under twenty-four hours, it had.

All unknown to Fighter Command's chief, Churchill, by now in Paris and again under heavy pressure from Reynaud, had agreed afresh to a reinforcement of ten squadrons—until at 11 p.m., on May 16, Sir Cyril Newall had staunchly vetoed it. Although squadrons from south-east England might rotate to French airfields in daylight hours, Newall conceded, "I do not believe that . . . a few more fighter squadrons . . . would make the difference between victory and defeat in France."

It was a crucial decision for the battle to come. Already in ten days fighting, 195 Hurricanes had been irretrievably lost.

For the ten Hurricane squadrons already based on French soil, their role from the first had been one of total and uncoordinated confusion. Each eighteen-hour day had seen every battle fought as an eleventh-hour emergency, attacks against bridges and light ack-ack, destined to do little more than boost the morale of the B.E.F; at Merville, near Arras, the brief sojourn of No. 79 Squadron, despatched on May 10, was climaxed by a sunlit flarepath of tool kits, petrol tins and blazing Hurricanes. By May 24 the remnants of the squadron were back at Biggin Hill.

At first, no man had cavilled at the rigours of life in the field: the sleeping in barns, the shaving in streams, that became the universal lot, where 'dispersal' now scaled down to no more than a field telephone and a ditch. Yet the sense of helplessness was everywhere apparent. On May 17, Sergeant James 'Ginger' Lacey was one of sixteen 501 Squadron

Many a battle have I won in France,/When as the enemy hath been ten to one:/Why should I not now have the like success?

(from *Henry VI, part 3*, William Shakespeare)

Wednesday 12 June

I had my first air action today when we were up on patrol by Le Havre. 3 Heinkel 111 were bombing shipping when we came out of the sun. I was in the first section to attack and as I fired smoke came out of the starboard engine. I broke away and made two other attacks. All the bombers were shot down, also another which was caught by another bloke. We were very badly shelled after on another patrol. It was most terrifying. I collected two bullet holes in the morning in my port wing and tail.

(from the diary of Pilot Officer Denis H. Wissler No. 17 Squadron)

left: PZ865 'The Last of the Many,' a Mk.IIC Hawker Hurricane of the Battle of Britain Memorial Flight, at West Malling in 1988.

I'm a lean dog, a keen dog, a wild dog, and lone;/I'm a rough dog, a tough dog, hunting on my own;/I'm a bad dog, a mad dog, teasing silly sheep;/I love to sit and bay the moon, to keep fat souls from sleep.

(*Lone Dog* by Irene R. MacLeod)

Hauptmann Adolf Galland in France, 1940.

pilots attacking German armour for the first time with their .303 machine guns.

"It was like shooting at elephants with a pea-shooter," Lacey complained later. "The tank commanders didn't even pay us the compliment of closing their turrets; they just ducked their heads as we came over and stuck them out again as soon as we'd gone past." The tanks, Lacey noted, rolled on completely unscathed.

Central to the thinking that would lead to the heaviest defeat ever inflicted on a French army in the field was the defensive concept of the 400-mile long Maginot Line, "like row upon row of sunken earthbound battleships," a line which left France both north and south naked to her enemies. It was to the south, where the heights of the Ardennes Forest had been reckoned "equal to the best fortifications," that the German armour had struck as early as the night of May 11, and this was of a piece with the seizure of Belgium's "impregnable" Fort Eben Emael by nine gliders soon after dawn on May 10, the devastation of the ancient fort of Sedan three days later. Early on May 15, as the *Wehrmacht* surged through the forty mile gap south and west of Sedan, sweeping for the Channel and cutting the Allies in half, Reynaud, calling from Paris, had appealed hysterically to Churchill, "We are beaten . . . we have lost the battle."

On May 19, four days after assuming office, the new Commander-in-Chief, General Maxime Weygand, summed up for history: "This war is sheer madness. We have gone to war with a nineteen eighteen army against a

German army of nineteen thirty nine.''

It was in essence, an epitaph for all those Hurricane squadrons that had from the first made part of the battle. The ill-fated "B" Flight of No. 56 Squadron, detached from North Weald, was written off within seven days; one who came back, Flight Sergeant 'Taffy' Higginson, reported, "It was sheer hell and terror from start to finish." At Lille-Seclin, where seventeen pilots were lost and only three pilots remained to No. 85 Squadron, one man, Sergeant 'Sammy' Allard, survived only through sheer fatigue, falling asleep three times over German-held territory, then collapsing afresh in the cockpit on landing. Finally, evacuated to England, he slept for a total of thirty hours.

All over France, in these disquieting days, the casualties, in terms of both men and machines, were mounting daily. At Le Mans, No. 501 Squadron were down to three planes; all but two were lost to No. 111 Squadron. The first into action, at Vassincourt, and among the last to leave, No. 1 Squadron, returned to England in a state of mind that was near pathological. "We were convinced that the Air Ministry were holding back the £60 due for kit replacement until we'd all got killed," Pilot Officer Peter Boot recalls wonderingly, "There was a real persecution complex throughout the squadron." Some squadrons, like No. 607, where twenty-six pilots were lost, had only their inheritors to speak for them. "Things were in an awful mess," remembers Squadron Leader James Vick, who took command of No. 607 at Tangmere, "It was quite a shock to walk in

33

Dunkirk, May, 1940.

and find that practically all of them were dead and to take over their huts and their old cars."

Few units pulled out under conditions more traumatic than No. 242, the all-Canadian fighter squadron. From early on, Flying Officer Russ Wiens had noted, "The war in the air today makes shows like *Dawn Patrol* look like Sunday School;" long slow weeks of attrition were to follow. Between May and June, every pilot of Flying Officer rank, all middle echelon officers, was lost over enemy territory. At Biggin Hill, the ultimate line of retreat, Pilot Officer Don Howitt spent almost all of his time re-addressing both the letters and the luggage of those who had gone missing. Not until June 14 did No. 242's rearguard, victualled only by two sacks of carrots, pull out for the coast at St Nazaire, and anxious moments followed even here. At Nantes, while their ground crews embarked, the pilots weighed in to refuel, re-arm and service their own aircraft.

Even the visiting firemen—those south coast squadrons which in daylight hours patrolled the Arras-Cambrai—Lille—St Omer sector—sensed danger in the air. "Land at Abbeville, refuel, hear dreadful stories, get very frightened," noted the diarist of Squadron Leader John Worrall's No 32 Squadron, "do a patrol, see nothing, feel better, do another, see nothing, feel much better, return to Biggin Hill, feel grand." Theirs was a charmed life. "Have just heard . . . that 605 Squadron were sent from here to cover the evacuation from Dunkirk," one flight commander wrote from Tangmere, ". . . The news has just come through that they have lost nearly all their

chaps on the first day including their C.O., George Perry."

That was on May 31, and six days earlier the Secretary of State for War, Anthony Eden, had authorised Lord Gort's British Expeditionary Force to deny the French High Command who were essentially their masters and effect a wholesale withdrawal to the coast, fighting back down a corridor fifty miles long by fifteen wide to the 1000-year-old port of Dunkirk. To heighten the crisis, on May 27, King Leopold of the Belgians, with three-quarters of his territory lost, had sought an armistice from midnight—leaving the whole left flank of the British Army open for some twenty miles. A mighty military evacuation was in the offing.

For Fighter Command this was a new and near insurmountable challenge. Ostensibly, squadrons like the Hornchurch-based No. 92 boasted a full complement of twenty-six pilots; the daily reality was a scant fourteen, young men still formally clad in the white flying overalls of peacetime, airborne in Spitfires as yet innocent of armoured plating. On any one patrol, the odds were weighted; between Calais and Dunkirk, on May 24, No. 54 Squadron, another Hornchurch unit, somehow survived an encounter with seventy German bombers and countless Messerschmitts.

It was thus no time for lone wolves. The lucky ones, like Pilot Officer Tony Woods-Scawen, limped back to Tangmere with his Hurricane's hydraulics shot to splinters, his cockpit bathed in oil, lacking even the pressure to put down his under-carriage, yet marvellously, indisputably alive. "How did you get on, sir?," his ground crew pressed him, "What was it like?," and Woods-Scawen had just one seraphic answer, "*Dee*-licious!."

Within days, Fighter Command's Dunkirk dilemma was plain: should they stage small patrols at frequent intervals, boosting the morale of the retreating troops, or larger sporadic patrols, in the hope of coming to grips with the German bombers? Of a Spitfire's two hours and twenty minutes flying time, only twenty minutes operational manoeuvres were feasible at full throttle; on one

day alone, May 30 the Hornchurch wing flew 68 sorties over Dunkirk, yet never once sighted an enemy plane. It was small wonder that the station commander, Wing Commander Cecil Bouchier, was to go on record: "The coverage of the beaches of Dunkirk was infinitely more exhausting and exacting than any part of the Battle of Britain."

After ten days of intensive operations, some squadrons had to be withdrawn from the line. The seven remaining planes of No. 54 Squadron under Flight Lieutenant James Leathart flew north for a well-earned rest to Catterick, Yorkshire, where a puzzled senior officer greeted them, "Which flight is this?" Replying, Leathart spoke at that moment for the whole hard-pressed R.A.F., "Flight, nothing. *This* is a squadron."

How a pilot viewed the shameful glory of Dunkirk depended, invariably, on temperament. For Flight Lieutenant John Simpson, a happy-go-lucky extrovert, what stood out was the holiday aspect: "I could see the *Brighton Belle,* and the paddle steamers, and the sort of cheerful little boats you see calling at coastal towns on Sunday. Hundreds of boats! Fishing boats and motor boats, and Thames river craft and strings of dinghies, being towed by bigger boats. All packed with troops, and people standing in the water . . . ." But Flying Officer Robert Stanford Tuck, a by then case-hardened realist of No. 92 Squadron, glimpsed a harsher picture, from 1,000 feet above the harbour—"shells exploding on the cluttered beach . . . raising tall white plumes in the shallow water . . . smouldering trucks and carriers, ruptured convoys, abandoned stores piled ready for burning . . . sandbags being filled for the last dour stand . . . ."

Probably no man, in the fleeting moments of patrol, could grasp the cold hard logistics of this victory-in-defeat: from a triangle less than 1,000 miles square, some 366,000 men would be ferried to safety by more than 1,000 vessels, ranging from sleek whippet-like destroyers to cockle boats from the Essex mud flats. Travelling in garbage trucks and on children's scooters, on tractors and astride dairy cattle, the remnants of an army were drawn by one landmark: the column of black smoke, visible from thirty miles away, that marked the beaches of Dunkirk.

These were military concerns. For the pilots, the lowering skies above twenty-three miles of sandy shelving shore now became a proving ground for R.A.F. and Luftwaffe alike—nor was this a challenge that the Luftwaffe, despite the battle scars of Spain

36

and Poland, viewed lightly. The veterans among them saw to that. At Wissant, near Calais, *Oberst* Theo Osterkamp, regional fighter commander for Air Fleet Two, gave due warning to one flight leader, *Hauptmann* Walter Kienzle, "Now we are going to fight 'The Lords,' and that is something else again. They are hard fighters and they're good fighters—even though our machines are better."

Some Germans learned this lesson by degrees. For *Hauptmann* Werner Mölders, leader of Fighter Group Fifty Three's First Wing, with fourteen confirmed "kills" from the Spanish Civil War, the first stages of the Battle of France had been almost tiresomely routine. No sooner did the hapless Hurricanes abandon an airfield than Mölders' acolytes, *Leutnant* Claus and *Oberleutnant* Kaluza, armed only with tommy guns, land in their

Fieseler-Storch and take over. "Keep a stiff upper lip, boys, even if you have to wedge it down with a matchstick." Mölders would rally them, though still knowing that morale was at its peak.

It was the bomber pilots who first gave the R.A.F. their due. "They were the real resistance, those fighters," acknowledges *Oberleutnant* Karl Kessel, of the Second Bomber Group's First Wing, "They came from above, and from below, from the sides, and from everywhere—and this was something we were meeting for the first time." *Leutnant* Otto Wolfgang Bechtle, of the Group's Third Wing, concurs. "We knew about the Spitfires and respected them even before the war," he recalls, and adds "We respected them even more after Dunkirk."

Ironically, for many German pilots, it was suddenly a cleaner battle once the R.A.F. entered the fray. Ground strafing the beaches from 300 feet *Hauptmann* Paul Temme of the 2nd Fighter Group's 1st wing felt nothing but revulsion—"just unadulterated killing . . . cold-blooded point blank murder." Hans Heinz Brustellin, of the 51st Group, felt the same. "It was an awful business if you looked too closely, a demoralising business for a fighter force," he says now. "Some got physically sick with the killing."

No Luftwaffe ace felt this more keenly than *Hauptmann* Adolf Galland, a Spanish Civil War ace credited with 17 victories, then part of the 27th Fighter Wing. "My first kill was child's play," Galland recalled of a one-sided combat with a Belgian piloting a beat-up Hurricane, "I had something approaching

a twinge of conscience." His first brush with the R.A.F. revealed a new kind of adversary— "Each relentless aerial combat was a question of 'you' or 'me'."

"Until then we'd always been army support planes," Galland explains, "Dunkirk gave us our first chance to prove ourselves." And he stresses with hindsight, "Dunkirk should have been an emphatic warning for the leaders of the Luftwaffe." One such alarm bell was sounded on May 29, when Galland, escorting the wing's commander, crusty old *Oberstleutnant* Max Ibel, was jumped by a gaggle of Spitfires. Although he came instantly to Ibel's aid, "blazing away with all I had," the Spitfires totally ignored this brash intruder. "Sure of their target," they streaked single mindedly after Ibel, who was lucky to survive a crash landing.

Tributes like Galland's would then have astonished the R.A.F. Trained to fly pre-war copybook attacks in rigid air display formation, the fluid weaving tactics of the Messerschmitts had them dazed. Flying Officer "John" Petre of No. 19 Squadron, a star pupil of the R.A.F. College at Cranwell, was on the tail of an ME 109 when he recoiled abruptly; an explosive bullet had torn into his cockpit, shattering his instrument panel.

Plunging into a spindive below the level of the swarm, Petre realised that he had never even seen the plane that hit him.

At this stage of the battle, as the R.A.F. saw it, sheer audacity rather than tactics saw them through. Squadron Leader Teddy Donaldson, of No. 151 Squadron, was closing a Heinkel over Dunkirk when he found his

The conventional way to start a Hurricane was to pour a flood of electricity into the engine from a trolley-load of accumulator batteries until its twelve cylinders began to fire. Alternatively it was possible to insert a starting handle on each side and, by winding furiously, coax the engine into life. This was blistering toil. The flies danced delightedly around the pilot's sweating heads. As each fighter poppled and crackled and finally roared, it was necessary for the pilot to nurse it until it would idle happily, then lock the brakes on, jump out, and go and help someone else. Quickly, before the first plane began to overheat. There was one great incentive in getting the propellors turning. They blew away those bastard, bloodsucking French flies.

(from *Piece of Cake* by Derek Robinson)

ammo exhausted; still, in cold fury, he rammed his Hurricane forward. His nerve gone, the pilot first jettisoned his bombs, then baled out minus his parachute.

On another such sortie, Robert Stanford Tuck, soon to command No. 92 Squadron, was exasperated beyond belief; the din of voices in his earphones testified not only to lack of radio discipline but to the total confusion then prevailing.

"Look out—here's another!"

"Watch that bastard—smack under-neath you, man, *under* you!"

"He's burning—I got him, I *got* him chaps!"

"Bloody hell, I've been hit . . ."

"Jesus, where are they all coming from?"

"For God's sake, *some*body . . .!"

This archetypal cry for help symbolised the bewilderment of all the novices; a gut re-action against judgments more fleeting than they had ever been called upon to make, in combats so dizzying as to defy gravity. "The ME 109s were quicksilver," points out Squad-

Dunkirk, June 4, 1940.

ron Leader 'Tubby' Mermagen, a portly teddy bear of a man, leading No. 222 Squadron out of Hornchurch, "It would have been ideal to come against them as a controlled formation, but the Germans always split up, so somehow you did, too."

To this Mermagen adds the bleak corollary, "It was every man for himself then—which was all right if you were good."

Barely a handful would have rated that accolade as Dunkirk dawned. Yet just as the Luftwaffe learned wariness and grudging re-

spect following their first encounters, Dowding's pilots too, grew more cunning. Over Dunkirk—just as later over London—the sure tactic was to ignore the gleaming arrowhead of Messerschmitts 4,000 feet above them. The secret was to carve into the bomber formations before they could ever reach their target.

Among the first to score, as Tuck would always remember, was his own squadron, No. 92. At 12,000 feet, inland from Dunkirk, they spied twenty Dornier 17s curving gently to starboard, lining up for their bombing run

Talk not of France, sith thou hast lost it all.

(from *Henry VI, part 3*, by William Shakespeare)

I took one draught of life,/I'll tell you what I paid,/Precisely an existence—/The market-price, they said.

(Further Poems by Emily Dickenson)

against the huddled troops. It was then that Flying Officer Anthony Bartley did, as Tuck put it "a rather extraordinary thing."

"He went down the starboard side of the stream, shooting them up one wing, and I distinctly saw him leapfrog over one 'vic', under the next, then up over the third—and so on. He did the whole side of the formation like that, and he tumbled at least one—maybe two—as flamers at that single pass. It was just about the cheekiest bit of flying I'd seen. The chaps in his section tried to follow him, but they managed only one or two of the 'jumps'. Tony made every one."

Most survivors later gave thanks to Dunkirk as a salutary baptism of fire. For on Saturday June 1st, the last full-scale day of the evacuation, they were almost 3,000 sorties wiser, and they were out for blood.

As early as 5 a.m. 4,000 feet above the target, the dawn patrol of three Spitfire squadrons saw the strength of the opposition: no bombers were in sight but the grey shapes of a dozen ME 109s and ME 110s were darting like sharks from cloud cover. By now even the fighters held no terror for them; within seconds battle was joined.

Flight Sergeant George Unwin, of No. 19 Squadron, looped so close beneath one Messerschmitt that it blew up above his head. Flying Officer Gordon Sinclair, attacking eight ME 110s in line astern, screamed after one victim in a dive so uncontrolled it took him within 50 feet of the shining water. Flight Lieutenant Douglas Bader of No. 222 Squadron, pouncing like a hawk on the first ME 109 he had ever engaged, watched the great

spurt of orange flame hose back at him like a blowtorch and thought naively, "It's true—they *do* have black crosses."

By 6 a.m., claiming a total bag of 15 German fighters, the dawn patrol was heading back for base.

Then, just as suddenly as it had begun, it was all over. On June 4, 13 days before 84-year-old Marshal Henri Phillipe Pétain, France's new premier, sought an armistice, a single flight of No. 242 Squadron was airborne over Dunkirk. More than 50,000 vehicles littered the beaches and the promenades, choking the inshore waters and smoke still billowed from the burning port, but not a soul moved in the streets. Only the white sail of a lone yacht, moving towards open sea, caught their attention.

There was nothing to indicate that the nine days of Dunkirk had cost Dowding 106 fighters and that only 283 planes then remained serviceable for the nation's defence.

Already the promises had been made, no less than the prophecies. On June 4, Churchill had pledged the nation to "fight on the beaches . . . on the landing grounds . . . in the fields and in the streets." On June 18, he warned: "The Battle of France is over. I expect the Battle of Britain is about to begin." It was General Sir Hastings Ismay, Assistant Secretary to the War Cabinet, who put it more starkly to the U.S. Military attache, General Raymond E. Lee.

"The future of our Western civilisation," he told Lee, "rests on the shoulders of the Royal Navy and about 5,000 pink-cheeked young pilots."

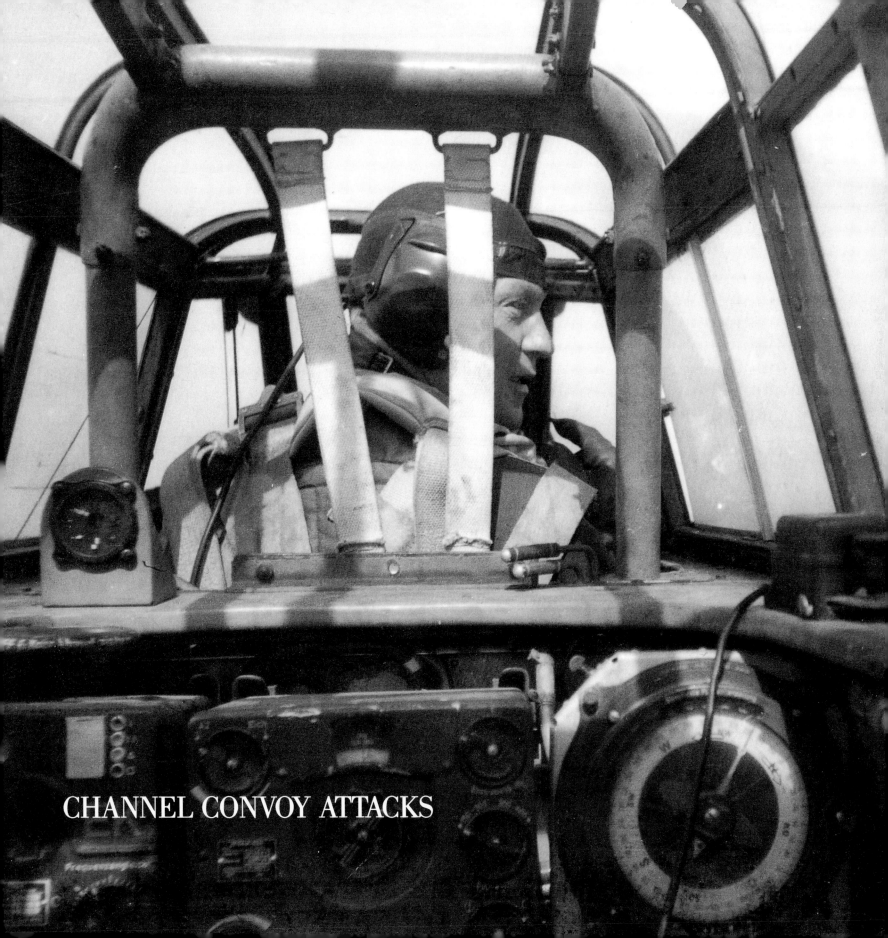

CHANNEL CONVOY ATTACKS

What General Weygand called the Battle of France is over. I expect that the Battle of Britain is about to begin . . . Let us therefore brace ourselves to our duties, and so bear ourselves that, if the British Empire and its Commonwealth last for a thousand years, men will still say, "This was their finest hour."

(—Winston Churchill, June 18, 1940)

EARLY ON WEDNESDAY June 5, two high-ranking Luftwaffe staff officers were picking their way through the detritus that littered the beaches east of Dunkirk: thousands of pairs of shoes discarded by fugitive soldiers, hundreds of bicycles, heavy guns silted over with sand, a blizzard of army papers stirring in the chill dawn wind.

Ahead of them loomed a glinting mountain of empty wine and whisky bottles, seemingly the remnants of a last officers' mess party. It was the cue for *General* Hoffman von Waldau, the junior of the two, to prod the bottles contemptuously with a highly polished boot, gesturing towards the Channel. "Here is the grave of the British hopes in this war!" he prophesied, "and these,"—with an arrogant, dismissive glance at the bottles—"are the gravestones!"

But his superior, *General* Erhard Milch, a dark and fleshy World War I veteran, and the Luftwaffe's Inspector General, shook a troubled head. "They are not buried yet," he remarked. Then, almost as if to himself, he added, "We have no time to waste."

It was a point that Milch was to stress urgently later that day to his chief, *Feldmarschall* Herman Goering, in his private train, a few miles from Dunkirk. Yet given the euphoria prevailing after the rout of the B.E.F., Milch was painfully conscious of being a spectre at the feast. And it was with mounting perplexity that Goering heard his deputy's recommendation: "I strongly advise the immediate transfer to the Channel coast of all available Luftwaffe forces . . . The invasion of Great Britain should begin without delay . . . I

warn you, Herr Feldmarshall, if you give the English, three or four weeks to recoup, it will be too late."

Goering's first reaction was a terse *Nicht lösbar* (It won't work), and at the topmost level, Hitler, already tendering peace-feelers through such sources as the Papal Nuncio in Switzerland and King Gustav of Sweden, was equally lukewarm. Not until July 16, when the British had stubbornly rejected all his offers, did the Führer issue his famous Directive No. 16: "As England, in spite of her hopeless military situation, still shows no signs of willingness to come to terms, I have decided to prepare, and if necessary to carry out, a landing operation against her." The code-name for this "exceptionally daring undertaking"—a fullscale thirteen-division invasion on a 225-mile front from Ramsgate, on the Kentish coast, to Lyme Regis, west of the Isle of Wight—was "Operation Sealion."

Inevitably, there were preliminaries. Seaways like the English Channel must be closed to shipping. Ports must be brought to a standstill. Above all, the directive stressed, "the British Air Force must be eliminated to such an extent that it will be incapable of putting up any sustained opposition to the invading troops."

The main attack plan—Adlerangriff, or Attack of the Eagles, to come into force on receipt of the codeword Adler Tag (Eagle Day)—was scattered along the whole invasion front, and by the yardstick of the Polish and French campaigns, the R.A.F. should be out of the picture in four days flat.

If the R.A.F. were still seen as formidable

adversaries, this was an unlooked for role. Despite the get-up-and-go tactics of Lord Beaverbrook's Ministry of Aircraft Production, the 283 fighters that were Dowding's standby when Dunkirk fell stood at no more than 600 by July. The other services were in worse shape still. Against Germany's 200 divisions, Britain could now muster but a score. At least ten divisions had left their heavy guns and howitzers gutted or strewn across the fields of Flanders. Out of 200 naval destroyers only 74 were out of dockyard hands.

The Atlantic U-boat war was fast becoming, in Churchill's words, "the only thing that ever frightened me." June alone had seen 300,000 tons of shipping lost to the torpedoes of *Konteradmiral* Karl Doenitz, whose 57 U-boat skippers would always remember this as Die Glückliche Zeit, The Happy Time. Since January their successes had been reflected on every British breakfast table—now limited to two ounces of tea a week, four of butter, half a

left: Generalfeldmarschall Albert Kesselring, Commander of Luftflotte 2, France, 1940; *above:* Junkers JU87 'Stuka' dive-bombers.

below: Reichsmarschall
Hermann Goering in
France.

pound of sugar.

The contention of the isolationist U.S. Ambassador, Joseph P. Kennedy, that "to suppose the Allies have much to fight with except courage is fallacious," drew a storm of protest in Foreign Office circles—"I thought my daffodils were yellow until I met Joe Kennedy," was one abrasive reaction. Yet Air Marshal Dowding, at Fighter Command, had been equally realistic: "The Germans could lay large areas of our big towns in ruins at any time they choose to do so."

A cartoon by David Low in the London *Evening Standard* summed up the mood of the nation: a steel helmeted Tommy shaking a defiant fist across a storm-tossed Channel,

below: Reichsmarschall Hermann Goering in France.

above the caption, "VERY WELL, ALONE!"

For the first time since the Napoleonic Wars, Britons felt consciously beleaguered and they responded to the challenge with zest. As early as May 14, Anthony Eden's radio appeal for what he privately called "a broomstick army," known as the Local Defence Volunteers, had been answered with alacrity by 500,000 men. Soon to be re-christened the "Home Guard" by Churchill—and known to a later generation as "Dad's Army"—the force consisted of any man not in uniform, aged between sixteen and sixty-five, committed to a minimum ten hours a week standing

guard duty or scouting for paratroops. Overnight, as they mustered on their first parades, the England they knew was becoming a honeycomb of ghost towns, as signposts, village signs and street names came down—an idea to fox potential invaders dreamed up by the thriller writer Dennis Wheatley in a strategic memo to the War Cabinet. In reality, it baffled few more truly than the 117,000 London school children evacuated to remote villages by the Great Western Railway.

Already pillboxes, three and a half feet of solid concrete bulked as tank traps in thousands of village streets. In thousands of back gardens, the citizens had prudently installed corrugated iron shelters, six feet long and four feet deep, topped with eighteen inches of rammed earth, named after their creator, David Anderson, as an overnight haven if Goering's bombers should come.

"We were all told to plug 'Hitler is irrevocably committed to invasion'," recalls Vera Arlett, one of a team of Ministry of Information lecturers touring the south coast but on one visit to Kent Edward R. Murrow, the tall immaculate head of the CBS network in Europe, saw few overt signs of disaster. "Most of the talk," he reported, "is about this year's hop harvest, the heavy oat crops, and the need for preserving fruit and vegetables for the winter . . . ."

As always, Murrow was reporting the mood truly: in a countryside that had abruptly harked back to the era of Thomas Hardy, the British were swift to adapt. At Cadborough Farm, Rye, Sussex, the mooted invasion area for Army Group A, the farmer,

Later than many, earlier than some,/I knew the die was cast—that war must come;/That war must come. Night after night I lay/Steeling a broken heart to face the day/When he, my son— would tread the very same/Path that his father trod. When the day came/I was not steeled— not ready. Foolish, wild Words issued from my lips—'My child, my child,/Why should you die for England too? He smiled:/'Is she not worth it, if I must?' he said. John would have answered yes—but John was dead.

(from *The White Cliffs* by Alice Duer Miller)

We left Howes at his dispersal hut and walked over to where our machines were being warmed up. The voice of the controller came unhurried over the loud-speaker, telling us to take off, and in a few seconds we were running for our machines. I climbed into the cockpit of my plane and felt an empty sensation of suspense in the pit of my stomach. For one second time seemed to stand still and I stared blankly in front of me. I knew that that morning I was to kill for the first time. That I might be killed or in any way injured did not occur to me. Later, when we were losing pilots regularly, I did consider it in an abstract way when on the ground; but once in the air, never. I knew it could not happen to me. I suppose every pilot knows that, knows it cannot happen to him; even when he is taking off for the last time, when he will not return, he knows that he cannot be killed. I wondered idly what he was like, this man I would kill. Was he young, was he fat, would he die with the Fuehrer's name on his lips, or would he die alone, in that last moment conscious of himself as a man? I would never know. Then I was being strapped in, my mind automatically checking the controls, and we were off.

(from *The Last Enemy* by Richard Hillary)

John Hacking, still escorted his wife Anne, to weekly dances, but in a horse drawn cart now that petrol was short. Two miles northwest of Hawkinge airfield, surely a priority target for the Luftwaffe, Earl Knight, the tractor driver at Ladwood Farm, worked on steadily as always with the new Fordson tractor. But now a galvanised iron canopy was rigged above his head to screen him from falling shrapnel, and he steered the tractor cautiously—intent on evading the long black poles, placed to repel anticipated glider landings, that jutted from the ripening wheat.

It was a time of exodus, even so. West of Folkstone, 100,000 sheep had been evacuated from the low-lying Romney Marshes. The children had gone, too, with Mickey Mouse gas-masks for the toddlers, to make it all seem a game. All along the Kentish coast, house after house stood empty, often abandoned so hastily that beds were left unmade and ham and eggs congealed on the stoves—"I never thought I'd see sights like that in my home town," marvels Mrs Lillian Ivory, who stayed resolutely put in her own hotel, the Mecca, at Folkestone.

It was a time of waiting, too. By noon on August 7, it was nine days since a destroyer, let alone a coastal convoy, had moved in the English Channel. At his headquarters in a stuffy omnibus at Cap Blanc Nez, near Wissant, *Oberst* Johannes Fink, the newly appointed *Kanalkampfführer*, or Channel Battle Leader, was more than content. He had fulfilled his task—to win and keep air superiority over the Straits of Dover—in exactly twenty-seven days.

In vain, fighter pilots like Adolf Galland had roamed above south-east England, using height and sun as they willed it, hoping to provoke a British reaction. But none was forthcoming. Even *lockvögel*—literally decoy birds, bombers acting as bait, had produced no results. "*Schweinerei*," says Galland, in retrospect, "but still they didn't come!"

Then quite suddenly, late on the night of August 7, they did.

The British had now accepted that they must "force" the Channel passage, and accordingly, at 9 p.m., C.W.9, a 25-strong convoy of merchantmen had set out from Southend, on the Thames Estuary, bound for the wharves of Portsmouth and Southampton. Their cargo formed part of the 40,000 tons of seaborne coal and coke which fuelled southern industry each week. Their escort by night was a small flotilla of *Hunt*-class destroyers; by day, the onus of their safety would rest on Dowding's Fighter Command.

But at 1.30 a.m. on August 8, long before daylight, an E-boat flotilla found them—fast 103-foot motor torpedo boats resembling American Coast Guard Cutters. What followed was inevitable, as Captain J.H. Potts of the collier, *Betswood*, 1,350 tons, would always recall. "They ravaged it like wolves from Beachy Head to the Nab Tower."

Another master, William Henry Dawson, of the 500-ton coaster *John M.*, took up the tale: "I saw a blinding flash, followed by a heavy explosion in the starboard column of the convoy. A second later the same thing happened out in the port column. The explosions . . . rocked the ships and I could smell the cordite fumes blown over on the wind. 'What the hell's happening now?' I thought.''

At first light, Dawson knew. Convoy C.W.9 was now a convoy in name only: nothing but tiny groups of ships, scattered beyond hope of re-assembly, all the way from Dover to St. Catherine's Point, the southernmost tip of the Isle of Wight. Before 9 a.m. news of their passage reached the Cherbourg headquarters of the Luftwaffe's 8th Flying Corps, and its commander, *Generalmajor* the Baron von Richtofen. A trigger-tempered disciplinarian, and the cousin of Manfred 'The Red Baron' von Richtofen, the World War I air-ace, the Baron invariably expected 100 per cent success from each sortie—akin to that which his Stuka dive-bombers had achieved at Dunkirk. His order was peremptory: "This convoy must be wiped out."

The Stukas needed no second bidding. As the *Betswood's* Captain Potts remembered it later: "The scene changed in an instant, from a perfectly flat sea to a typhoon." Somehow, despite the maelstrom of churning water, the *Betswood* steamed on unscathed, her sole armament a single Lewis gun on her bridge, but few other merchantmen were so lucky. "Away to starboard another flight was diving down," Captain Dawson recalled. ". . . Swallowing hard, I saw them come . . . then this salvo crashed. The first one hit the water near the starboard bow, the other was a near-miss amidships . . . Down came more bombs, flinging up great columns of water nearly one hundred feet high . . . I saw one water column, green between me and the sun, smash over the forecastle head and sweep the

two gunners off their feet . . . In the middle of the party, the mate dashed into the wheelhouse, shoved the man away from the wheel, and shouted, "For God's sake, let me do *something.*"

It was now, from Hornchurch in the east to Middle Wallop in the west, that Fighter Command's six sector controllers alerted their squadrons, although one unit, Squadron-Leader John Peel's No. 145 Squadron, was already in position. At 16,000 feet above St. Catherine's Point they had sighted the Stukas streaking for the shipping at the moment John Peel, appropriately, gave the huntsman's cry, "Tally, ho!"

As if on cue, twelve hump-backed Hurricanes altered course, heading not for the shattered convoy but for the brassy ingot of the sun that swam above them. If they dived from the sun, Peel knew, the Germans' vision would be dazzled from the start.

Soon they were 18,000 feet above the water and again Peel's voice rasped through the intercom—"Come on chaps, down we go!"—and suddenly, as the Hurricanes swooped, ninety-six .303 Browning machine-guns were chattering as one, marking the first shots, many sources maintain, to be fired in the Battle of Britain.

It was the rankest injustice, reflected Captain Dawson later, that their appearance was at once hailed by his Lewis gunner above the wheelhouse: "Here come the Spitfires!" The legend of 'invincible Spitfires' would be a long time a-dying.

From the bridge of the *John M.*, Dawson now had a ringside view of "the grandest sight

So looks the pent-up lion o'er the wretch/And so he walks, insulting o'er his prey,/And so he comes, to rend his limbs asunder.

(from *Henry VI, part 3*, by William Shakespeare)

Saturday 13 July

We were at readiness all morning but nothing happened. Then as soon as we sat down to lunch we were told to take off for Martlesham. We did one patrol over the sea and up the E. coast but we saw nothing, although we were guided to where 3 bombers were meant to be. We returned about 8 and, on arriving back at Debden were instructed to do some formation flying so that photographers from "Life" could get some shots. I never felt less like formation and it wasn't really good.

(from the diary of Pilot Officer Denis H. Wissler No. 17 Squadron)

I have ever seen . . . the sky was simply full of whirling aircraft and falling flaming black streaks of crashing dive bombers . . . ." And high above the zig-zagging convoy, the pilots of 145 Squadron were equally conscious that luck was with them. Days earlier, Flight Lieutenant Roy Dutton had broken a carpal bone in his right hand, an injury so painful he could barely press the starter button. Yet twice he found himself positioned behind slow-moving Stukas, with just enough strength to press the firing button for four long seconds, time enough to see them spin like spent bullets for the sea. This was Dutton's all-too-brief taste of battle: for six months after that his right hand was encased in plaster.

Even a novice like nineteen-year-old James Storrar, now a Cheshire veterinarian,

felt himself a world-beater; opening fire on a Stuka, he barely realised that he had hit it until he saw the rear machine-gun tilting skywards and the gunner lolling dead. Convinced that they had knocked down 21 German planes single-handed, the squadron that night threw an all-ranks party to end them all—as Storrar recalled it, "The floor literally swam in beer." With quiet satisfaction, John Peel inscribed one swastika in his log-book. The old World War One adage, "Beware of the Hun in the sun," had once again been proven true; the battle seemed almost over.

But scores of Dowding's pilots, on August 8, had never seen "the Hun in the sun." The canny tactics of 145 Squadron had quite eluded them. Flying Officer Edward Hogg, of 151 Squadron, still remembers this day;

Luftwaffe ground crewmen in France keeping score on the tail fin of a JU88 bomber.

weaving his Spitfire above the foundering convoy, he had to break from combat time and again without firing a shot. However high he climbed, there were always ME 109s still higher—and all the time the sun struck at his eyes like white fire.

To most pilots aloft, it seemed that the Luftwaffe held the sky. And even at mid-afternoon, von Richtofen's third and last sortie, an umbrella of planes filling the sky all the way to Cherbourg, struck Pilot Officer Frank Carey, of 43 Squadron, as "a raid so terrible and inexorable it was like trying to stop a steam roller." The simile was valid. Within minutes, with two pilots wounded, and two seriously injured, 43 Squadron was out of the combat.

In retrospect, the lesson was plain. Every squadron over southern England had been scrambled too late and too low. As yet, few Sector Controllers realised that height, above all, was what the squadrons needed—and while the Germans were timing each sortie to strike with the sun behind them, the Sector Ops Rooms did not even plot the position of the sun on their boards.

Thus Pilot Officer D.H. 'Nobby' Clarke, a Coastal Command pilot surveying the wreckage of C.W.9 from an ROC target-towing plane above the Isle of Wight, thought in terms of a total Luftwaffe victory: "The wreckage stretched in every direction . . . tables, chairs, timber, hatches, spars . . . coke-vast rafts of it: grey-black against the dark blue of the sea . . . patches of oil, too, silver-grey in the sun . . .," and ships, "empty shells of red-glowing coal."

This was not an estimate shared by *Hauptmann* Werner Andres, an ME 109 pilot of *Major* Max Ibel's 27th Fighter Group, a hapless casualty of von Richtofen's last sortie. Swimming steadily in the choppy waters, 30 miles north-west of Cherbourg, Andres had never even seen the plane that had hit him—but the equation of the day's battle was to him as chilling as the icy Channel.

To be sure, 300 planes—the 8th Flying Corps, plus Ibel's fighters—had crippled or sunk twenty-two merchant ships, 70,000 tons of shipping, but all this had been achieved at a loss of thirteen Luftwaffe planes. A battle timed to last four days now loomed as a deadly war of attrition, until each side groped bloodily to a standstill.

At HQ Fighter Command, pacing his high Georgian office facing south towards the spire of Harrow Church, Air Chief Marshal Sir Hugh Dowding knew the same sense of perturbation. The losses of August 8—nineteen planes—was the highest that Fighter Command had ever been called upon to bear.

So if Goering, newly appointed Reichsmarshall, decided to step up the pressure, what could Dowding do? Exactly twenty-three squadrons existed to defend southern England, but if their losses reached a constant drain of twenty aeroplanes a day, could Beaverbrook's M.A.P. keep pace? A *Collier's* magazine article by the Anglophile American war correspondent, Quentin Reynolds, proclaimed, "It's still Churchill's Channel"—but was it?

For thousands the battle had barely started, and Dowding could not know.

Dr. Carrot

51

HITTING THE
RADAR CHAIN

HAUPTMANN Walter Rubensdörffer was a deeply preoccupied man on the morning of Tuesday August 12. As his colleague, *Oberleutnant* Otto Hintze, would later recall, Rubensdörffer, a tall dynamic Swiss, aged thirty, with an infectious sense of humour, was in no mood for small talk as he sipped his breakfast coffee at Calais-Marck airfield. That morning, Rubensdörffer's 28-strong unit, Erprobungsgruppe (Test Group) 210 had been assigned to what most pilots knew could be the battle's most crucial mission.

A onetime Stuka pilot, Rubensdörffer had long nurtured the theory that fighters—whether ME 109s or ME 110s—were not only capable of carrying bombs but of hitting their targets. Faced with the profound scepticism of most Luftwaffe chiefs—foremost among them *Generalfeldmarschall* Albert Kesselring, Chief of *Luftflotte Two* Rubensdörffer had still persisted. At Rechlin, on the Baltic, he and his group of hand-picked pilots, had spent long weeks of trial and error and finally seen their perseverance pay off.

As recently as yesterday, Rubensdörffer's mixed force of 109s and 110s had swooped on a convoy code-named 'Booty', fifteen miles south-east of Harwich, to attract only sporadic ack-ack: fighter planes, the British had plainly reasoned, could do little harm to shipping. Yet Test Group 210 had scored mortal hits on two large freighters with 250-kilo bombs, then once again, engaged by 'Sailor' Malan's 74 Squadron from Hornchurch, resumed their role as fighters. The element of surprise had been all; two of Malan's pilots did not return.

Do not believe the tale the milkman tells;/No troops have mutinied at Potters Bar./Nor are there submarines at Tunbridge Wells./The B.B.C. will warn us when there are.

(—A. P. Herbert, May, 1940)

left: A standard 360' Chain Home transmitter tower of the British Radio Direction Finding (radar) system.

53

right: The plot table at HQ No. 11 Group, Uxbridge; *below:* a page from an Uxbridge controller's notebook.

SECTOR CONTROLLED INTERCEPTION.

Requirements are :—

1. An adequate bomber track

2. An estimate of time lag.

3. Quick, broad vectors.

The aim is to bring the Fighter ahead of the Bomber on the Bombers track.

Time lag varies enormously. From 30 secs on a GCI plot to 5 mins on Army DF.

Filter lag is about 2-3 mins (roughly 1½-2 squares)

The simplest Interception is for Fighter and Bomber to converge along two equal sides of an Isosceles △. thus :—

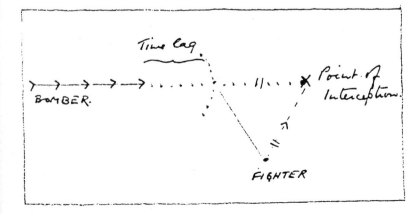

Ironically, Test Group 210 was now Kesselring's most cherished unit; the man nicknamed "Smiling Al" was prone to arrive on unofficial visits with a jeroboam of champagne. And that morning Kesselring's hopes rode exceedingly high, for Test Group 210 were charged to knock out four key radar stations—then known as R.D.F. (radio direction finding) stations—on the Kent and Sussex coasts. (A fifth, at Ventnor, on the Isle of Wight, had been assigned to fifteen JU88s).

Set down amid the apple orchards and the flat salt marshes that girdled the south coast, the brick-built stations, in tightly-guarded six-acre sites, were a mystery to all except the screened personnel who lived and worked there. Isolated units in a chain of 20 stations, that stretched from the Shetlands to the Isle of Wight, they were at all times markedly conspicuous through their sinister latticeworks of towers, steel towers rising 350 feet for the transmission aerials, wooden towers 240 feet high for the receivers. Already the sites had prompted a formidable crop of rumours. Along the coast, many countrymen swore that they were geared to cut out a hostile aircraft's engine at one flick of a switch.

The truth, if more prosaic, spelt equal danger to the Luftwaffe. Once the echo of an approaching aircraft showed as a V-shaped blip of light on the glass screen in the station's Receiver Block, the news passed within 40 seconds along a formidable chain of command: by landline from the detector station to the Filter Room of Fighter Command, 42 feet below ground at Stanmore Middlesex, to the Ops Room next door, known mysteriously as

'Room 24', from thence to the Ops Rooms of No. 10, 11 and 12 Groups, and on to such sector stations as North Weald, Biggin Hill, Kenley and Middle Wallop.

The entire labyrinthine structure of "Stuffy" Dowding's Fighter Command stood or fell by this high-pressure plotting, which from the first blip on a radar screen to a squadron's frantic "scramble" had a time-lapse of exactly six minutes.

At 9 a.m. on August 12, no one was later to recall any discernible sense of tension. In Fighter Command's Filter Room, the WAAF plotters, alerted through telephone headsets plugged into jack sockets in the table's edge, were readying their magnetic 'rakes' to position counters, coloured red, yellow and blue, representing Luftwaffe formations; every five minutes these would be changed, enabling the controller to see the 'age' of a plot. The atmosphere was much the same in that morning's target stations: Pevensey, hard by Eastbourne, Dover, Dunkirk, near Canterbury, and Rye, close to the old Kentish seaport.

Corporal Daphne Griffiths, one of the morning watch of four at Rye, who had just taken over the screen in the flimsy wooden Ops hut, was already, at nineteen, a veteran of the Receiver Block. Like all of her intake at Bawdsey Manor, on the Suffolk coast, Daphne had toiled through the long eight hour watches, coped with time checks, plotted "friendlies" up the Channel and already—she had to admit it—thought of Rye as 'home'.

As they settled to their tasks that morning, wholly absorbed in a system that each of them took entirely for granted, few realised that five years back, when most were teen-agers, no such system had even existed.

*

On another historic Tuesday—February 26, 1935—four men were anxiously scanning the sky from a hummocky pasture at Weedon, Northamptonshire, four miles from the powerful Daventry radio transmitter which the B.B.C. had erected in 1925. They were awaiting what one Fighter Command expert was later to call "the most critically-watched aircraft in the history of British aviation."

Heading the party was Robert (later Sir Robert) Watson-Watt, a plump—"tubby if you want to be unkind"—42-year-old Scot, Chief of the National Physical Laboratory's Radio Research Station at Slough, Buckinghamshire. Together with his junior scientific officer, Arnold 'Skip' Wilkins, lean and laconic, their driver, Mr Dyer, and Albert P. Rowe, of the Air Ministry's Directorate of Scientific Research, Watson-Watt was on time for a rendezvous with a bomber.

The aircraft they awaited, a lumbering Heyford night bomber laid on by the Royal Aircraft Establishment at Farnborough, had been briefed to fly at 6,000 feet along a fixed track of twenty miles, up and down the Daventry fifty-metre beam. To the pilot, Squadron Leader Bobbie Blucke, it was a totally boring assignment; he assumed, as he later allowed, it was "some B.B.C. job."

When the first drone of the Heyford's engines became audible, the men, surprisingly, abandoned their vigil. All four hastily repaired inside a biscuit-coloured Morris caravan, to fix their eyes on the screen of a cathode-ray oscillograph, much like an ordinary television set. In the very centre of the screen, a bright green spot was glowing.

Steadily, the Heyford droned nearer. With equal steadiness, the green spot grew to an inch in length, then, as the engine-throb receded, shrank once more. A moment passed, then Watson-Watt broke the silence. "Britain," he said, "has become an island once more."

The demonstration, suggested by the prudent Air Vice Marshal Sir Hugh Dowding, then Air Member for Research and Development, had pointed the way to the brightest of futures: a £10,000 Treasury subsidy.

For fully three years, Britain's nakedness in the event of an air war had been a cause of grave concern to the prescient few. As far back as November, 1932, a former and future Prime Minister, Stanley Baldwin, had gloomily written off Britain's chances of survival: "The bomber will always get through." On February 7, 1934, the Member for Epping, the Rt. Hon. Winston Churchill, although a loner in the political wilderness, had yet conjured up to the House of Commons, a vision of "the crash of bombs exploding in London . . . the cataracts of masonry and fire and smoke," concluding, "We are vulnerable as we have never been before." Four months later, a search by Albert Rowe of the Air Ministry's dusty files revealed only fifty-six that covered air defence.

"Unless science evolves some new method of aiding our defence," he warned his

Monday 29 July

Up at 4:30 and forward to Martlesham Heath. I was with F/L Bayne and F/O B-Wilson and after one uneventful patrol we met a HE111 which was being half-heartedly attacked by Spitfires. We made a head on attack and then an astern attack. Pieces and oil coming out in all directions. The E/A slowly went down to the water. I thought it was trying to get away low down and made another head on attack. This time it went into the water.

(from the diary of Pilot Officer Denis H. Wissler No. 17 Squadron)

The BOOK of the W·A·A·F

1/3

chief, Harry Wimperis, "we are likely to lose the next war if it starts within ten years."

Wimperis, an urbane Scot, now turned to his old friend and fellow-Scot, Watson-Watt: was a Death Ray, then unknown outside the B-movie world of Boris Karloff, in any way feasible? The problem, passed for evaluation to Arnold Wilkins, came up against a blank wall: no aircraft would linger long enough in the most intense beam of radio energy the scientists could produce to knock out its engine. "Well," Watson-Watt mused, "I wonder what we can do to help them."

Although Watson-Watt was later hailed as "the Father of British Radar," Wilkins, his chief always claimed, was "the Mother." It was Wilkins who had recalled how Post Office engineers so often complained that radio reception was disturbed when aircraft flew close to their receivers.

Then might not an aircraft's electromagnetic energy be visually depicted by use of the cathode-ray apparatus? The pathway to Weedon had been charted.

Until this moment, Britain's resources had been primitive in the extreme. The sole detector system then centred on the Romney Mirror, a concave concrete block 200 feet long and 25 feet high, facing across the Channel on Romney Marsh, in Kent. Given ideal conditions, the microphones dotted along its length could give rough bearings of an aircraft eight miles distant, but height and range were outside the Mirror's scope. Motor cars, boats, flights of birds, could make even bearings dubious. The Mirror's one back-up system was the 30,000 members of the Observer Corps—

58

left: The W.A.A.F.'s guide; *above:* an Operations room telephone, believed to have been used at Debden during the Battle of Britain.

duly rechristened the Royal Observer Corps by 1941—who, equipped with binoculars, armbands and helmets, could spot planes only after they had crossed over the coast line, an arrangement which Churchill derided as 'Early Stone Age'.

After Weedon, events moved swiftly. On May 13, 1935, an R.D.F. experimental unit, under Watson-Watt, was set up on the Suffolk coast at Orfordness, equipped with a 75-foot radio aerial. By September, Orfordness was tracking aircraft 58 miles away. Urged on by Wimperis, the Air Ministry invested £24,000 in acquiring nearby Bawdsey Manor from Sir Cuthbert Quilter, a telephone pioneer, whose family motto, appropriately, was FIRST IN THE FIELD. Bawdsey was now the focal point of a £100,000 project, the world's first radar station, soon capable of locating aircraft at a range of 150 miles, at heights of up to 30,000 feet.

It was, Wimperis noted in a memo to Dowding, a system "which will be independent of mist, cloud, fog or nightfall . . . at the same time . . . vastly more accurate than present methods."

By 1937, Bawdsey had become a magnet, attracting such scientific luminaries as Sir Henry Tizard, Chairman of the Committee for the Scientific Survey of Air Defence, Albert Rowe, who took over from Watson-Watt in 1938, and Professor Patrick Blackett, a Nobel Prize winner. Under their surveillance, the first of the Air Ministry Experimental Stations (AMES)—later called Chain Home Stations—were rising at 25-mile intervals along the coastline of Britain: Bawdsey itself by May 1937, three months after the first training school for radar ops was opened, Dover by July of that year, Canewdon, in Essex, by August. A dedicated community of 50 physicists, who dispensed with nine-to-five routines, the 'Bawdsey Soviets' talked radar from breakfast to bedtime, evolving the streamlined plotting techniques that were to become known as 'the Tizzy Angle'.

Inevitably, from March 1935 on, with the new Luftwaffe a reality, the Germans grew curious—and none more so than *General* Wolfgang Martini, Commanding General of German Signals and Radar. In May, 1939, and again in August, Martini reactivated the giant airship LG 127 *Graf Zeppelin*, despatching her across the North Sea to Bawdsey. From Good Friday, 1939, the day that Mussolini invaded Albania, the Chain Home link had begun a twenty-four hour watch that would not cease until war's end—yet with the *Zeppelin's* radio receivers emitting nothing but static, 'the Tizzy Angle' remained an unplumbed mystery.

Were those tall towers the eyes of The Few? Their ears? Martini didn't know—but before the Luftwaffe launched *Adler Angriff*, the Attack of the Eagles, on August 13, a prelude to the seaborne invasion, Rubensdörffer's task was to neutralise them for good and all.

*

At 9.25 a.m. on August 12, Daphne Griffiths, in the Receiver Block at Rye, was suddenly alerted. A V-shaped blip of light had registered off northern France. Promptly she

O love, they die in yon rich sky,/they faint on hill or field or river;/Our echoes roll from soul to soul,/And grow for ever and for ever./Blow, bugle, blow, set the wild echoes flying,/And answer, echoes, answer, dying, dying, dying.

(from *The Splendour Falls* by Alfred, Lord Tennyson)

reported, "Hello, Stanmore, I've a new track at 30 miles. Only three aircraft—I'll give you a plot." Abruptly, the thought crossed her mind: were other stations plotting the same planes? But the Filter Room reassured her; she alone had registered them. Could they please have a height?

Although height was one of the teething-troubles many radar operators had yet to master—most pilots added an extra 5,000 feet to their estimates to avoid being 'bounced'—Daphne reported confidently, "Height, 18,000." She noted, too, that the range was fast decreasing; if the planes contin-

ued on course, they would pass directly over-head. "Stanmore," she queried, "is this track still unidentified?" The Filter Room seemed unperturbed. The plot had been marked with an X, signifying doubtful, to be watched and investigated further.

As the steep chalk cliffs of Dover loomed ahead, *Hauptmann* Walter Rubensdörffer knew no doubts whatsoever; visibility over the Straits was good, and all were geared for action. "*Achtung*, No 3 Staffel," he signalled into his microphone, "Dismissed for special mission. Good hunting!" Promptly *Oberleut-nant* Otto Hintze and his section swung east

AVM Keith Park controlled No. 11 Group during the Battle of Britain from this underground Ops room at Uxbridge. This photo was made on November 11, 1942.

Think in the morning. Act in the noon. Eat in the evenings. Sleep/in the night.

(from *Proverbs of Hell* by William Blake)

towards Dover. *Oberleutnant* Martin Lutz and his men streaked for Pevensey. Rubensdörffer himself set course for Dunkirk, near Canterbury. The towering aerials at Rye were thus the target for *Oberleutnant* Wilhelm Roessiger.

In Rye's Receiver Block, the station adjutant, Flying Officer Smith, now recalled that the Ops hut was protected only by a small rampart of sandbags. "I think it would be a

good idea," he told Corporal Sydney Hempson, the NCO in charge, "if we had our tin hats." Simultaneously, the voice of Troop Sergeant Major Johnny Mason, whose Bofors guns defended the site, seemed to explode in their headsets: "Three dive bombers coming out of the sun—duck!"

Mindful that this was the Glorious Twelfth, Assistant Section Officer Violet Hime,

A young pilot of
Erprobungsgruppe 210
(Experimental) relaxing
with his mascot in France,
1940; *left:* derelict
remains on the Chain
Home R.D.F. site above
Ventnor, Isle of Wight;
inset: a bomb crater on
the Isle of Wight, as seen
in 1988.

the WAAF administrative officer, muttered a dry aside, "They've mistaken us for grouse."

Still glued to her set, Daphne Griffiths heard a faint faraway voice in her headphones, barely audible above the snarling whine of Roessiger's engines: "Rye, what's happening? Why don't you answer me?" Still mortified that her plot had been relegated to an 'X', Daphne replied quite coldly, "Your 'X' raid is bombing *us*, Stanmore, and it's no wonder you can't hear me, we can't hear ourselves either!"

It seemed at first that Rubensdörffer's split-second timing had paid off. At Rye, the Ops hut shuddered convulsively; glass and wooden shutters toppled; chunks of chalk were blasted 400 feet high to bespatter the steel aerials. Beneath the table, Daphne and her fellow-plotters, Helen McCormick and Brenda Hackett, watched chairs and tables spiralling above them like a juggler's fast-flying balls, and the same confusion prevailed everywhere. At Pevensey, tons of gravel swamped the office of Flight Lieutenant Marcus Scroggie, the C.O., only minutes after he had left it. At Dunkirk, one Rubensdörffer bomb literally shifted the concrete transmitter block by inches; at Dover, one of Hintze's bombs sheared past the recumbent operators to bury itself beneath the sick quarters.

Yet in all instances, although the tall towers swayed palpably, they remained intact.

At Ventnor, on the Isle of Wight, it was a different story. Pounded by 15 Junkers 88 dive bombers, the station was swept by a curtain of fire, and the Fire Brigade, pumping up water through 560 yards, were barely able to

cope. All this was narrated to Fighter Command's Filter Room in a frenzied running commentary from an NCO on site, who lamented repeatedly that a WAAF named "Blondie" was missing. This was so stirring to Pilot Officer Robert Wright, Dowding's personal assistant and a pre-war screenplay writer that he shattered the Filter Room's cathedral calm by seizing a microphone and yelling, "Well, where are the rest of you?"

At once a disdainful colleague reproved him, "Don't get *too* Hollywood," so infuriating Wright he forgot whose side he was on. "You English make me sick," he blazed back.

On the coast there was less excitement; most of the personnel were too stunned to react. At Rye, Violet Hime, groping shakily from the floor of the Ops hut, her eyes and nostrils choked with grit, found Corporal June Alderson, a striking blonde, diffidently profering a cigarette. "I'll light it for you, too, ma'am," she promised, "if my hand isn't shaking too much."

When Violet Hime saw no trace of a tremor in the Corporal's hand, she knew a moment of pure triumph. Some days earlier, the camp's flight sergeant had enquired casually how soon RAF operators would be replacing the WAAF; if an invasion was imminent, a clutch of hysterical airwomen would badly affect morale. Within hours of the raid—which delivered forty bombs on Rye in exactly four minutes—he was back to offer abject apologies: "We're proud to have the WAAF on the station with us."

At Calais-Marck airfield, Rubensdörffer and his team were quietly exultant; every squadron had scored triumphantly. Pevensey was already reported silent; at Rye, Roessiger had accurately reported ten hits, not realising that he had demolished ten empty barracks and that the main installations had gone un-scathed. By contrast, *General* Wolfgang Martini was a bitterly disappointed man. By mid-afternoon every station except Ventnor, inoperative for the next eleven days, was reported back on the air, operating with stand-

The Junkers JU87 assembly line.

65

O, it's a snug little island!/A right little, tight little island!

(The Snug Little Island by Thomas Dibdin)

by diesels. It now seemed unlikely that the radar stations could be silenced for more than a few hours at a time, and three days later, Goering made the same point to his *Luftflotte* commanders at Karinhall. "It is doubtful whether there is any point in continuing the attacks on radar sites," he summed up, "in view of the fact that not one of them attacked has so far been put out of operation."

In fact, only two more attacks were ever launched: at Rye once more, on August 15, as well as Dover and Foreness, and at Poling, on August 18, when 90 bombs so badly damaged the station that a mobile unit was brought in to fill the gap.

Even though the commanders-in-chief shrugged off this setback, the rank-and-file were far from content. As the then *Major* Adolf Galland, commanding JG 26, was to complain, "We had no fighter control at that time, and no way of knowing what the British were doing with their forces as each battle

progressed." Radar, he grumbled, seemed to give the British "superbinoculars" that could see across the Channel.

With this verdict, "Stuffy" Dowding fully and wholeheartedly concurred. "Where would we have been without R.D.F. and all that went with it?" he asked once, "We could never have maintained the vast number of standing patrols that would have been necessary if we had not had that magic sight." Given that Dowding began the Battle in August with exactly 708 serviceable aircraft and 1434 battle-worthy pilots—half the complement of an average post-war airline—that conclusion was inescapable.

Almost twenty years after the Battle, in July, 1959, the Duchess of Gloucester was to unveil a plaque in Bawdsey's Officers Mess that paid final tribute to those pioneering days. It was, perhaps inevitably, a masterpiece of British understatement.

IN THE YEAR 1936 AT BAWDSEY MANOR
ROBERT WATSON-WATT
AND HIS TEAM OF SCIENTISTS
DEVELOPED THE FIRST AIR DEFENCE
RADAR WARNING STATION
THE RESULTS ACHIEVED BY THESE
PIONEERS PLAYED A VITAL PART IN
THE SUCCESSFUL OUTCOME OF THE
BATTLE OF BRITAIN IN 1940

What have I done for you,/England, my England?/What is there I would not do,/England, my own?

(*England, My England* by W. E. Henley)

far left: At Pevensey Castle, Sussex, an unusual example of field defence pillbox design; *left:* one of the few remaining structures at the Pevensey Chain Home site, as photographed in 1988.

Assistant Section Officer Edith Heap of the Women's Auxiliary Air Force. She joined the W.A.A.F. in 1939 as an M.T. driver, later became a plotter and, finally, an intelligence officer debriefing bomber crews. Her fiance, Pilot Officer Denis H. Wissler, one of The Few, was killed in action on November 11, 1940. Extracts from the diary he kept during that year appear throughout this book.

THE WOMEN'S AUXILIARY AIR FORCE

The Women's Auxiliary Air Force was formed on June 28th, 1939, by Royal Warrant. At the outbreak of the Second World War on the 3rd, September, 1939, there were less than 2,000 women on strength. Its object was to replace R.A.F. men, where practicable, freeing them for other active service.

When war was declared, an appeal for recruits for the W.A.A.F. was broadcast by the BBC, and from all walks of life hundreds of women immediately volunteered. But to begin with, the W.A.A.F.s had very little uniform or

equipment, inadequate accommodation, little proper training, and no clear rules or traditions of their own. They had to contend with difficult, makeshift conditions during the severe first winter of the war, as well as with prejudice from some of the R.A.F. who felt that women had no part to play in the Service, and that they would panic under bombardment.

The first recruits were given a choice of only five trades, as Cooks, Drivers MT, Equipment Assistants, Clerks or Orderlies. But as the war progressed and the Service grew, this choice increased, until by 1943 there were twenty-two officer branches and seventy-five trades, with nearly 182,000 women employed. Without this participation by the W.A.A.F., the R.A.F. would have required 150,000 more men.

Working side by side with the R.A.F. at home and overseas, throughout the war, the W.A.A.F. won many honours and awards, including six Military Medals for "Gallantry in the face of the enemy," and thousands of "Mentioned in Despatches."

The great majority, however, worked with no reward. Their hours were long, conditions sometimes harsh, their life dull and their duties unglamourous, whilst their work could be both dirty and dangerous.

They earned the full admiration and gratitude of the R.A.F. And the Air Council stated: "It is the view of the Air Council that an essential operational factor of the R.A.F. would be missing if there was no W.A.A.F."

And a Group Captain in command of the Fighter Station during the Battle of Britain, declared: "I had cause to thank goodness that this country could produce such a race of women as the W.A.A.F. on my Station."

IN A SENSE, the raid was symbolic of the Luftwaffe's entire conduct of the Battle.

The timing was perfect—7.02 a.m. on Tuesday August 13—and caught everyone unawares, as a good raid should. "Raid 45 is bombing Eastchurch drome," intoned the Bromley Observer Corps' Controller, Brian Binyon, at the moment that fifty bomb-aimers of Bomber Group 2 bent to the five complex readings of their sights. Across the airfield, reactions were traumatic, which again was exemplary. In the N.C.O's quarters, Sergeant Reginald Gretton, of No. 266 Squadron, a devotee of the mess' shepherd's pie, cried out shrilly: "They're dropping bombs. They're dropping bombs on *us*!" Eastchurch, a haven of good home cooking, was suddenly and unforgivably in the front line. The C.O., Group Captain Frank Hopps, was more prosaic. "My God," he thought, "this station's worth millions—some accountant's got a job to do writing off this lot."

There was formidable devastation—precisely what *Oberst* Johannes Fink, the bomber commander, would have wished. Five Bristol Blenheim night fighters were written off, plus the twelve Spitfires of No. 266 Squadron, which were on overnight transit to Hornchurch. The Operations Block was untenable, all electricity and telephone lines had been severed, and vital petrol supplies destroyed. Yet Sergeant Gretton's surprise was wholly legitimate. Eastchurch was a Coastal Command Station, whose patrols kept watch for German naval raiders over the North Sea. It was in no way part of the Fighter Command network that must be neutralised prior to

Across the fields of yesterday/He sometimes comes to me,/A little lad just back from play—The lad I used to be.

(from *Sometimes* by T. S. Jones)

Though not a part of the Battle of Britain, this watch office at Tangmere presents a highly evocative image from the war years. *below:* Flt. Lt. Richard Reynell.

71

Certainly it was typical of our English weather that in a normal summer it is quite impossible to get fine weather for one's holidays, and yet in war time, when every fine day simply plays into the hands of the German bombers, we had week after week of cloudless blue skies.

(—Flight-Lieutenant D. M. Crook, D.F.C.)

Fortune favors the bold.

(—Virgil, Aeneid, X)

"Operation Sea-Lion."

Later, that same day, the Luftwaffe scored again—one of the few occasions in the Battle where the overrated Stuka dive-bombers triumphed. At 4 p.m., the teabreak, eighty-six of them achieved total surprise at Detling airfield near Maidstone, Kent, wrecking the runway, torching the hangars, demolishing the ops block, destroying twenty aircraft on the ground and claiming fifty lives—so bloodily that a local undertaker, Wallace Beale, needed only the five-foot coffins reserved for unidentified remains. For almost a day, Detling was non-operational, but this, too, was a Coastal Command airfield,

where Dowding's writ did not run.

Yet one day earlier at Manston, Kent, Fighter Command's 530-acre forward base, codenamed Charlie Three, the bomb-laden ME 109s and ME 110s of Hauptmann Rubensdörffer's Test Group 210, had achieved a victory—more decisive by far than the inconclusive sortie against the radar stations. As Rubensdörffer's pilots peeled off in their dive, the Spitfires of No. 65 Squadron, caught at the second of take-off, were powerless to act, taxiing blindly through clouds of choking smoke. Overhead, Flight Lieutenant Al Deere, on that day leading No. 54 Squadron, was equally nonplussed by "a cloud like white

Typical Fighter Command Sector Station plan, 1940. *right:* Pilot Officer J.G.P. Millard of No. 1 (R.A.F.) Sq. *below:* Pilot Officer C.H. MacFie of Nos. 616 and 611 Squadrons.

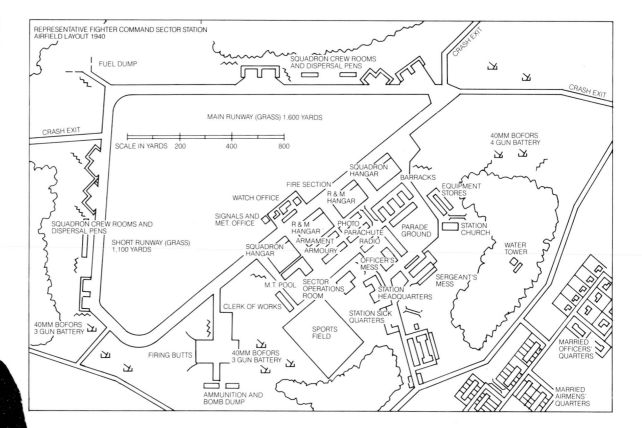

REPRESENTATIVE FIGHTER COMMAND SECTOR STATION AIRFIELD LAYOUT 1940

pumice rising over the drome . . . it was like a shroud over everything." Not realising that it was chalk dust swirling from more than 100 craters, Deere thought that Manston was on fire. Flying Officer Duncan Smith, of No. 600 Squadron, returning from leave in an old Tiger Moth biplane, was also flummoxed as he circled the drome, pondering, "Who's been spreading fertiliser?"

An all-grass field, lacking runways, Manston was in many ways an anachronism, a base dating back to 1916, when Germany's frontier had been the Rhine. Manned by a largely civilian staff, who kept strictly peacetime hours, Manston was still a station where things were done by the book: hard-pressed mechanics seeking a spanner, remembers Flight Sergeant John Wright, of 600 Squadron, "had to produce the right form at Main Stores—or else." The pilots of 32 Squadron, had similarly bitter memories. On one occasion, refused transport to the mess because they lacked a form 658, they had commandeered a tractor at gun point—only to find that the chef had gone home and locked up the food. "The station was deeply resentful when I shot the lock off the larder," relates Squadron Leader John Worrall, "but we ate."

Thus, at Manston, not surprisingly, nerves broke early and stayed broken; the civilian stance was all too infectious. On August 12, the airfield was at once a thundering horde of blue-clad men seeking shelter, bound for the deep chalk caves that wound like catacombs beneath the drome. Here hundreds, despite their officers' exhortations, were to stay for days on end, contracting out of the battle for the duration.

Attacks like these made total sense to fighter commanders like Adolf Galland. "The enemy air force must be wiped out while still grounded," he would emphasise, following the tenet of the Italian General Giulio Douhet, the bombers' champion, for what Galland envisaged was the clinical elimination, one by one, of Fighter Command's airfields. But soon it was plain that the Luftwaffe's Abteilung 5, the intelligence arm, directed by a mere major, Josef 'Beppo' Schmid, made no distinction between Fighter Command's airfields and others in southern England. Nor had Schmid, a non-operational officer who spoke no foreign language, had any liaison with General Wenniger, Germany's air attaché in London until the spring of 1939.

Were the radar stations vital or were they not? Which of Fighter Command's airfields most merited attack, and when attacking them, which targets mattered most—the hangars and buildings or planes on the ground? None of these questions had been adequately studied or thought through by Schmid and his staff.

Another forward base, Hawkinge, inland from Folkestone, was so scientifically pounded by Junkers 88 bombers on August 12 that it closed down for the rest of the day. Yet on August 15, when another attack, this time by Stukas, put Hawkinge out of action for two more days, other mass attacks were directed at secondary targets: once more at Eastchurch, and at the Short Brothers Aircraft Factory at Rochester, Kent, whose final assembly line was producing not fighters but

Friday 16 August

I did a lot of flying today 4.30 hours in all, and am I tired. We had two squadron flaps which came to nothing. Just as I was writing the above . . . I heard a Hun over head and two bombs dropped in Ipswich direction. I hope to get 48 hours leave tomorrow, and I haven't phoned home this week yet. We have now been taken off convoy patrols and are essentially a flap squadron. We hadn't heard this for more than a minute when the air raid siren went.

(from the diary of Pilot Officer Denis H. Wissler No. 17 Squadron)

73

top left: A crumbling North Weald hangar in 1986; *top right:* scars of bomb blast fragments still evident on these hangar doors at North Weald; *right:* the Tangmere station sign, now part of the Tangmere Military Aviation Museum.

top: A view across the long derelict aviation fuel dump at Hawkinge; *far left:* at North Weald; *left:* A Debden hangar survives in 1988.

75

right: In an image recorded by the brilliant aviation photographer Charles E. Brown at Tangmere in July, 1940, Squadron Leader Max Aitken is seen at left (wearing a Mae West), and, at far right, Flight Lieutenant Willie Rhodes-Moorehouse, in white overalls, as their Hurricanes are being refuelled and rearmed; *below:* Pilot Officer Noel Agazarian of No. 609 Squadron.

Britain's first four-engined bomber, the then massive Stirling.

Within this timespan, the naval air stations at Gosport, Ford and Lee-on-Solent were attacked as if the fate of Fighter Command depended on them.

Had the Luftwaffe struck at every Fighter Command base as consistently as at Manston, 'Sea-Lion' might have been closer to fruition. On August 18, two squadrons of Test Group 210 harassed them yet again, though this time an unexpected resistance greeted the invaders; angered by the craven conduct of those skulking below ground, the officers and men of No. 600 Squadron had been working overtime. A Bristol Blenheim night fighter squadron, grounded by day, they had banded together, regardless of rank, to fill the gap—contriving such primitive armament as 'The Sheep Dipper', a spare set of Browning machine guns rigged on a pole, and 'The Armadillo', a truck converted with concrete facings to a rudimentary armoured car with a machine-gun fixed amidships. Now, as sixteen ME 110s launched the second all-out attack, a withering curtain of fire arose to meet them.

Crouched on an improvised fire-step of trestles, Pilot Officer Henry Jacobs was one of six squadron air gunners determined to hit back against the Germans. As the swooping 110s shrank to slim pencils in their gun sights, fire from 'The Sheep Dipper's' dismantled Brownings went hammering up the sloping roof of No. 600 Squadron's crew-room. Then, as the 500-pounders came whistling, blast tore all six gunners from the trestle in a blasphemous tangle of arms and legs.

76

What though the field be lost?/All is not lost; th' unconquerable will,/And study of revenge, immortal hate,/And courage never to submit or yield.

(*Paradise Lost*, Milton)

right: This low retaining wall remains today between two fighter blast pens at Exeter airport; a watch office at Stapleford Tawney; *below:* the Officer's mess at R.A.F. Kenley.

It was a short-lived resistance, even so; within six days, morale at Manston was at lowest ebb. To the pilots of No. 266 Squadron, operational flights from Charlie Three spelt frustration from the first; the first devastating Eastchurch raid had cost them their Mae Wests and parachutes, and at Manston no storeman had come on duty to replace them. One flight commander, Flight Lieutenant Dennis Armitage, spent a murky half-hour groping through the labyrinth of caves, vainly seeking the station electrician he had entrusted to do a job. Finally, emerging into the strong sunlight, Armitage completed the job himself.

Across 500 deserted acres every officer could tell the same story. At 600 Squadron's dispersal, Pilot Officer Jacobs found it hard to repress his laughter; the station's accounts officer had wandered disconsolately by yet again, weighed down by two bags of silver. Although it was Sunday, he sought in vain enough airmen above ground to organise a pay parade.

By August 18, four all-out raids had ensured that few buildings were even habitable. With all water cut off, men shaved—if they shaved at all—at the pre-war swimming pool. Many were overwrought to the point of collapse. Only in the nick of time did Squadron Leader James Leathart, of No. 54 Squadron, stop a technical officer firing blind down a shelter to flush out the deserters, and Manston's Chaplain, the Reverend Cecil King, acted as promptly. When an officer burst into the mess, brandishing a revolver, threatening to finish off himself and every man present, King led him gently from the room, keeping

top: The blast wall entrance to the Sector F Operations block still standing at Debden; *below:* in 1988, the Croydon airport terminal building. *below:* Flying Officer A.R. Edge of No. 609 Squadron.

So we must part, my body, you and I/Who've spent so many pleasant years together./'Tis sorry work to lose your company/Who clove to me so close.

(from *Any Soul To Any Body* by Cosmo Monkhouse)

79

up an anodyne flow of pleasantries until the man broke down, surrendering his gun.

By now the end was very near. "Manston was literally taken from us piece by piece," recalls Henry Jacobs bitterly, for it had needed more than the brave archaic armament of No. 600 Squadron to stop the Luftwaffe. On August 18, when more ME 110s burst from the sun, Flying Officer David Clackson and six others dived beneath the mess billiard table, emerging to find that bullets had sheared the baize from the slate, as cleanly as a knife might have done. All of them believed then that the Germans had meant to do it, and were engulfed with a sense of powerlessness.

There were more vital airfields for the Luftwaffe to tackle—but again on the haphazard basis of a chance spin of the coin. At lunchtime on August 18, thirty-one Dorniers of *Oberstleutnant* Fröhlich's Bomber Group 76 were assigned, by sheer chance, to strafe two of Fighter Command's most vital sector stations, covering the southern approaches to London—Kenley in Surrey, and Biggin Hill in Kent. Further to fox the radar stations, a spearhead of five Dorniers was to fly at wavetop height, homing in on both stations at nought feet, in precise concert with the high level raids.

This now became a split-second decision for Kenley's controller, Squadron Leader Anthony Norman; although the Observer Corps had spotted the low level Dorniers, heading for the white chalk quarry that marked out Kenley, HQ 11 Group had ordered no "scramble." So Norman acted on his own initiative. "Get them into their battle bowlers

. . . tin hats everybody," he ordered the floor supervisor, then, to Squadron Leader Aeneas MacDonell's 64 Spitfire Squadron: "Freema Squadron, scramble, patrol base, angels twenty."

Over Kenley, 64 Squadron were at first at a loss, until MacDonell's voice, high-pitched with urgency, ordered "Freema squadron, going down." Sergeant Peter Hawke remembers thinking, "Why down? We need all the height we can get," until he saw the black corona of smoke pulsing from Kenley's hangars: the low level raid had arrived in advance of the high level strike. Seeing a flash like exploding helium from a Dornier, Hawke recalls: "I just felt, My God! Did I do that? Then I thought, Well, this was what I was trained to do."

Fifty feet above the airfield, the Hurricanes of Squadron Leader John Thompson's No. 111 Squadron, scrambled from nearby Croydon, were almost casualties themselves. No one had warned them that the station defences were firing P.A.C (parachute and cable) rockets at the raiders—electrically fired rockets snaking upwards at forty feet a second to grapple the wings with steel wire. Now Thompson thought in anguish, if one of those hits us we're finished.

For this risky exploit, Bomber Group 76 paid dearly: fully six Dorniers and their crews, and four of the JU 88 bombers that had accompanied them. But in their turn they had scored with painful accuracy. Ten hangars had been shattered, and six more damaged; the Ops Room was out of action and many buildings had been reduced to trembling shells.

Only one factor had saved Kenley from total destruction: many bombs from the low level raid had landed horizontally and they had failed to explode.

At Biggin Hill, the bulk of the 500 bombs dropped had landed wide, on the airfield's eastern perimeter, but the C.O., Group Captain Richard Grice, still paraded the station personnel to issue a timely warning: "What happened at Kenley today can well happen here, so don't think that you've escaped." WAAFs like Corporal Elspeth Henderson recall standing consciously taller: already their shoulders were bruised and aching after compulsory hours on the range with Lee-Enfield rifles, and now they were truly in the front line.

At Fighter Command, Dowding's personal assistant, Pilot Officer Robert Wright, recalls widespread consternation: did the Germans plan to concentrate the might of their bombers against the sector stations? In truth, as *General* Paul Deichmann, the Chief of Staff to the 2nd Flying Corps, was later to record, this fear was groundless. Never at any time did the Luftwaffe High Command suspect that Kenley and Biggin Hill—or, for that matter, Hornchurch, Tangmere and Middle Wallop—*were* sector stations, the nerve-centres of Dowding's command.

"We all thought priority command posts would be sited underground, away from the centre of operations," Deichmann explained, "not in unprotected buildings in the centre of the airfields. And not all of them had sand-bags or blast walls!"

Incredibly, *Major* Schmid had no liaison

The thing that numbs the heart is this:/That men cannot devise/Some scheme of life to banish fear/That lurks in most men's eyes.

(*Fear* by James Norman Hall)

Heinkel HeIIIs raiding an English target.

I looked up again, and this time I saw them—about a dozen slugs, shining in the bright sun and coming straight on. At the rising scream of the first bomb I instinctively shrugged up my shoulders and ducked my head. Out of the corner of my eye I saw the three Spitfires. One moment they were about twenty feet up in close formation; the next catapulted apart as though on elastic. The leader went over on his back and ploughed along the runway with a rending crash of tearing fabric; No. 2 put a wing in and spun around on his airscrew, while the plane on the left was blasted wingless into the next field. I remember thinking stupidly, 'That's the shortest flight he's ever taken,' and then my feet were nearly knocked from under me, my mouth was full of dirt, and Bubble gesticulating like a madman from the shelter entrance, was yelling, "Run, you bloody fool, run!" I ran. Suddenly awakened to the lunacy of my behaviour, I covered the distance to the shelter as if impelled by a rocket and shot through the entrance while once again the ground rose up and hit me, and my head smashed hard against one of the pillars. I subsided on a heap of rubble and massaged it.

(from *The Last Enemy* by Richard Hillary)

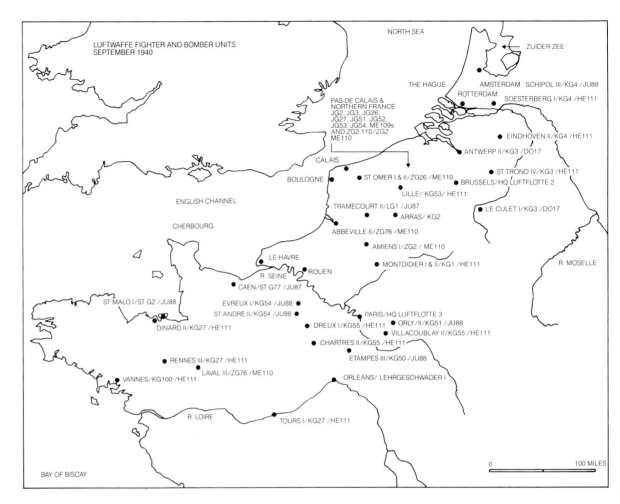

LUFTWAFFE FIGHTER AND BOMBER UNITS
SEPTEMBER 1940

NORTH SEA

ZUIDER ZEE

THE HAGUE

AMSTERDAM   SCHIPOL III/KG4 /JU88
ROTTERDAM
SOESTERBERG I/KG4 /HE111

PAS DE CALAIS &
NORTHERN FRANCE
JG2, JG3, JG26,
JG27, JG51, JG52,
JG53, JG54, ME109s
AND ZG2 110/ZG2
ME110

EINDHOVEN II/KG4 /HE111

ANTWERP II/KG3 /DO17

CALAIS

ST TROND IV/KG3 /HE111

BOULOGNE   ST OMER I & II/ZG26 /ME110   BRUSSELS/HQ LUFTFLOTTE 2

ENGLISH CHANNEL   LILLE/ KG53/ HE111

LE CULET I/KG3 /DO17

TRAMECOURT II/LG1 /JU87
ARRAS / KG2

CHERBOURG   ABBEVILLE II/ZG76 /ME110

AMIENS I/ZG2 / ME110

LE HAVRE   MONTDIDIER I & II/KG1 /HE111   R. MOSELLE
R. SEINE   ROUEN

CAEN/ST G77 /JU87

ST MALO I/ST G2 /JU88   EVREUX I/KG54 /JU88
                    ST ANDRE II/KG54 /JU88   PARIS/HQ LUFTFLOTTE 3
                    DREUX I/KG55 /HE111   ORLY /II/KG51 /JU88
DINARD II/KG27 /HE111   VILLACOUBLAY II/KG55 /HE111

CHARTRES II/KG55 /HE111

RENNES III/KG27 /HE111   ETAMPES III/KG50 /JU88
          LAVAL III/ZG76 /ME110
VANNES/KG100 /HE111   ORLEANS/ LEHRGESCHWADER I

R. LOIRE   TOURS I/KG27 /HE111

0   100 MILES

BAY OF BISCAY

officers either with the fighter groups in the Pas de Calais or the bomber groups centred on Brittany; given this mix of ignorance and random planning, Manston was still seen as as good a target as any. By August 24, all efforts to hold it had proved in vain. As twenty JU dive bombers, with a fighter escort, swept in over the drome, Pilot Officer Henry Jacobs, relaying a blow-by-blow commentary to HQ 11 Group, heard a hollow note like a gong echo up the wire; a bomb, striking the telephone and teleprinter links, had severed 248 circuits at one blow. Dashing from 600 Squadron's Ops Room, Jacobs saw the East Camp guardhouse had now vanished, swallowed into a chalky crater, forty feet deep.

Fire swept all those buildings still standing, and Leading Fireman Herbert Evans, of Margate Fire Brigade, arriving on a motor cycle as the spearhead of the main fire force, never forgot the spectacle that met his eyes— "I was appalled at the damage done. The hangars were ablaze, planes on the field were blazing, and in pieces . . . there was . . . not a soul to be seen except an R.A.F. officer who stood gazing at the scene . . . pipe in mouth and hands in pockets, with tears streaming down his face. On seeing me, he turned away and I never saw him again."

On the same day, the bulk of the station personnel were moved out, while Flight Sergeant John Wright hastily filled a 600 Squadron truck to overflowing with spare parts. Already civilians were moving in to loot tools and live ammunition from the main store: the shame of Manston was complete.

At Fighter Command, there was growing concern: would the panic prove contagious? Aircraftman Thomas Mackay recalls how at Hawkinge "it was so bad some boys took their blankets out and slept under the hedges . . . Some were in such a state of nerves they didn't come back but stayed away all the time." At length, Mackay recalls, senior NCOs armed with revolvers were sent to flush them out like beaters at a shoot. At North Weald, too, the first bombs of August 24, saw men surging like frightened sheep from the main gates, bound for the glades of Epping Forest, until the powerful brogue of Wing Commander Victor Beamish, the Irish C.O, boomed out through the tannoy loudspeaker: "Any officer, N.C.O. or airman who leaves his post on duty is a coward and a rat—and I shoot rats on sight." There was no further panic at North Weald.

And for the most part calm did prevail. Edward R. Murrow, the CBS commentator, painted a graphic word picture of WAAFs coming on duty at Kenley a few hours after the raid of August 18—"Most of them were girls with blond hair and plenty of makeup. They marched well, right arms thrust forward and snapped smartly down, after the fashion of the Guards . . . Some of them were probably frightened, but every head was up . . . most of them were smiling." At many airfields, which underwent random bombing, like Warmwell, Dorset, the personnel viewed the vast German onslaught almost with detachment—"Have you ever seen anything so cool, so damned cool," Aircraftman Lawrence James remembers applauding from a slit trench. "What efficient bastards they are!"

Tuesday 20 August

I took off from Debden at about 10:15 and flew to Tangmere. I navigated my way o.k. but being on the coast this wasn't very hard. Tangmere is in a shocking state, the buildings being in an awful shambles, several 1000 lb bombs having fallen. We were put to 30 mins at 1, and did nothing for the rest of the day. The dispersal hut is most cozy and puts ours at Debden to shame.

(from the diary of Pilot Officer Denis H. Wissler No. 17 Squadron)

top left: A locator map showing the principal Luftwaffe units in France, July, 1940; *left:* Pickett-Hamilton forts now at Tangmere Military Aviation Museum.

COLUMBIA

3644
(CO 316

(There'll Be Bluebirds Over)
THE WHITE CLIFFS OF DOVER
Fox Trot - Vocal Chorus by
Harry Babbitt and Glee Club
-Burton-Kent-
KAY KYSER and
his ORCHESTRA

I believe this plan (raiding RAF airfields and British aircraft factories) would have been very successful, but as a result of the Führer's speech about retribution, in which he asked that London be attacked immediately, I had to follow the other course. I wanted to interpret the Führer's speech about attacking London in this way. I wanted to attack the airfields first, thus creating a prerequisite for attacking London . . . I spoke to the Führer about my plans in order to try to have him agree I should attack the first ring of RAF airfields around London, but he insisted he wanted to have London itself attacked for political reasons, and also for retribution.
I considered the attacks on London useless, and I told the Führer again and again that inasmuch as I knew the English people as well as I did my own people, I could never force them to their knees by attacking London. We might be able to subdue the Dutch people by such measures but not the British.

(Hermann Goering International Military Tribunal Nuremberg, 1946)

Tangmere airfield in 1988.

Some survivors believe that the airfield attacks brought about a new sense of cohesion. "At first the airmen hated us for wearing their uniform," says Rosemary Inness, a WAAF plotter at North Weald, "and the Chief Controller . . . removed all WAAF from the Operations Room when unidentifiable plots appeared on the board . . . But finally . . . when the 'Ops Room' received a direct hit . . . he so appreciated his WAAF who remained steadfastly plotting away with their tin hats on over their headsets that he allowed us special passes."

Towards August's end, there was need for such cohesion at all the fighter airfields. At first, 'The Few' in the sky had monopolised all the glory: now heros and heroines became commonplace on the ground. When nine Junkers 88 dive bombers streaked for Biggin Hill on August 30, cutting off all electricity, water and gas, killing or injuring sixty-five, more than forty WAAFs sheltering in a trench were engulfed by tons of chalk and stones, but some were on duty the next day—still chuckling at the WAAF Flight Sergeant Gartside's outraged complaint: "My God, they've broken my neck—and they've broken my false teeth, too!" Among them was Corporal Elspeth Henderson, who worked on next day until a 500-pound bomb from a second raid tore through the Ops Room roof—one of only six WAAFs to be awarded the Military Medal during the entire war.

Now the main London-Westerham telephone cable connecting Biggin Hill with the outside world was severed: the onus now lay on Hornchurch Sector Station, covering the

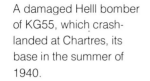

A damaged HeIII bomber of KG55, which crash-landed at Chartres, its base in the summer of 1940.

Thames Estuary, to control Biggin's squadrons and satellites, Gravesend and Redhill as well as its own, Rochford. Six squadrons were to be manoeuvred in combat over 5,000 square miles of sky—and on August 30, Hornchurch, too, was decisively blitzed.

At 1.15 p.m., Wing Commander Cecil Bouchier had been first on the scene, to find more than 100 craters pitting what he saw as *his* airfield. Promptly, all leave passes were cancelled and Bouchier himself led the working parties filling in the holes with pick and shovel, placing yellow cardboard cones to mark the sites of unexploded bombs. "Whatever your rank you were in there pitching," remembers Pilot Officer Henry Jacobs, who had moved up from Manston with 600 Squadron, and Aircraftman George Stokes, Al Deere's cherished flight mechanic, remembers the spirit of those times. "The C.O. put out an appeal for all nearby civilians for help. They came in their dozens with spades and shovels . . . they worked so hard that everything was back to normal in four hours."

But could even such concerted teamwork prevail against a determined Luftwaffe? After

numerous false starts they were learning to strike hard where it counted most, so that even the most sanguine of pilots had cause to wonder. On September 1, raid followed raid with the deadly precision of a hammer driving home nails: Hawkinge, Detling, Lympne, Biggin Hill, then Debden, Rochford, North Weald and Biggin Hill yet again. And at Warmwell, Flight Lieutenant David Crook, of 609 Squadron, happened to remember the Duke of Wellington's words at Waterloo: "Hard pounding this, gentlemen; let's see who will pound longest."

Their deliverance, when it came, surprised nobody more than the Imperial General Staff. On the afternoon of Saturday, September 7, a meeting called by their Chief, General Sir John Dill, was just under way when Brigadier Leslie Hollis entered with a message. Dill, after studying it anxiously, still recognised that 4 p.m. was the hour of Winston Churchill's catnap.

"I think we should inform the Prime Minister," he said. "Will he be awake yet?"

Even in the weekend silence of Whitehall, the sound of explosions could be clearly heard. "If he wasn't before, he is now," Hollis replied. "I'll go and tell him that they're bombing London."

On the ethics of shooting at aircraft crews who have baled out in parachutes—

Germans descending over England are prospective Prisoners of War, and, as such, should be immune. On the other hand, British pilots descending over England are still potential combatants. Much indignation was caused by the fact that German pilots sometimes fired on our descending airmen (although, in my opinion, they were perfectly entitled to do so), but I am glad to say that in many cases they refrained and sometimes greeted a helpless adversary with a cheerful wave of the hand.

(ACM Sir Hugh C. T. Dowding from his despatch to the Secretary of State for Air, 20 August 1941)

DEFENCE VERSUS OFFENCE

AS THE BATTLE gathered pace, the growing concern of Dowding and his commanders would have puzzled the Luftwaffe's top fighter aces—men like Werner Mölders and Adolf Galland. Day by day, it was plain that their onslaught was being slowly but decisively repulsed. On one visit to Mölders, at the headquarters of Fighter Group 51, *Major* Fritz von Forell found his old friend in despair following yet another abortive conference with Goering. "It will turn out all right," Mölders mimicked the Reichmarschall's lusty optimism. "Everything's been all right so far." Then he ended gloomily: "So far! I wonder if Goering is really the general, politician and strategist that we need."

Although Mölders was reluctant to acknowledge it, the Luftwaffe was as unequal to the task of neutralising the R.A.F. as Lord Gort's British Expeditionary Force had been to check the relentless advance of the panzers from the west.

All along, the Luftwaffe's main role had been to support the army in the field, as in Poland and France. Its strength had always lain in short-range fighters, like the ME 109, which the old hands called 'Emil', divebombers like the Stukas that had wrought such havoc at Dunkirk, and twin-engined level-flight medium-weight bombers. On paper this was the world's largest air force, with 4,093 first-line aircraft (with 3,646 operational) yet at the outbreak of war it had lacked night bombers, bombs larger than 1,000 pounds, air torpedoes, modern mines, modern armament and bombsights.

From Karinhall, his vast feudal estate

Actually, once you have done a few hours' flying in a Spitfire and become accustomed to the great power and speed, then it is an extraordinarily easy machine to fly and it is absolutely marvellous for aerobatics. Practically everybody who has flown a Spitfire thinks it is the most marvellous aircraft ever built, and I am no exception to the general rule. I grew to like it more than any other machine I have flown. It is so small and compact and neat, yet it possesses devasting fire power, and it is still probably the best and fastest fighter in the world. The new fighters which will soon be coming into service will have to do very well to equal the Spitfire's amazing record of success.

(—Flight-Lieutenant D. M. Crook, D.F.C.)

And now I see with eye serene/The very pulse of the machine;/A being breathing thoughtful breath,/A Traveller between life and death; the reason firm, the temperate will, Endurance, foresight, strength and skill;/A perfect Woman, nobly planned,/To warn, to comfort, and command; And yet a Spirit still, and bright/With something of angelic light

(from *She Was A Phantom Of Delight* by William Wordsworth)

Courage is the price that Life exacts for granting peace./The soul that knows it not/Knows no release from little things: Nor mountain heights where bitter joy can hear The sound of wings. How can life grant us boon of living, compensate/For dull gray ugliness and pregnant hate/Unless we dare/The soul's dominion? Each time we make a choice, we pay/With courage to behold the resistless day, And count it fair.

(—*Courage* by Amelia Earhart)

preceding spread: 'Looking for Trouble' by Frank Wootton; *above and right:* women building Spitfire fighters at the Supermarine factory, Castle Bromwich.

forty miles north-east of Berlin, Goering had thus far run the Battle as his own private war, without reference to either the Army or the Navy. Euphoric on a daily intake of thirty paracodeine tablets, a mild drug to which he was addicted, the Commander-in-Chief of the Luftwaffe, lived in a world of fantasy, where the trappings of a *nouveau-riche* quite eclipsed the battlefront of the Pas de Calais: an art gallery packed with Renoirs, a bowling alley, a private cinema, gold-plated baths and canary cages shaped like divebombers. As a thrusting Minister of Aviation from 1935 on, Goering had brought the Luftwaffe to its peak, but he now so disdained technical detail that Erhard Milch, as Inspector-General, was granted an audience once every three months.

It was thus in keeping that Goering pinned most of his faith in two planes supremely unfitted for the combat. Pride of place was given to the twin-seater, twin-engined ME 110, known as *Zerstörer* (destroyer), an escort fighter designed to clear the way for mass bomber attacks, with a maximum cruising range of 680 miles. But the ME 110, when loaded, outweighed the streamlined ME 109 by almost 10,000 pounds. In the French campaign, it had won easy laurels, but its lack of manoeuvering and speed were a byword with the pilots.

In combat their stock tactic was what the R.A.F. called "the circle of death," a defensive gambit which had the machines circling warily, each guarding the other's tailplane. ("They broke formation and formed a great big circle," Sergeant John Burgess, a Spitfire pilot remembered. "I'm not sure that forty

91

And thou art dead, as young and fair/As aught of mortal birth:/And form so soft, and charms so rare,/Too soon returned to Earth!

(from *And Thou Art Dead* by George Gordon, Lord Byron)

right: The control column and instrument panel of a Hawker Hurricane in restoration at Duxford. *below:* Pilot Officer George Barclay, No. 249 Squadron.

were in the circle, but certainly a part of them was.'') It was a tactic that *Major* Hennig Strümpell, an ME 109 commander for Fighter Group 2, viewed with distaste. Early in the battle he had found himself, like Burgess, in the middle of one such circle, dog-fighting with a Spitfire, while ME 110s blasted tracer at both of them impartially.

Yet to all arguments against their use, Goering remained obdurate: "If the fighters are the sword of the Luftwaffe, the ME 110 *Zerstörer* is the point of that sword." Goering's resolute faith in the Stuka troubled his commanders, too. When the Luftwaffe held the sky, the JU 87 Stuka had been unrivalled for precision bombing and close infantry support; in recognition of this, they now made up one-third of the Luftwaffe's bomber force. Yet their disastrous losses in the convoy attack of August 8 had presaged the shape of things to come, and twice within ten days, on August 12 and August 18, the pattern was repeated. The Stukas, their speed throttled back by air brakes, streaked for their target at 310 m.p.h.; lacking any such brakes, the ME 109s protecting them screamed past at 375 m.p.h., so that time and again the R.A.F. picked off the Stukas with unerring accuracy.

The sortie of August 18 was no exception. Briefed to attack targets round Portsmouth harbour in the hope of drawing up British fighters, *Major* Paul Hozzel joked incredulously: "But that's just like showing a dog a sausage." In the melee that ensued, Hozzel was proven right: many of his Stukas blew up like fantastic fiery rockets with their bombs still on board. *Oberleutnant* Kurt

Scheffei crash-landed near Caen so weak from loss of blood that the ground crews had to lift him from the plane. One wing commander, *Major* Walter Enneccerus, limped back to complain bitterly to the top brass: "They ripped our backs open right up to the collar."

At his Cherbourg headquarters, even the 8th Flying Corps' martinet commander, the Baron von Richtofen, was appalled by the news: eighteen out of twenty-eight Stukas had been lost or severely damaged. His diary entry was succinct: "A Stuka wing has had its feathers well and truly plucked." From this moment, the Stukas—280 aeroplanes—were virtually withdrawn from the battle.

A bitter bone of contention then with Goering's pilots was the role of the ME 109. As fast as a Spitfire (its maximum speed was 354 miles an hour) and faster than a Hurricane, it could out-dive and out-climb both, and its worth had been more than proven in the Spanish Civil War. Yet in the Battle, more often than not, it was forced to play nurse-maid to the lumbering bombers—all of them, from slim pencil-shaped Dorniers to slow scantily armed Heinkel 111s were dubbed 'furniture vans' by the fighter pilots. Often 120 fighters were assigned to protect a bomber formation 40 miles long—"as frustrated as polo ponies," commented the war correspondent Leonard Mosley, "acting as outriders on a herd of slaughterhouse steers." The ME 109s with an operational radius of 125 miles and a tactical flying time of ten minutes, were thus severely hampered. If the R.A.F. chose to fight, they were left with eight minutes combat time before breaking away.

Soon, as with Dowding's crews, every Luftwaffe pilot was feeling the stress. Each found himself watching his fuel gauge anxiously in the interval of scanning the sky; the red warning bulb on the instrument panel that showed fuel running low prompted a code cry: "Trübsal" (distress). As *Oberleutnant* Hans von Hahn reported in a letter home, "There aren't many of us who haven't made a forced landing in the Channel in a badly shot-up plane or without a propeller."

Although Goering could scarcely ignore the mounting *Zerstörer* losses—for its fifty-three feet span as against the 109's thirty-two feet always led the R.A.F. to single it out—he now reached an incredible decision. From 16 August, every *Zerstörer* must be shepherded into battle by an escort of ME 109s—a fighter in the farcical predicament of itself needing fighter protection.

Few of the wing commanders summoned to Karinhall felt comfortable in Goering's presence. Away from the fighting front, hemmed in by natty staff officers with white and raspberry striped trousers, Adolf Galland felt ill-at-ease, and the ritual of 'the cigar game' particularly bothered him: all Goering's favourites covertly tucked stolen Havanas up their sleeves, and the Reichsmarshall, pounding their forearms in farewell, would break the cylinders, hooting with laughter, before making good the loss. Mölders, on at least one occasion, had doubts concerning Goering's sanity. Following his release from a Toulouse prison camp, once France fell, Mölders had been dining at Karinhall when Goering, without warning, had clapped an empty wine glass on the tablecloth. "Look Emmy," he hailed his wife, shaking with crazy laughter. "Look what I've got! A flea! A present from Mölders' from captivity!"

Strangely, neither Air Fleet commander, attempted to wean Goering from his world of fantasy. *Feldmarschall* Hugo Sperrle, whose 300-pound bulk earned him the nickname 'The Monocled Elephant', remained remote from the conflict in Air Fleet Three's Paris HQ; as the one-time commander of the Condor Legion, Sperrle was a specialist in low-level saturation bombing and thus to some extent out of his depth. By contrast, *Feldmarschall* Albert Kesselring, abandoning Air Fleet Two's HQ in Brussels, had installed himself in 'The Holy Mountain', a bombproof HQ forty steps below ground at Cap Blanc Nez, determined to check on the triumph or failure of every plane that took off. Neither man had much contact with Goering, who was once surprised in his Paris hotel suite by his signals chief, *General* Wolfgang Martini, clad only in a sky-blue silk dressing gown and describing by telephone to Emmy how he was at that moment on the cliffs at Calais, overseeing the squadrons that thundered towards England.

One of the few men to voice a caution was *Oberst* Werner Junck, Air Fleet Three's regional flight commander. If the ME 109 was to be employed increasingly as a bodyguard, he suggested, serious thought should be given to stepping up fighter production, since only 320 ME 109s had rolled from the assembly lines during July. At the current rate of attrition, the Luftwaffe would need to shoot down four British fighters for every one they lost. But

Goering saw any such move as fatal to home front morale. "I must take your pulse to see if you are all right physically," he told Junck, a patronising hand outstretched, "It seems you have taken leave of your senses."

It was at this time, too, that Goering issued an order which beggared belief: it had come to his attention that the *Zerstörers* called their tactical manoeuvre 'the circle of defense', and this was expressly forbidden. It would be 'the offensive circle', in keeping with Luftwaffe belly-fire, from now on. "Ah," sighed *Oberleutnant* Friedrich Vollbracht, whose *Zerstörer* Group had been wiped out by mid-September, "it's still the same old circle."

Through black misfortune, the R.A.F., too, had their *Zerstörer* counterpart, a twin-seater fighter, the Boulton Paul Defiant. As far back as May 29, the Defiant had confounded all the sceptics with a 'kill' of thirty-seven Stukas over Dunkirk; ten days later, their 'bag' had risen to sixty-five, as the Germans, mistaking No. 264 (Defiant) Squadron for hump-backed Hurricanes, had been mown down by the withering fire from the rear gunners. At Kirton-in-Lindsey, on the Lincolnshire fens, 100 miles from the battleline, Spitfire pilot John Burgess remembers 264 well; "They were a little full of their own importance and they'd done well over Dunkirk and they were

He that fights and runs away/May live to fight another day./But he that is in battle slain/Will never rise to fight again.

(from *History Of The Rebellion, 1749* by J. Ray)

left: Pilots of No. 19 Squadron, Duxford, 1940; *above:* Pilot Officer R.H. Holland of No. 92 Squadron.

expected to wipe the Luftwaffe from the skies." Soon after breakfast on August 20, their C.O., Squadron Leader Philip Hunter, signalled the walkover. "Just stuff a toothbrush in a parachute bag," he briefed them confidently. "Don't worry about kit."

The severe mauling that another Defiant squadron—No. 141—had undergone in mid-July was thus conveniently forgotten.

This was no oversight on the part of Dowding or of Air Vice Marshal Keith Park, commanding No. 11 Group. For Dowding, after four years at Stanmore, Fighter Command had become his life, with no salient detail escaping him. A vegetarian and a near-teetotaller, who also dabbled in spiritualism, Dowding was never once known to enter the officers' mess; his entire day was a punishing routine at his desk broken only by quick breaks for lunch and dinner at 'Montrose', the rambling villa nearby where his sister Hilde kept house. Although his austere demeanour hid a sardonic sense of humour—"It makes me look like a gloomy newt peering from under a stone," he commented on his official photograph—he somehow never achieved rapport with the pilots known as "Dowding's Chicks." When Squadron Leader John Ellis, commanding No. 610 Squadron, broached the wastage of novices downed on their first flight, the C-in-C, on a visit to Biggin Hill, was frosty. If twelve planes were serviceable, twelve pilots would at all times be airborne.

"They're really nothing but passengers who never check on their tails," Ellis volunteered, but beyond his first pronouncement, Dowding refused to be drawn.

97

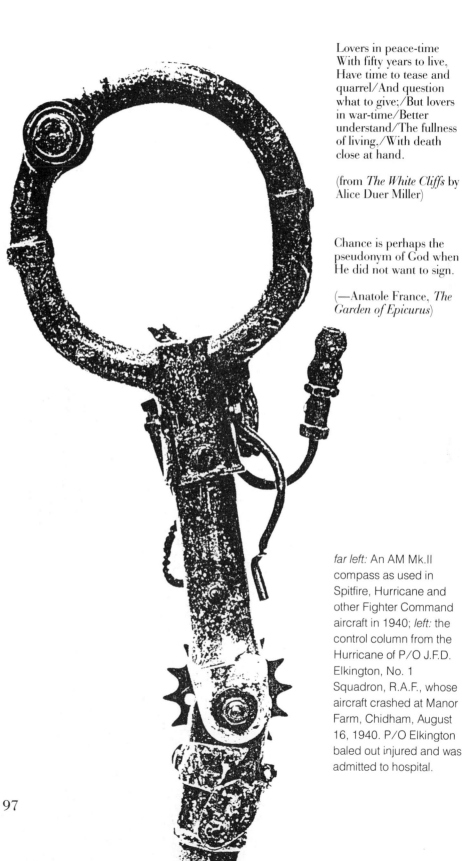

Lovers in peace-time With fifty years to live, Have time to tease and quarrel/And question what to give;/But lovers in war-time/Better understand/The fullness of living,/With death close at hand.

(from *The White Cliffs* by Alice Duer Miller)

Chance is perhaps the pseudonym of God when He did not want to sign.

(—Anatole France, *The Garden of Epicurus*)

far left: An AM Mk.II compass as used in Spitfire, Hurricane and other Fighter Command aircraft in 1940; *left:* the control column from the Hurricane of P/O J.F.D. Elkington, No. 1 Squadron, R.A.F., whose aircraft crashed at Manor Farm, Chidham, August 16, 1940. P/O Elkington baled out injured and was admitted to hospital.

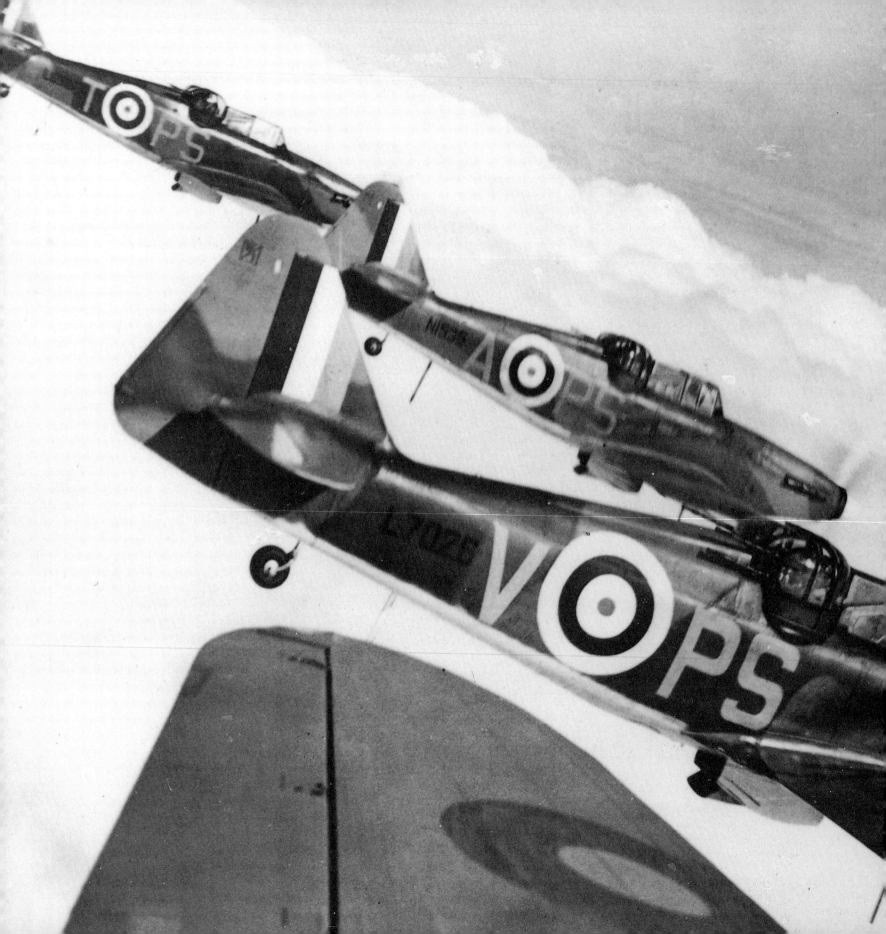

At HQ 11 Group, Uxbridge, Keith Park, a canny New Zealander, and not one to suffer fools gladly, was equally aware of the Defiants' vulnerability: direct and informal, Park, as his P.A., Flying Officer Donald Wiseman knew, had made 'going round his men' a speciality, open to the views of everyone from ground crews to ops room staff. Yet by August 21, neither Park nor Dowding could see any other way; six squadrons had been pulled from the battleline, 426 aircraft had been written off and 222 were undergoing repairs. The breach was wide open and No. 264 Squadron would have to fill it.

What followed, as every squadron survivor would testify, was stark slaughter: with the Defiants it was gunners like Pilot Officer Freddie Sutton and Flight Lieutenant Clifford Ash who called the tune and by now the Luftwaffe knew it. Lacking all forward armament with a maximum speed of 304 miles an hour, the pilots relied solely on their gunners' verbal instructions to manoeuvre into a firing position. The aerial twentieth century equivalent of cannon fodder, they were powerless against frontal attack, as one novice, Flight Lieutenant E. W. Campbell-Colquhoun, promoted to pilot after one flight, soon discovered. Unable even to identify the buttons and switches on his instrument panel, he mistakenly joined up with three ME 109s, whose cannon shells exploded his Very cartridges. Choking with smoke, his Defiant alive with bouncing coloured balls, he touched down at Manston and pelted for a slit trench. This five-minute skirmish cost the squadron six men and three machines, and on August 25, tangling with more

Man goeth to his long home.

(—Old Testament, Ecclesiastes, XII, 5)

A speck of dirt on your windscreen could turn into an enemy fighter in the time it took to look round and back again. A little smear on your goggles might hide the plane that was coming in to kill you.

(from *Piece of Cake* by Derek Robinson)

preceding spread: A Spitfire low over the English country-side in 1988; *left:* Boulton-Paul Defiants of No. 264 Sq., Kirton-In-Lindsey. The Defiants were extremely vulnerable turret fighters and proved utterly unsuited for that role. They were ultimately relegated to a night fighter assignment.

than fifty ME 109s over Herne Bay three more were lost.

By August 28, after only four days in action, the massacre of the Defiants was complete: eleven aircraft had been sacrificed, and fourteen lives, among them Squadron Leader Philip Hunter. Flight Lieutenant Campbell-Colquhoun telephoned his wife to drive him back to Kirton-in-Lindsey. His hands were shaking so badly that it was impossible to light a cigarette, let alone grip the steering wheel of their car.

In the last resort, the Battle of Britain was to resolve into an unremitting combat of Hurricanes and Spitfires against ME 109s, with the public's affections, perversely, centred on the Spitfires. As early as August 8, the merchant skippers of the Channel convoy had hailed their Hurricane-saviours as Spitfires. As late as September 15, a German pilot, shot down by a Hurricane near Maidstone, had added his tribute, "Well done, Spitfire." Two years later, on the Battle's second anniversary, the movie epic, *The First of the Few*, starring Leslie Howard in the role of the Spitfire's creator, Reginald J. Mitchell, set the seal on the legend.

Yet sheer logistics gave that legend the lie. All told only nineteen Spitfire Squadrons took part in the Battle; at peak, on August 30, exactly 372 Spitfires were ready for operations. By contrast, Hawker Hurricane squadrons totalled thirty-three, with a total of 709 planes available for front line operations on August 30.

The Spitfire legend began, by sheer chance, on Wednesday, July 10, one month

Having mastered the cockpit drill, I got in and taxied out on the aerodrome, sat there for one moment to check that everything was o.k., and then opened up to full throttle. The effect took my breath away. The engine opened up with a great smooth roar, the Spitfire leapt forward like a bullet and tore madly across the aerodrome, and before I had realized quite what happened I was in the air. I felt as though the machine was completely out of control and running away with me. However, I collected my scattered wits, raised the undercarriage, and put the airscrew into coarse pitch, and then looked round for the aerodrome, which to my astonishment I saw was already miles behind.

(—Flight-Lieutenant D. M. Crook, D.F.C.)

The Spitfire Mk.1A of the Lindsay Collection, at Booker where it is maintained by Tony Bianchi, Personal Plane Services.

103

below: In August, 1940, airmen of the Royal Air Force are given physical training in their preparation as new pilots; *right:* a Spitfire showing its beautifully formed elliptical wing.

before battle was finally joined. It was then that a broadcast made on Beaverbrook's behalf by Lady Reading, chairman of the W.V.S. (Women's Voluntary Services for Civil Defense) exhorted all British housewives to yield up "everything made of aluminium, everything that they could possibly give to be made into aeroplanes . . . cooking utensils of all kinds . . . if you are doubtful, give our aeroplanes the benefit of the doubt and please be generous . . . ."

The response was overwhelming. One W.V.S. official, leaving Broadcasting House minutes later, saw women hurrying to the collecting depot with saucepans still warm from the stove. The Princesses Elizabeth and Mar-

garet Rose donated miniature teapots and kettles forgotten from the nursery. At Oxted, Surrey, one Home Guardsman was put to work with a sledgehammer demolishing all the aluminium articles in a garage thirty feet long. One old lady, handing in a frying pan, set the keynote: it was to go towards a Spitfire, which she felt had the edge on a Hurricane. Ten months later—when the Battle was virtually over—the appeal had yielded 1,000 tons of metal, yet as one Beaverbrook aide, David Farrer commented caustically: "It is doubtful if the gift of pots and pans created a single Spitfire or Hurricane . . . but to a considerable number of people . . . (Beaverbrook) had given a sense of purpose."

The reality as most front-line veterans knew, was different. To some pilots, like Pilot Officer Eugene 'Red' Tobin, no aircraft ever sang a blither tune than the Spitfire's 1,000 h.p. engine—"the sweetest little ship I've ever flown," he had written in a letter home. Others in turn would rhapsodise over the eight powerful .303 Browning machine guns, the rate of climb (2,530 feet a minute), the maximum speed (at 19,000 feet) of 355 miles an hour. Some are still uncompromising. "All the Hurricanes couldn't have won the Battle of Britain," says Norman Ryder, a flight commander on No. 41 Squadron. "All the Spitfires could. A Hurricane was virtually useless at 23,000 feet and a lot of fighting was going on above that height." Flight Lieutenant Finlay Boyd, of No. 602 Squadron, who turned down command of a Hurricane squadron, agrees. "From a fighting point of view, as a dogfighter, they were never surpassed."

Do unto the other feller the way he'd like to do unto you,/an' do it fust.

(*David Harum* by E. N. Westcott)

Snap back the canopy,
Pull out the oxygen
tube,/Flick the harness
pin/And slap out into the
air,/Clear of the machine.
You knew that you must
float/From the sun above
the clouds/To the gloom
beneath, from a world/Of
rarefied splendour to
one/Of cheapened dirt,
close-knit/In its effort to
encompass man/In
death.

(from *Parachute Descent*
by David Bourne)

DO. 17 & 215

top left: An R.A.F. Air
Diagram, the Mk.II
reflector gunsight; *top
and centre right and far
right:* the Messerschmitt
Bf 109, Gloster Gladiator
and Junkers JU88
respectively, as depicted
in a children's aircraft
book; *right:* during the
Battle of Britain only a few
R.A.F. air-sea rescue
launches were in service.
They later came into use
in great numbers as a
result of lessons learned
during the air actions of
1940 over the English
Channel.

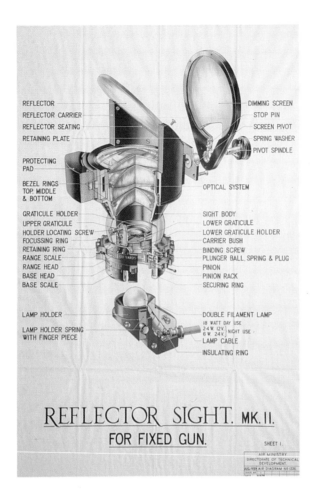

REFLECTOR SIGHT. MK. II.
FOR FIXED GUN.

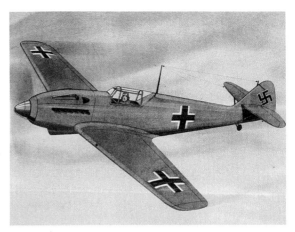

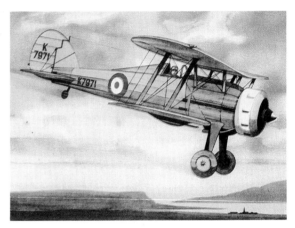

They plough the 'drome and scatter/The Hurricanes around: "Well what the hell's the matter/If I came in too near the ground?"/Then comes the Flight Mechanic/Upon the scene to mourn,/And to him says the dimwit/"I didn't hear the horn!" A spot of work, and out she goes,/I hope we'll pack up now,/Another bastard's on his nose—Why did I leave the plough!!/So out again with lots of rope,/(We'd like to use it on the dope!)/We find him smoking "Players Please"/As we wade in mud up to our knees. A still, small voice within us sings/If only we could have your wings,/And you the spanners, drivers, screw—/We'd see that you had lots to do./Dear Lord, who gives the angels wings—/We pray you so to order things/That wingless creatures like the erk/Shall not be done to death with work.

(from *A Fitter's Lament* by Jack Ashford)

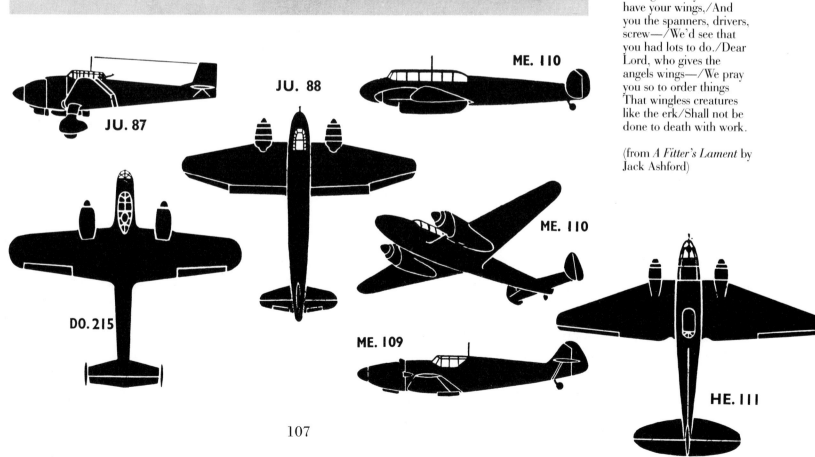

JU. 87

JU. 88

ME. 110

DO. 215

ME. 110

ME. 109

HE. 111

Other 'aces' more consciously weigh the pros and cons. "The Spitfire was better than the 109," allows Al Deere, "Except in a straight dive, we could do anything they could do and better." "Without question, the Spitfire was better at altitude than the Hurricane," says Geoffrey Page, "so we knew when flying Hurricanes that the ME 109 could out-dive us . . . The Hurricane was a more rugged aeroplane . . . (It) would take in more punishment when hit by enemy fire."

To its credit, the Spitfire, with "its classic elliptical silhouette . . . and beautiful thin wings" matched up to a pilot's definition: "If it looks right, it is right." Almost all the survivors' evaluations stress a feminine comparison. A bulldog and a greyhound is the simile that occurs to Geoffrey Page; to Pilot Officer Glen Niven, of 602, it was "like driving a racing car as opposed to a truck." For Robert Doe, himself a violinist manqué, "it was a musician's aeroplane." Yet even admirers conceded that the stressed-metal Spitfire, less resistant to exploding cannon-shells needed the care of special servicing units at designated "Spitfire bases."

Most pilots who acknowledged the Hurricane's supremacy at first did so grudgingly. For Robert Stanford Tuck, his first encounter, on September 9, was with "a flying brick, a great lumbering stallion." Robert Doe's appraisal, after time on Spitfires is earthier: "a brick-built shithouse." Yet both men at widely divergent times, confessed themselves won over by the fighter's indomitability. "She was solid," Tuck admitted freely. "She was steady as a rock and was a wonderful gun platform

left: Factory production of Helll bombers; *above: Generalfeldmarschall* Hugo Sperrle, Luftflotte 3 Commander during the Battle.

109

. . . My God, the punishment those Hurricanes could take." "It was strong," Doe amplifies. "It could turn on a sixpence . . . It was a brutal machine where the guns were really fixed firmly." John Burgess was another Spitfire pilot attesting to the Hurricane's worth. "Because the Spitfire was reckoned to be a better match for the 109s . . . the Hurricanes were usually vectored to the bombers."

Flight mechanics echoed that enthusiasm: the Hurricane, with its traditional construction of wood and fabric stiffened by a metal tube framework and its powerful 1,030 h.p. Rolls Royce Merlin engine, was a ground crew's dream. It was a "go anywhere, do anything plane," in one man's estimate, "a defensive fighter, a work-horse," in the words of its historian Paul Gallico. Eric Marsden remem-

bers how at Westhampnett "We could turn our Hurricanes in 145 Squadron round—turn the whole flight and, on occasions, the squadron in eight minutes ... the whole thing was rather like a modern pit stop in Grand Prix car racing."

It was a classic case of the plane meeting the need of the hour: by 1941, the Hurricane now reduced to a fighter-bomber role, was

Yes; quaint and curious war is!/You shoot a fellow down/You'd treat if met where any bar is,/Or help to half-a-crown.

(*The Man He Killed* by Thomas Hardy)

Hellls raiding England;

obsolete in fighter-to-fighter encounters. Yet the Hurricanes which took part in the Battle made 80 per cent of the "kills" claimed by Fighter Command. One such was claimed over Southampton on August 16, when 23-

year-old Flight Lieutenant James Nicholson, until then a stranger to combat, was, surprisingly, jumped by a ME 110 *Zerstörer* at 18,000 feet and hit by four cannon shells. One shell tearing through the perspex hood, peppered his left eye with splinters and blinded him with blood. A second shell struck his reserve petrol tank and in one searing moment his plane took fire. More shells tore away his trouser leg, disabling his left heel.

But Nicholson was piloting a Hurricane, and although his cockpit was now an inferno, the instrument panel "dripping like toffee," it continued to fly straight and true, closing on the ME 110 at 400 m.p.h. as his right thumb, boiling with white blisters, pressed the gun button. Afterwards he swore—perhaps partisan testimony—that although the *Zerstörer* twisted and turned to evade the bullets, his Hurricane, "as though by an instinct of her own, was following the evasive action."

The Hurricane held its course long enough for Nicholson to see the *Zerstörer* fall smoking for the sea, then, at 5,000 feet, with flames lapping at his trousers, he baled out. His was just one of 1,715 Hurricanes involved in the Battle, yet three months later, when it was all over, Flight Lieutenant Nicholson was the one pilot in Fighter Command to be awarded the Victoria Cross.

Downed in combat near English coastal cliffs, a virtually intact Messerschmitt 109.

EAGLES

SATURDAY, AUGUST 17 was a day of sullen overcast. On both sides of the Channel, Fighter Command and Air Fleet Two reported only reconnaissance flights. At the airfields the pilots, after nine days of frenetic activity, caught up with domestic chores. In a farmhouse at St Inglevert, near Boulogne, *Oberleutnant* Hans-Otto Lessing, aged twenty-three, of the 51st Fighter Group, was one of several writing home for the first time since the Battle began.

"My dear parents," he wrote, ". . . At last I have some time to write to you . . . Of course we have a lot to do every day . . . sometimes two to three sorties . . . Usually we are in the vicinity of London—if you look at the map, you'll see the distance between the French coast and Dover. With a flying time of 1½ hours and air battles as well—and a fuel shortage—you can imagine how difficult it is to get back."

For all that, Hans-Otto had one triumph to record. "Yesterday I shot down my fifth enemy plane . . . not very much if you think of the many opportunities we get, but unfortunately not every plane we shoot at falls from the sky . . . Another time I had very bad luck, having got to a good position I found I had no ammo left, but one gets experience even in running away . . . My enemy plane was the hundredth enemy plane of the group.

"The English pilots seem to get less and less these last few days," Hans-Otto reported, "but those few are fighting very well. The Spitfires sometimes give us the most astonishing aerial aerobatic display. I watched with great interest how one tore about among 30 MEs without getting hurt himself. These are exceptional ones."

Regretfully, Hans-Otto Lessing brought his letter to a close: "Well, this is a short report—one would have to write a book in order to give the whole picture." But this, too, had to be said: "For me this is the most exciting time of my life—I wouldn't wish to change places with a king. Peacetime will seem very dull after this."

Predictably, few pilots took time from the wheeling chaos of the combat to set down their thoughts like *Oberleutnant* Lessing. The way they felt was more often expressed in a casual aside, a verbal shorthand shared only by initiates. Those with few doubts shared the ebullience of Pilot Officer George Bennions of No. 41 Squadron at Hornchurch: "My God, life wouldn't seem right if you didn't go up to have one scrap in the morning and another in the afternoon." The more introspective felt the same misgivings as Flight Lieutenant Tom Hubbard, of 601 Squadron, Tangmere: "We all knew it was like a game of roulette, backing black all the time. Our luck wouldn't come up forever."

The few who kept diaries revealed little of their true emotions, in entries as terse as telegrams: "Had a scramble today but they went home," noted Pilot Officer Eugene 'Red' Tobin on August 30. "Did some practice flying and we were lousy. Went to Andover and drank. Then home." Pilot Officer Patrick Barthropp of No. 602 Squadron, faced on September 15, with a German armada stretching beyond the horizon, noted succinctly: "Thousands of them." Following the afternoon sortie, he noted again: "*Still* thou-

below: Flight Lieutenant James B. Nicholson, Fighter Command's first and only recipient of the Victoria Cross; *left:* the identity discs of Flying Officer R.P. Plummer, No. 46 Squadron.

Fame is the perfume of heroic deeds.

(— Socrates quoted by Plato)

115

TEN of MY RULES for AIR FIGHTING

1 <u>Wait until you see the whites of his eyes.</u>
  Fire short bursts of 1 to 2 seconds and only when your sights are definitely 'ON'.

2 Whilst shooting think of nothing else; brace the whole of the body; have both hands on the stick; concentrate on your ring sight.

3 Always keep a sharp lookout. "Keep your finger out"!

4 Height gives <u>You</u> the initiative.

5 Always turn and face the attack.

6 Make your decisions promptly. It is better to act quickly even though your tactics are not the best.

7 Never fly straight and level for more than 30 seconds in the combat area.

8 When diving to attack always leave a proportion of your formation above to act as top guard.

9 INITIATIVE, AGGRESSION, AIR DISCIPLINE, and TEAM WORK are words that MEAN something in Air Fighting.

10 Go in quickly – Punch hard – Get out!

sands of them."

Both sides were anxious to prove themselves, but the R.A.F. were at first more conscious of their limitations. Flying Officer Dudley Williams of 152 Squadron recalls that before his first combat he had twice been allowed to fire his eight Browning machine guns into the sea for practice—and barely 10 per cent of Dowding's pilots had undergone more stringent training. Most, unaccustomed to sighting their guns, opened fire at 600 yards, then, at 200 yards, a surer range, broke from combat. All had been schooled to fly in rigid air display formation, and to home in on bombers in one of four standard Fighter Command attacks. "No one had told us that was the most stupid thing on earth to do!" says Robert Doe, then a Pilot Officer with No. 234 Squadron at Middle Wallop. ". . . The change of tactics came purely by knowing that the one laid down was wrong . . . I learned that I had to fly an aeroplane through the gunsight . . . I really concentrated on learning how to shoot, and when you're flying an aeroplane through the gunsight, you do what's needed to keep the gunsight where you want it."

As Doe recalls it, his first victory against an ME 110, over Swanage, Dorset, bore that lesson out: it was the first time he had ever peered through his reflector gunsight or even touched the red-painted firing button at the apex of his control column. It was then that the only advice his flight commander, the Australian Pat Hughes, had ever offered him came abruptly back to him—"Get as close as you can and you can't miss"—and in this moment he barely gave a thought to his ad-

Flight Lieutenant
Adolphus G. 'Sailor'
Malan, No. 74 Squadron;
left: Malan's code of
conduct for aerial
combat.

Little is the luck I've had,/And oh, 'tis comfort small/To think that many another lad/Has had no luck at all.

(*Last Poems* by A. E. Housman)

Do not despair/For Johnny-head-in-air;/He sleeps as sound/As Johnny underground. Fetch out no shroud/For Johnny-in-the-cloud;/And keep your tears/For him in after years. Better by far/For Johnny-the-bright-star,/To keep your head,/And see his children fed.

(from *For Johnny* by John Pudney)

versary, the rear gunner, hosing back fire until he baled out, only 1,000 feet above the water. And it was then that Doe felt 'suddenly invincible'—although as a survivor he "retained the knowledge that you could be shot down very easily, and you're always shot down by the one you don't see."

Another Spitfire pilot, John Burgess, recaptures the psychology of the moments succeeding the two-and-a-half minutes that it took No. 222 Squadron to scramble from Rochford: "You got that horrible feeling down in the pit of the stomach . . . and when you were climbing you still had that sort of peculiar tummy feeling. But once action started you were too busy and all you were interested in was avoiding getting killed or trying to shoot down the other aircraft. It was rather like a dare to some degree. You wanted to see how far you could go without . . . coming to any harm."

A relative latecomer to the Battle, Burgess still developed by degrees a veteran's psychology. "If you got caught and shot at and had to do a forced landing, you lived to fight another day . . . I think that the spirit of the successful fighter pilot was to "look everywhere" and to never be intimidated by the number of enemy aircraft that were around because you didn't realise at the time that they were more frightened than you were . . . They were miles away from home, deep into enemy territory . . . If they were caught alone, they were finished."

Every Luftwaffe fighting man would have echoed those sentiments. In the Pas de Calais, it seemed at times that the pressure

was stepping up almost hourly. At Audembert, the new commander of the 26th Fighter Group, *Major* Adolf Galland, told his younger brother, Wilhelm, a trainee artillery officer, "Things can't go on much longer like this. You can count on your fingers when your time will come." *Oberst* Carl Viek, chief of staff to the regional commander for Air Fleet Two, remembers that no rest-days were permitted, no rotation of frontline units. The watchword always was " 'The last man shall go again!'."

Other Air Fleet Two pilots testify to that sense of strain. Towards August's end, few worried as they would have done earlier if combat was not joined: that anxious eye on the fuel gauge made things all too fraught. *Oberleutnant* Hans-Ekkehard Bob, 54th

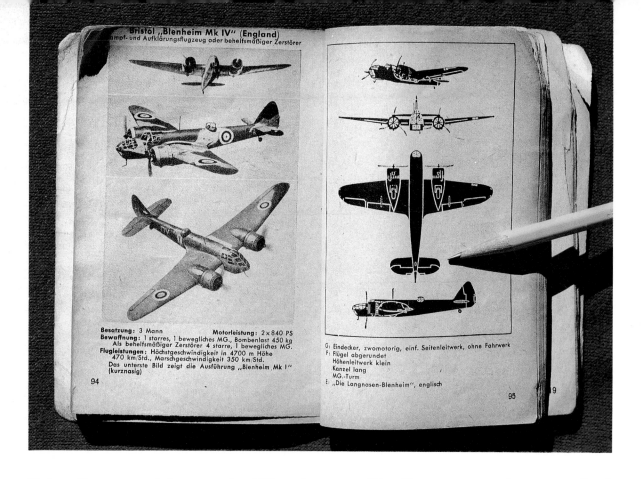

The image within the photograph contains German text:

Bristol „Blenheim Mk IV" (England)
Kampf- und Aufklärungsflugzeug oder behelfsmäßiger Zerstörer

Besatzung: 3 Mann   Motorleistung: 2×840 PS
Bewaffnung: 1 starres, 1 bewegliches MG., Bombenlast 450 kg
Als behelfsmäßiger Zerstörer 4 starre, 1 bewegliches MG.
Flugleistungen: Höchstgeschwindigkeit in 4700 m Höhe
470 km/Std., Marschgeschwindigkeit 350 km/Std.
Das unterste Bild zeigt die Ausführung „Blenheim Mk I"
(kurznasig)
94

G: Eindecker, zwomotorig, einf. Seitenleitwerk, ohne Fahrwerk
F: Flügel abgerundet
   Höhenleitwerk klein
   Kanzel lang
   MG.-Turm
E: „Die Langnasen-Blenheim", englisch
95   9

Monday 26 August

We had another crack today when we were brought to readiness from 30 mins available, and sent off. As we took off a HE111K waffled across the aerodrome at about 1500 feet. F/L Bayne put us in line astern and we went roaring after it. However it was already being attacked by Spitfires and its undercart was down. We gave it a good burst each and it turned back for land crashing by Ford aerodrome. A Spitfire and Hurricane landed minus U/C.

(from the diary of Pilot Officer Denis H. Wissler No. 17 Squadron)

Fighter Group, put it humorously: "Blessed are they who leave space behind them, for they will see the Fatherland again." *Leutnant* Erich Hohagen saw it more starkly: "The Channel's a blood-pump—all the time draining away our strength." *Hauptmann* Walter Kienzle, of Galland's staff, remembers a growing air of unreality with each successive sortie: "You were only thirty minutes away from your base . . . you saw the planes on the ground, the bend in the Thames, the puffs of flak . . . and you felt 'I don't belong here'." And *Leutnant* Johannes Steinhoff, of the 52nd Fighter Group, a future Inspector-General of the post-war Luftwaffe, thought more than once: "The R.A.F. seem so hesitant—perhaps they never realise how scared to death we are."

The flimsy green combat reports flooding in to Fighter Command's headquarters showed the punishment the pilots and planes routinely took. At one airfield alone, North Weald, three pilots of No. 56 Squadron had astonishing escapes. Pilot Officer 'Scruffy' Joubert, who was blown clean through the side of his Hurricane when his radiator exploded, mercifully pulled his ripcord just in time. Flight Sergeant 'Taffy' Higginson, skid landing at 100 miles an hour near Whitstable, Kent, vacated his burning plane so fast he fell face down in a cowpat and broke his nose. Flight Lieutenant 'Jumbo' Gracie, joked for days that his neck must be broken, since he could no longer crane round in the cockpit, then returned from the X-Ray department

top left and right: A German guide to military aircraft recognition. From 1940.

119

Fighter Command pilots wait for the call to "scramble" in a dispersal crew room on an English airfield in 1940.

white and shaken: "My God, it *is* broken."

But all such encounters were the small change of battle, stories to be capped, in time, by any long-term survivor. For the chosen few there were apocalyptic moments, encounters which even the participants, in retrospect remembered with awe. Some called for a resourcefulness few men had realised they possessed. Flying Officer Jimmie Coward,

left: A wounded German pilot brings his bomber back to its French base; *above:* a KG55 presentation plate.

123

top left: Major Hannes Trautloft, JG54; *top right: Leutnant* Gordon Gollub, JG3; *right:* a Heinkel crew in France.

"Alone in the silence of the hour before dawn/I speak my sorrow. For now of the living/None is left, none to learn,/To know of things hidden in my soul's heart.

(from *The Wanderer* Anonymous)

top: A JU88 crew preparing for an attack on England; *far left: Leutnant* Hans Beisswenger, JG52; *left: Hauptmann* Walter Nowotny, III Gruppe; *above:* the grave in England of Obergefreiter Reuhl, rear gunner on a Junkers 88A-1 of 3(F) 123, which was shot down over Southwestern England on September 27, 1940, by P/O Eric Marrs of No. 152 Squadron.

of No. 19 Squadron, was airborne from Fowlmere in one of the R.A.F's few cannon-equipped Spitfires, heading for a flight of Dorniers. Abruptly two things happened: his cannons jammed and his Spitfire shuddered all over. Briefly he felt a dull pain 'like a kick on the shin in a Rugger scrum', then he saw his bare left foot lying on the cockpit floor, severed from the damaged leg by all but a few ligaments.

To bale out proved no problem, but the agony of his foot spinning crazily by its ligaments spurred him to action. Floating to earth from 20,000 feet, he could see blood jetting from his tibial artery, vanishing in thin swirls below. Unable to reach the first aid kit in his breast pocket, since the slipstream had sucked away his gloves from his icy hands, Coward somehow contrived a tourniquet from the radio lead in his flying helmet—raising his left leg almost to his chin and binding the lead tightly round his thigh.

Within an hour of drifting across Duxford airfield, he was in Addenbrookes Hospital, Cambridge, where a doctor amputated his leg below the knee.

A few men unwittingly qualified for membership of the Caterpillar Club: those who had somehow made it to earth by unorthodox use of a parachute. One such pilot, David Bell-Salter, of No. 253 Squadron, was jumped by a formation of ME 109s, over the Sussex coast; struggling from a Hurricane he could no longer control, he was 1,800 feet above the whirling kaleidescope of fields before he braced both legs against the cockpit floor and pitched clear into the buffeting air-

126

The gentlemen got up betimes to shoot,/Or hunt: the young, because they liked the sport— The first thing boys like after play and fruit;/The middle-aged, to make the day more short;/For ennui is a growth of English root,/Though nameless in our language:—we retort/The fact for words, and let the French translate/That awful yawn which sleep cannot abate.

(from *Don Juan, Canto XIII* by George Gordon, Lord Byron)

In the early stages of the fight Mr. Winston Churchill spoke with affectionate raillery of me and my "Chicks." He could have said nothing to make me more proud; every Chick was needed before the end.

(ACM Sir Hugh C. T. Dowding from his despatch to the Secretary of State for Air, 20 August 1941)

far left: Pilot Officer R.F.T. Doe, Nos. 234 and 238 Squadrons; *inset:* Wing Commander (ret.) Doe in 1988; *left:* the Spitfire Mk.1A of the Lindsay Collection.

A Sergeant Pilot in the cockpit of his Spitfire in 1940; *right:* a combat report of the type filed in 1940 by Fighter Command pilots for every combat sortie flown.

flow. Before he had even pulled the ripcord of his parachute he had lost consciousness.

A hundred feet above the ground, he came to, albeit groggily, to find himself upside down, hanging by one leg suspended by a single rigging line caught behind his knee. Above him the parachute was flapping wildly, and dimly he could see a long rent across its canopy—yet the speed of his fall, 175 feet a second, had stripped the harness from his body. Now the ground rose up very fast to meet him, and before he could twist himself into a better position, he struck the Sussex farmland so violently that he crushed several vertebrae, dislocated both shoulders and one knee, and smashed his right heel.

But how had his parachute opened at all? The ripcord ring was still in its pocket when he was found unconscious by two railway workers and hastened to hospital. Had the pack been ripped open by his aerial mast or by the tail of his Hurricane as he was swept away from the cockpit? Even today, Bell-Salter, a successful Manhattan import agent, has no answers to those questions: he only knows that he lived to tell the story.

Other pilots owed their lives to the vigilance of others, among them Flying Officer Paul Le Rougetel, a darting dynamic Channel Islander, nicknamed 'Blackbird'. A Blenheim night fighter pilot from No. 600 Squadron, at Hornchurch, Le Rougetel and his radar operator, Sergeant St. James Smith, were hit at night and forced to ditch over St. Margaret's Bay, Kent. Now their fates were in the lap of the gods, for while the Luftwaffe maintained a force of some thirty Heinkel 59 aeroplanes for

F/LT KENT.

COMBAT REPORT.

Sector Serial No. (A)	
Serial No. of Order detailing Flight or Squadron to Patrol (B)	
Date (C)	9/9/40
Flight, Squadron (D)	Flight: A Sqd
Number of Enemy Aircraft (E)	40 Bombers & Nume
Type of Enemy Aircraft (F)	JU 88,HE 111,ME 10
Time Attack was delivered (G)	18,00 hours
Place Attack was delivered (H)	Nr.Beachy Head
Height of Enemy (J)	20,000 ft.
Enemy Casualties (K)	1 ME 110 Destroye 1 JU 88 Damaged.
Our Casualties Aircraft (L)	Nil
Personnel (M)	Nil

GENERAL REPORT (R)

I took off from Northolt to join up with No.1 Canadian Squadron at 2000 I was leading the Squadron - 12 Hurricanes. We were vectored in a South direction, climbing all the time. When we got not far from the Coast a 11,000 ft, I saw many A/C - ME's and Spitfires probably, at 20,000 ft. turned N.W. I saw some aircraft cross below the Canadians.

Suddenly out of the sun came about 40 Bombers going South. We were 13,000 ft. I watched No.1 Canadian to see what they were going to do. seemed to be sending off a section or two, and I lost them in the sun. turned off after the Bombers, but we were too late to make good contact I only the leading Section did so. I caught up with one straggler, and started to dive into cloud, just South of the Coast. I followed and op fire at 500 yds. Meanwhile I was being chased up by two or three ME 10 which were kept off my tail by Red 3 (F/O Henneberg) who was doing cros behind me. After my third burst at about 400 yds - his tracer had been under me - the rear gunner stopped firing. I gave another short burst saw a lot of pieces come off his starboard engine, and it began to pour dense clouds of smoke. He turned slightly to the right as he went into cloud. I followed down into the clouds, and came out over the Channel. It was very dark and hazy under the clouds. I could see no sight of th As I was circling round I saw another A/C at about 1000 ft flying towar France. I approached to investigate, and was surprised to find it was with our camouflage, and had yellow mark on the side of the fuselage. juncture I think the rear gunner fired. I decided to attack.

P.T.O.

Signature   F/Lt.Kent.
                    Red
O.C   Section
                    Flight

rescue work, the R.A.F. had only eighteen high-speed rescue launches to cover the entire coastline of Britain.

Although Sergeant Smith had baled out within wading distance of the beach, Le Rougetel had landed fully 1½ miles out in the bay. A strong swimmer, he could have easily made the shore, but on the pitch-dark night of August 9, all unknowing, he was swimming out to sea. By degrees, a slow chill invaded his loins, and he lost consciousness. Only by sheer chance did the tiny luminous dial of his wrist-watch catch the keen eye of the Margate Life-boat's Coxswain Dennis 'Sinbad' Price, and as Le Rougetel came to, the crew were hauling him aboard, remarking "These R.A.F. boys are tough. This one must have been in the drink for at least two hours." For medical reasons, they next dosed him with naval rum, and Le Rougetel, for happier reasons, lost consciousness all over again.

Back at Hornchurch, the cold had so penetrated his body that the medical orderlies kept him packed for hours with twenty-four hot water bottles to counteract the paroxysms of shivering, but two days later he was completely fit again. "Ever since then I've tried to get the most out of life because I still feel I've cheated and am living on borrowed time."

Two men at least, on the afternoon of September 15, took risks that later turned them cold to think about. Above Maidstone, Pilot Officer Mike Cooper-Slipper, of No. 605 Squadron, felt something jar the undercarriage of his Hurricane and realised that the plane had caught fire. At the same moment, dead ahead, he saw three Dorniers closing in and came to a sudden clinical decision, "I'll ram them."

As he now recalls, his main preoccupation was to ram the middle plane; all thoughts of death and pain had completely passed him by. When the impact came, Cooper-Slipper recalling a former automobile accident, thought judiciously, "It's quite different. It's not a big bump at all. It's just a swishing and a swooshing." He was just conscious of his Hurricane's port wing, catapulting away into space, but smoke had enveloped the centremost Dornier and that, too, was falling steeply away. At 20,000 feet, ripping three fingernails from his right hand, Cooper-Slipper baled out—at almost the same moment that Pilot Officer Paddy Stephenson of No. 607 Squadron was reaching the same decision over Appledore, Kent. He, too, had seen two Dorniers approaching, too fast for the copy-book gunsight tactics approved by Robert Doe. "Well, I knew I couldn't take aim at them and that in

Glad that I live am I;
That the sky is blue;
Glad for the country lanes,/And the fall of dew.

(*A Little Song Of Life* by Lizette W. Reese)

left: P/O J.R.B. Meaker, No. 249 Squadron; *below:* P/O B.E. 'Paddy' Finucane, No. 65 Squadron.

that case they would probably get *me*, so I decided to charge them."

In that unrepeatable moment, Stephenson became perhaps the only Battle of Britain pilot to bring down two German aircraft without firing a shot; rocked by the impact from the left and right wings of his Hurricane, he saw both Dorniers burst into flame as they spiralled into space. Then, with the realisation that both his port and starboard wings were severed at the roots, Stephenson, like Cooper-Slipper, baled out at 20,000 feet, to land with a force that concussed him against the high brick wall of the local lunatic asylum.

When a pilot's oxygen feed jammed, it was tacitly acknowledged that he broke for home base. To climb to 25,000 feet without oxygen was to court disaster. But on August 25, above the four-mile channel of the Solent connecting Portsmouth with the Isle of Wight, Eugene 'Red' Tobin, finding his oxygen supply blocked, still flew on in support of No.

609 Squadron. Thus, he, too, joined the select company of those who had faced death as though in a mirror.

On that day he had broken all the rules, streaking in pursuit of one ME 110 he had already riddled with tracer—"Don't follow them down," the veterans counselled. "Your own tail will be wide open"—and as he banked steeply, at 370 miles an hour, 18,000 feet above the water, he blacked out.

In that moment the thrust of G was forcing him deep against the aluminium bucket seat, bending his backbone like a bow, forcing his chin downward into his chest. An inexorable centrifugal force was driving the blood from his head towards his feet, turning it to the weight of molten lead. For a second his brain was no longer working; his jaw sagged like a cretin's and a yellow-grey curtain swam before his eyes. Then, drowsily, he found his head clearing, and he was flying absolutely level only 1,000 feet above the water, to return

left and right: graves
of German airmen
downed in the Battle,
Tangmere churchyard.

132

left: German pilots as prisoners of war in Canada after having been shot down in the Battle, together with the principal Luftwaffe medals;
top: Heinkel bombers dispersed in a wood on their French airfield in 1940.

top: Sgt. J.H. 'Ginger' Lacey; top right: the 609 Squadron 'state' board, Warmwell; next - Sgt. J.H.H. Burgess, No. 222 Squadron; far right: F/L W.J. Harper and F/O G.R. Bennette, No. 17 Squadron.

hastily to Warmwell and excuse himself, "I blacked out colder than a clam."

In the warm smoky twilight of the pubs they frequented—The White Hart, at Brasted for Biggin Hill pilots, The Thatched House at Ingatestone for North Weald, the Black Swan at Monxton, otherwise "The Mucky Duck," for Middle Wallop men—such stories were now common currency. Expertise was freely traded because the lives of others depended on it. Never take off in wet boots—even at 35,000 feet your feet could freeze to the rudder pedal. A sliced potato rubbed over the bullet-proof windscreen was a sure way to stop it icing up, avowed 'Sandy' Johnstone and the pilots of 602.

Use your mirror to watch your rear like a canny motorist. They were not yet incorporated in fighter planes but wise men fitted their own. Always see that the last fifty rounds

in your guns were glinting tracer, the sure way not to run short. In the mess at Hornchurch, newcomers listened in reverent silence to the dead-shot of No. 41 Squadron, Pilot Officer George Bennions: "You want to be slightly above them or just under their bellies, lad—dead astern, at two hundred yards range, and you just can't miss—."

But, of course, you could miss, and in their heart of hearts all of them knew it: the 'certainties' were no more than whistling in the dark. To live through your first three sorties was to achieve some tenuous hold on immortality, but as 'Red' Tobin always said, tapping the wings on his tunic: "I reckon those are a one-way ticket pal."

That was the way it was with Hans-Otto Lessing, marked *'gefallen'* in the 51st Fighter Group's Record Book, one day after his first letter home.

"It was no picnic despite what anyone might say later . . . Most of us were pretty scared all the bloody time; you only felt happy when the battle was over and you were on your way home, then you were safe for a bit, anyway."

(—Colin Gray, fighter pilot, 54 Squadron)

His life was gentle, and the elements/So mix'd in him that Nature might stand up,/And say to all the world "This was a man!"

(—Shakespeare, Julius Caesar, V, 5)

Squadron Leader Terence G. Lovell-Gregg, Commanding Officer of No. 87 Squadron, Exeter. On August 15, 1940, S/L Lovell-Gregg led 87 Sq. into action with a force of German fighters estimated at 120 + . He was badly wounded and his burning Hurricane crashed in a wood at Abbottsbury, Dorset at about 6 p.m., killing the New Zealander. *inset:* Gordon Dunford witnessed the crash on his father's farm.

top: Lovell-Gregg's Hurricane struck this tree in a wood near the Abbottsbury swannery; *far left:* his bullet-riddled burning body was found near his aircraft on this path; *left:* his grave stone at Warmwell.

The Queen and I offer you our heartfelt sympathy in your great sorrow.

We pray that your country's gratitude for a life so nobly given in its service may bring you some measure of consolation.

George R.I

top: Pilot Officer Denis Wissler at Debden; *below:* The bullet-holed rear vision mirror from the Hurricane of Flight Lieutenant R.F. Rimmer, resulting from an air action of September 11, 1940.

SHETLAND ISLANDS

SUMBURGH

FAIR ISLE

FOULA

ORKNEY ISLANDS

CAITNIP

NETHER BUTTON

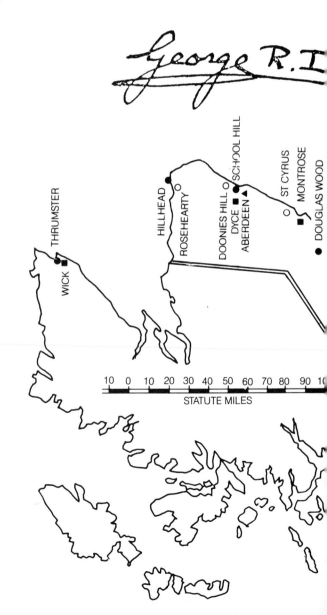

THRUMSTER

HILLHEAD

ROSEHEARTY

DOONIES HILL

DYCE

ABERDEEN

SCHOOL HILL

ST CYRUS

MONTROSE

DOUGLAS WOOD

WICK

10 0 10 20 30 40 50 60 70 80 90 10

STATUTE MILES

FIGHTER COMMAND LAYOUT
JULY 1940

far left: An expression of
Royal sympathy to the
families of R.A.F. pilots
lost in the Battle; *below:*
the layout of R.A.F.
Fighter Command in July
1940.

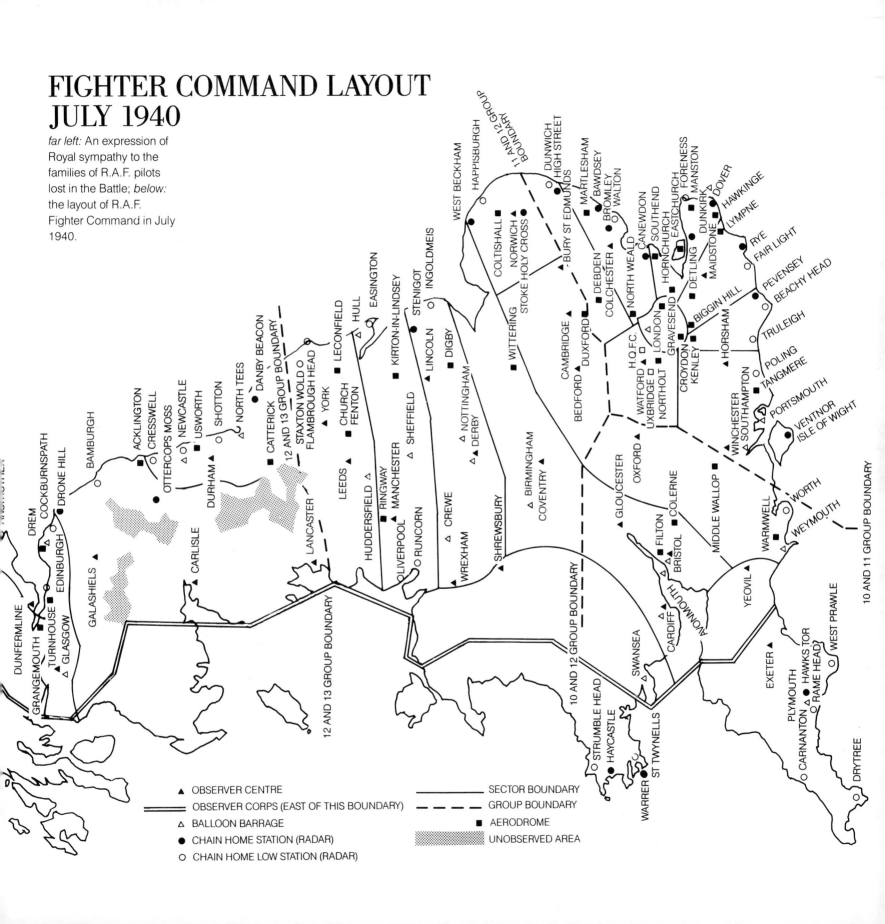

OBSERVER CENTRE

OBSERVER CORPS (EAST OF THIS BOUNDARY)

BALLOON BARRAGE

CHAIN HOME STATION (RADAR)

CHAIN HOME LOW STATION (RADAR)

SECTOR BOUNDARY

GROUP BOUNDARY

AERODROME

UNOBSERVED AREA

'B' flight, No. 145 Squadron on 'stand-by' at Westhampnett in August, 1940; *far right:* a bell used during the Battle to call a squadron to a "scramble" take-off.

AFTERWARDS, WHEN THEY looked back to that summer, the scene was archetypal. A dozen or more pilots would be mustered at dispersal, overtly relaxed in deck-chairs, and on canvas cots, or stretched out on the cool grass. They wore flying overalls, sometimes pulled on hastily over pyjamas, or rolltop sweaters if the day was chilly. Almost all had silk scarves for comfort: in combat the neck would swivel constantly. These men were at Readiness, with Mae Wests—lifejackets—duly adjusted. Those on standby, were already in their cockpits, facing the wind, engines ready to turn over. Only the fortunate few had drawn Avail-

SCRAMBLE

able status, with twenty minutes leeway before they took off.

Conversation was essentially sporadic. A few, like No. 603 Squadron, at Hornchurch, kept the demons at bay with Mah-Jong, a Chinese game played with chips and bamboo counters, or darts or shove ha'penny. Others leafed through magazines—*Illustrated, Picture Post*—or checked on Jane's state of undress in the current *Daily Mirror.* Only the ground crews rooted on terra firma, could concentrate on paperbacks; at Biggin Hill, Aircraftman Harold Mead was engrossed in the pulp thriller *No Orchids For Miss Blandish,* while one Debden flight sergeant gave his mechanics a crash course in *Lady Chatterley's Lover.* Music, too, was a potent aid to distraction; *Sweet Violetta* for 603 at Hornchurch, Dorothy Lamour's *These Foolish Things,* revolving endlessly on a tinny gramophone for 66 at Kenley. Only later would it be time for ribald ditties—*Bang Away Lulu, O'Riley's Daughter, The Ball o'Kirriemuir*—thumped out on the mess piano at night.

These were survivors' songs, songs for the fortunate who had lived through that day's scrambles.

Pilot Officer Geoffrey Page of No. 56 Squadron, would recreate one of those scrambles with almost total recall, even to the date and the time—5.20 p.m. on August 12—and for the best of reasons: it was a scramble that almost cost him his life, and was to involve nineteen operations on atrociously burned face and hands. Thus he remembered that the scramble took place at Rochford airfield, the old Southend Flying Club, the satellite for

North Weald sector station. At Rochford, as at most satellites, chairs and tables were unknown luxuries. Apart from a large bell tent, the one item of furniture was the field telephone, linking No. 56 to North Weald: the Scramble telephone.

The sounds of that day were largely subliminal. No one any longer heard the thump-thump of the petrol bowsers' delivery pumps dinning in their ears. But Page remembered quite vividly the screeching brake drums of the waggon that delivered the heavy Thermos flasks of tea, the hunks of cut bread-and-butter, the communal jar of strawberry jam. It was in the midst of a childish game with the jam, poising a spoonful above a crawling wasp, that Page had felt his hand tremble violently, and seen the jam spill wide. The telephone rang, and his flight commander, Flight Lieutenant E. J. 'Jumbo' Gracie had lunged for it, before struggling to his feet: "Scramble . . . seventy-plus approaching Manston . . . angels one-five."

Then, as always, Page felt the sense of sickness drain away. As he sprinted the fifty yards to his waiting Hurricane, neatly inscribed 'Little Willie,' his mind was growing clear and alert. His right foot slipped into the stirrup step, his left foot gained the port wing. One short move then brought his right foot to the step inset in the fuselage. Now he was secure in the cockpit, and his rigger was deftly passing the parachute straps across his shoulders, then the Sutton harness straps. His mask was clipped across and oxygen switched on.

Then Page had primed the engine, adjusting the switches, and now his thumbs went

". . . After a scrap I usually drink my tea through a straw."

(from *Piece of Cake* by Derek Robinson)

The first bang came as a shock. For an instant I couldn't believe I'd been hit. Two more bangs followed in quick succession, and as if by magic a gaping hole suddenly appeared in my starboard wing.

Surprise quickly changed to fear, and as the instinct of self-preservation began to take over, the gas tank behind the engine blew up, and my cockpit became an inferno. Fear became blind terror, then agonizing horror as the bare skin of my hands gripping the throttle and control column shrivelled up like burnt parchment under the intensity of the blast furnace temperature. Screaming at the top of my voice, I threw my head back to keep it away from the searing flames. Instinctively the tortured

right hand groped for the release pin securing the restraining Sutton harness.

"Dear God, save me . . . save me, dear God . . . I cried imploringly. Then, as suddenly as terror had

above: A Hurricane pilot of No. 249 Sq; *right:* an aircrew room of No. 66 Sq. at Digby.

up in signal to the mechanics. The chocks slipped away, the Rolls-Royce Merlin engines roared into life, and now No. 56 Squadron was heading for Manston, otherwise Charlie Three, the dancing grass flattening beneath the slipstreams.

Now, in this classic scramble, the voice of Wing Commander John Cherry, the North Weald controller was filling their earphones: "Hullo, Yorker Blue Leader, Lumba calling. Seventy-plus bandits approaching Charlie Three, angels one-five. At once Gracie's voice acknowledged: "Hullo, Lumba, Yorker Blue Leader answering. Your message received and understood. Over."

142

The cockpit panel of the Lindsay Collection Spitfire Mk.1A; *right:* pilots of No. 249 Squadron-at left, P/O George Barclay, top, P/O 'Ginger' Neil, at right, F/O Lohmeyer, and 'Pipsqueak.' *p146:* fighter blast pens remaining at Exeter.

About 100 miles southwest, over Warmwell airfield in Dorset, Pilot Officer Eugene 'Red' Tobin, one of three American pilots serving with No. 609 Squadron, heard an equally bizarre ukase from Squadron Leader Gavin Anderson, controlling Middle Wallop sector: "Hullo, Sorbo Leader, this is Bandy. Patrol Portland angels twenty. Many many bandits." As a typical pilot, Tobin's mind responded automatically: Is my manifold pressure too high? Will the guns work? Is the oil pressure dropping?

Yet was there truly such a thing as a typical pilot? All told, some 1,434 of them would be airborne some time after August 8, from the sensitive 20-year-old Page, who had contended with fear all his life, to the devil-may-care 'Red' Tobin, a 23-year-old real estate operator's son from Los Angeles. On the surface, these two had little in common, yet like most of 'Dowding's Chicks', they and the others shared one attribute: an intense individuality. Few were aces, in the Tuck-Bader-Malan tradition, but all of them in the phrasing of a later generation, "did their own thing." This alone was the common bond uniting a fraternity as diverse as Rodolphe, Comte de Grune, a Belgian Condor Legion veteran, now fighting against his onetime allies with the pilots of 32 Squadron, and Squadron Leader Aeneas MacDonnell, official head of the Glengarry Clan; that linked Derek Boitel-Gill, the Nizam of Hyderabad's former personal pilot with Randy Matheson, the ex-Argentine gaucho, Johnny Bryson, the Canadian Mountie, and Hugh Percy of No. 264 Squadron, a former Cambridge undergradu-

ate who kept his logbook in Greek.

Fully fourteen squadrons were made up of auxiliaries, wealthy weekend fliers who defied all conventions on principle. Thus, Flight Lieutenant Sir Archibald Hope's 601 (County of London) Squadron at Tangmere, sported scarlet silk linings to their uniforms because the R.A.F's powder blue depressed them; a poker game with 601 was usually £100 a stake. Before No. 602 (City of Glasgow) Squadron, accepted 'Sandy' Johnstone as their C.O., they plied him with enough liquor to fell a lesser man: a gentleman must be able to hold his drink. When 'Big Jim' McComb's No. 611 (West Lancashire) Squadron, ap-

overtaken me, it vanished with the knowledge that death was no longer to be feared. My fingers kept up their blind and bloody mechanical groping. Some large mechanical dark object disappeared between my legs and cool, relieving fresh air suddenly flowed across my burning face. I tumbled. Sky, sea, sky, over and over as a clearing brain issued instructions to outflung limbs. "Pull the ripcord—right hand to the ripcord." Watering eyes focused on an arm flung out in space with some strange meaty object attached at its end.

More tumbling—more sky and sea and sky, but with a blue clad arm forming a focal point in the foreground. "Pull the ripcord, hand," the brain again commanded. Slowly but obediently the elbow bent and the hand came across the body to rest on the chromium ring but bounced away quickly with the agony of contact.

More tumbling but at a slower rate now. The weight of the head was beginning to tell.

Realizing that pain or no pain, the ripcord had to be pulled, the brain overcame the reaction of the raw nerve endings and forced the mutilated fingers to grasp the ring and pull firmly.

It acted immediately. With a jerk the silken canopy billowed out in the clear summer sky.

It was then that I noticed

the smell. The odor of my burnt flesh was so loathsome that I wanted to vomit. But there was too much to attend to, even for that small luxury. Self-preservation was my first concern, and my chance for it looked slim. The coastline at Margate was just discernable six to ten miles away. Ten thousand feet below me lay the deserted sea. Not a ship or a seagull crossed its blank, grey surface.

Still looking down I began to laugh. The force of the exploding gas tank had blown every vestige of clothing off from my thighs downwards, including one shoe. Carefully I eased off the remaining shoe with the toes of the other foot and watched the tumbling footwear in the hope of seeing it strike the water far beneath. Now came the bad time.

The shock of my violent injuries was starting to take hold, and this combined with the cold air at the high altitude brought on a shivering attack that was quite uncontrollable. With that the parachute began to sway, setting up a violent oscillating movement with my teeth-chattering torso acting as a human pendulum. Besides its swinging movement it began a gentle turn and shortly afterwards the friendly shoreline disappeared behind my back. This brought with it an idée fixe that if survival was to be achieved, then the coast must be kept in sight. A

proached an airfield, they flew, as a perverse tradition of their own, in perfectly defined swastika formation.

All through the battle, a behind-the-scenes army had backed their endeavours from the first: the riggers, fitters, flight mechanics, instrument repairers and armourers, were known generically as the 'ground crews'. "We lived rough and ready," says Corporal Ernest Wilson, who saw service with No. 17 (Hurricane) Squadron at Debden, and Leading Aircraftman (L.A.C.) Eric Marsden, a veteran of No. 145 Squadron at the Tangmere satellite, Westhampnett, supplies unpalatable detail: "There were no beds for us . . . I made

my bed from a couple of hedge stakes which I laid on some bricks which I scrounged and I used a Hurricane rigging mat." Many had worked under such conditions since June 24, when the squadrons Dowding withheld from France had been converted from two-pitch to constant-speed (variable pitch) propellers for maximum take-off and flight speed. To ensure the changeover, the mechanics had worked all night in blacked-out hangars, making do on ten-minute coffee-breaks.

Far from being automatons, they, too, were individuals used to "doing their own thing." Following the example of Flying Officer Robert Lucy, No. 54 Squadron's engineer

officer, they improvised. On one occasion, Lucy wrenched the armour plating from the back-seat of one written-off Spitfire, coaxed a Hornchurch garage to fashion it into two stout fishplates and used them to patch another Spitfire's badly holed starboard wing root. "I took the fairing off each night to make sure it was bearing the strain," Lucy recalls, "but it was still flying in October." In this same tradition, Aircraftman Harold Mead, faced with an eighteen-inch gash in a Spitfire's wing, cut a slice from a petrol can and tacked it into place with four rivets. Time, the ground crews knew, was always of the essence. At Duxford, L.A.C. William Eslick and his crew once saved themselves precious minutes by switching the access point to the compressed air bottles powering the guns—from an inaccessible trap in the cockpit floor to a point behind the pilot's seat, with easier access through the sliding hood.

As L.A.C. Eric Marsden recalls it, theirs was a lonely life—" 'Parochial' is about the best way to describe the whole set up . . . We didn't mix . . . The people in 'B' Flight didn't know the people in 'A' Flight . . . We lived a very narrow existence." It could be a fraught existence, too, as when 'B' Flight's commander, Adrian Boyd, once returned to Tangmere seething with anger: the enemy aircraft he had been "chasing . . . all over France . . . turned out to be specks in the bottom of the windscreen." In no short order, Marsden relates, "we got cleaning rags and . . . perspex polish after that, so that we were able to keep things absolutely top line."

On some of the outlying stations, the mechanics— after consultation with their combination of agonized curses and bleeding hands pulling on the shrouds finally brought about the desired effect, and I settled back to the pleasures of closing eyes and burnt flesh.

Looking down again I was surprised to find that the water had come up to meet me very rapidly since last I had taken stock of the situation. This called for some fairly swift action if the parachute was to be discarded a second or two before entering the water. The procedure itself was quite simple. Lying over my stomach was a small metal release box which clasped the four ends of the parachute harness after they had passed down over the shoulders and up from the groin. On this box was a circular metal disc which had to be turned through 90°, banged, and presto! The occupant was released from the chute. All of this was extremely simple except in the case of fingers which refused to turn the little disc.

The struggle was still in progress when I plunged feet first into the water. Despite the beauties of the summer and the wealth of warm days that had occurred, the sea felt icy cold to my badly shocked body. Kicking madly, I came to the surface to find my arms entangled with the multiple shrouds holding me in an octopus-like grip. The battle with the metal disc still had to be won, or else the

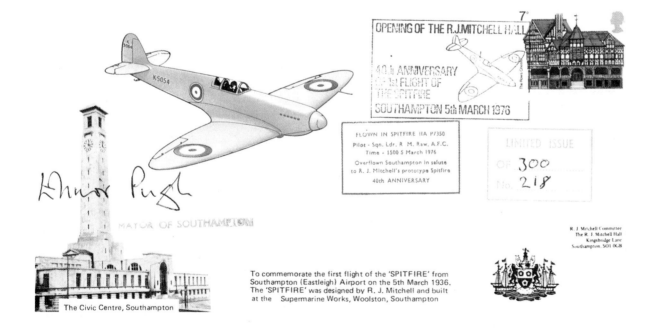

OPENING OF THE R.J.MITCHELL HALL
40th ANNIVERSARY
1st FLIGHT OF THE SPITFIRE
SOUTHAMPTON 5th MARCH 1976

FLOWN IN SPITFIRE IIA P/350
Pilot - Sqn. Ldr. R. M. Raw, A.F.C.
Time - 1500 5 March 1976
Overflown Southampton in salute
to R. J. Mitchell's prototype Spitfire
40th ANNIVERSARY

LIMITED ISSUE
OF 300
No. 218

MAYOR OF SOUTHAMPTON

The Civic Centre, Southampton

To commemorate the first flight of the 'SPITFIRE' from Southampton (Eastleigh) Airport on the 5th March 1936. The 'SPITFIRE' was designed by R. J. Mitchell and built at the Supermarine Works, Woolston, Southampton

R. J. Mitchell Committee
The R. J. Mitchell Hall
Kingsbridge Lane
Southampton, SO1 0GB

147

water-logged parachute would eventually drag me down to a watery grave. Spluttering with mouthfuls of salt water I struggled grimly with the vital release mechanism. Pieces of flesh flaked off and blood poured from the raw tissues.

Desperation, egged on by near panic, forced the decision, and with a sob of relief I found that the disc had surrendered the battle.

Kicking away blindly at

pilots—mocked up the legends that adorned the planes, legends that laid stress on the don't-give-a-damn spirit. Many were Disney-oriented. "Big Jim" McComb's Spitfire, operational from the Duxford satellite, Fowlmere, from September 11, had "Snow White" on its fuselage; other 611 men, according to temperament, were "Grumpy," "Sneezy" and "Dopey." Hurricane pilot Ian Gleed, of 87 Squadron, based at Exeter, had Figaro, with the diminutive cat swatting a swastika, as blithely as a mouse. Willie McKnight, of

Douglas Bader's No. 242 Squadron, had a sharp-edged scythe dripping blood, to symbolise death, the grim reaper. The Fleet Air Arm's Sub-Lieutenant Jimmie Gardner—one of sixty-eight Fleet Air Arm pilots on loan to the R.A.F., and slow to discard their starched white collars—had "England Expects," but spelt out in flags, to affirm his naval status.

Few men tilted so irreverently at superstition as Flying Officer D. H. Ward of No. 87 Squadron, a New Zealander who did not survive the Battle: his Hurricane coat-of-arms

was made up from a figure 13, a broken mirror, a man on a ladder and three on a match captioned, "So what the hell?"

In support of the pilots who made the scrambles, were the station commanders who turned the blindest of eyes to protocol and red tape. At Biggin Hill, Group Captain Richard Grice laid on crates of beer for all pilots returning from a day's last sortie; on one occasion, when Sergeant Ronnie Hamlyn, 610 Squadron, was three times scrambled during a disciplinary hearing, Grice finally met him at dispersal to "officially admonish" him for a careless landing. (That day's toll of five vic-

the tentacles that still entwined arms and legs, I fought free and swam fiercely away from the nightmare surroundings of the parachute. Wild fear died away and the simple rules of procedure for continued existence exerted themselves again.

No. 601 (County of London) Squadron pilots sprint to their Hurricanes for a "scramble".

"Get rid of the 'chute, and then inflate your Mae West," said the book of rules, "and float about until rescued."

"That's all very well," I thought, "but unless I get near to the coast under my own steam, there's not much chance of being picked up." With that I trod water and extricated the long rubber tube with which to blow up the jacket. Unscrewing the valves between my teeth, I searched my panting lungs for extra air. The only result after several minutes of exertion was a feeling of dizziness and a string of bubbles from the bottom of the jacket. The fire had burnt a large hole through the rubber bladder.

Dismay was soon replaced by fatalism. There was the distant shore, unseen but positioned by reference to the sun, and only one method of getting there, so it appeared. Turning on my stomach I set out at a measured stroke. Ten minutes of acute misery passed by as the salt dried about my face injuries and the contracting strap of the flying helmet cut into the raw surface of my chin. Buckle and leather had welded into one solid mass, preventing removal of the head-gear.

Dumb despair then suddenly gave way to shining hope. The brandy flask, of course. This was it—the emergency for which it was kept. But the problem of undoing the tunic remained, not to mention that the

WOMEN! Farmers can't grow all your vegetables

You must grow your own. Farmers are growing more of the other essential crops — potatoes, corn for your bread, and food for the cows. It's up to *you* to provide the vegetables that are vital to your children's health — especially in winter. Grow all you can. If you don't, they may go short. Turn your garden over to vegetables. Get the older children to help you. If you haven't a garden ask your local council for an allotment. DO IT NOW.

DIG for Victory

ISSUED BY THE MINISTRY OF AGRICULTURE

top: The Hawkinge perimeter track; *left:* Eric Marsden was a flight mechanic on Hurricanes at Westhampnett and Tangmere during the Battle; *top right:* a 'state' board still on the wall in a Maycrete hut at Rochford (Southend) in 1986; *right:* a field defence pillbox at Warmwell, Dorset.

tims earned for Hamlyn the DFM). North Weald's C.O., Victor Beamish, would leap through his office window rather than miss a scramble. At Northolt, Group Captain Stanley Vincent's Station Defence Flight—a lone Hurricane—had been formed to get him air-borne whenever possible.

By common concensus, the doyen of station commanders was Wing Commander Cecil Bouchier, the bright, peppery C.O. of Hornchurch, who kept morale at peak with non-stop commentaries on the Ops Room's tannoy loudspeakers. At mealtimes in the officers' mess, Old Sam, the chef, with his tall white cap, kept up his soothing flow of patter at Bouchier's behest. "Don't say you can't touch a bite, sir . . . Just a shaving of the roast beef now . . . some of the underdone." At night, Bouchier even dispensed with electricity, importing candles from Harrods' at his own expense, a softer light for the taut, strained boyish faces. "You always tried to wear your best blue for 'Daddy' Bouchier's candlelight dinners," recalls Flying Officer 'Razz' Berry of No. 603.

There were valid reasons for this solicitude. Those outsiders who saw most of the game—from commanders like Bouchier to flight mechanics like Eric Marsden—realised as no civilian ever could, the strain that The Few were undergoing, the accumulation of fear, fatigue and tension that mounted daily with each scramble.

Although few could have settled for a finite date, the crisis had peaked on July 10, when Professor Frederick Lindemann (later Lord Cherwell), Winston Churchill's scientific

tight-fitting Mae West covered the pocket as another formidable barrier. Hope and joy were running too high to be deterred by such mundane problems, and so turning with my face to the sky I set about the task of getting slightly tipsy on neat brandy. Inch by inch my ultra-sensitive fingers worked their way under the Mae West towards the breast pocket. Every movement brought with it indescribable agony, but the goal was too great to allow for weakness. At last the restraining copper button was reached—a deep breath to cope with the pain—and it was undone. Automatically my legs kept up their propulsive efforts while my hand had a rest from its labors. Then gingerly the flask was eased out of its home and brought to the surface of the water. Pain became conqueror for a while and the flask was transferred to a position between my wrists. Placing the screw stopper between my teeth, I undid it with a series of head-twists and finally the great moment arrived—the life-warming liquid was waiting to be drunk. Raising it to my mouth, I pursed my lips to drink. The flask slipped from between wet wrists and disappeared from sight. Genuine tears of rage followed this newest form of torture, which in turn gave place to a furious determination to swim to safety.

After the first few angry strokes despair returned

adviser, faced with a dearth of trained pilots and a glut of operational machines, had seen no option but to reduce drastically the pilots' operational training—from six months to four weeks. In the belief that the monthly output of pilots could be boosted from 560 to 890, Lindemann had asked: "Are not our standards of training too high? The final polish should be given in the squadrons."

From August 8 onward, as all the participants knew, more and more had acquired 'the final polish', through a cruel baptism of fire. No sooner had many pilots taxied in than

they slumped forward in their cockpits, as dead to the world as men under morphia. At Hawkinge, Pilot Officer Peter Hairs, a Hurricane pilot of No. 501 Squadron, was a case in point—"after eight scrambles in a day, you came to write up your logbook . . . and you just couldn't remember beyond putting down the number of times you'd been up . . . you couldn't remember at all . . . I had nightmares about blazing planes crashing all around me."

Many soon came to cushion their fears with liquor. "If you weren't in the air," recalled Squadron Leader John Worrall, of No.

in full force ably assisted by growing fatigue, cold and pain. Time went by unregistered. Was it minutes, hours or days since my flaming Hurricane disappeared between my legs? Was it getting dark or were my eyes closing up? How could I steer towards the shore if I couldn't see the sun? How could I see the sun if that rising pall of smoke obscured it from sight?

That rising pall of smoke . . . that rising pall of smoke. No, it couldn't be. I yelled. I splashed the water with my arms and legs until the pain brought me to a sobbing halt. Yes, the smoke was coming from a funnel—but supposing it passed without seeing me? Agony of mind was greater than agony of body and the shouting and splashing recommenced. Looking again, almost expecting that smoke and funnel had been an hallucination, I gave a fervent gasp of thanks to see that whatever ship it was, it had hove to.

All of the problems were fast disappearing and only one remained. It was one of keeping afloat for just another minute or two before all energy failed. Then I heard it—the unmistakable chug-chug of a small motor boat growing steadily louder. Soon it came into sight with a small bow wave pouring away to each side. In it sat two men in the strange garb peculiar to sailors of the British

Merchant Service. The high revving note of the engine died to a steady throb as the man astride the engine throttled back. Slowly the boat circled without attempting to pick me up. A rough voice carried over the intervening water. "What are you? A Jerry or one of ours?"

My weak reply was gagged by a mouthful of water. The other man tried as the boat came full circle for the second time. "Are you a Jerry, mate?"

Anger flooded through me. Anger, not at these sailors who had every reason to let a German pilot drown, but anger at the steady chain of events since the explosion that had reduced my tortured mind and body to its present state of near-collapse. And anger brought with it temporary energy. "You stupid pair of fucking bastards, pull me out!!"

The boat altered course and drew alongside. Strong arms leaned down

top: Wing Commander (ret) Geoffrey Page, in 1988. *right:* a drawing of Page by Frank Wootton.

32 Squadron, frankly, "you were plastered. It was as simple as that." At the Square Club, in Andover, where the pilots from Middle Wallop congregated, stupefying mixtures were soon the norm—everything from vodka and apricot brandy to brandy and port. The station M.O. at Warmwell, Wallop's forward base, Flight Lieutenant 'Monty' Bieber, still remembers mixing up 'harmless' pink drinks to quieten morning-after stomachs—"it was absolute alcohol, which clinched the hangover effect and gave an excuse to keep them off flying." But one unlucky pilot, Flying Officer Roland Dibnah of No. 1 (R.A.F.) Squadron, was now allergic to liquor. The tension was so great that merely one measure drove Dibnah vomiting to the lavatory.

Every man on the sidelines of the battle had his own personal yardstick of impending catastrophe. At Tangmere, a thin black line in the mess ledger that recorded each pilot's mealtimes was ruled beneath name after name. Mess Steward Joseph Lauderdale, at Middle Wallop, remembers that his pilots often died too soon to qualify for a change of sheets. Aircraftman George Perry, attached to No. 56 Squadron at North Weald, recalled how "boys came back men after an eighty minute sortie . . . faces would be grey . . . there'd be yellow froth round their mouths."

On August 17, when Fighter Command's thinning ranks were once more stiffened with many Fairy Battle pilots and Army Cooperation Command pilots, the training period was slashed once again—this time from a month to a bare two weeks. On the following day, twenty-seven planes were written off, eighteen

154

THE STORY OF THE PLANE THAT BUSTED THE BLITZ!

SPITFIRE

and dragged my limp body over the side and into the bottom of the boat. "The minute you swore, mate," one of them explained, "we knew you was an R.A.F. Officer."

The sodden dripping bundle was deposited on a wooden seat athwart ships. A voice mumbled from an almost lifeless body as the charred helmet was removed. One of the sailors leaned down to catch the words. "What did you say, chum?"

The mumble was more distinct the second time. "Take me to the side. I want to be sick."

The other man answered in a friendly voice, "You do it in the bottom of the boat, and we'll clean up afterwards."

But habit died hard and pride wouldn't permit it, so keeping my head down between my knees, I was able to control the sensation of nausea. Allowing me a moment or two to feel better, the first sailor produced a large clasp knife. "Better get this wet stuff off you, mate. You don't want to catch your death of cold."

The absurdity of death from a chill struck me as funny and I chuckled for the first time in a long while. To prove the sailor's point the teeth chattering recommenced. Without further ado the man with the knife set to work and deftly removed pieces of life jacket and tunic with the skill of a surgeon. Then my naked

pilots were hospitalised and ten pilots embarked on their last scramble.

Yet the steady induction of novices into the firing-line only saw the losses mounting. "I'm sorry, but I'm afraid you'll have to go in today," Squadron Leader John Thompson of No. 111 Hurricane Squadron remembers greeting two grass-green sergeants at Debden on August 24, "you see, we're so terribly short." And one of the sergeants, Raymond

Sellers, remembers it, too; he later awoke in hospital so deeply in shock that even his own name escaped him. Fifteen days earlier, on August 11, he had proudly noted twenty minutes dog fighting practice in his log book.

It is a story that Sellers recounts in humiliation, for his fellow sergeant had died, and at teatime that day the old car they shared was still parked outside the mess with their gear unpacked, but in truth he was in

body was wrapped up in a blanket produced from the seat locker.

One of them went forward to the engine and seconds later the little boat was churning her way back to the mother ship. The other sailor sat down beside me in silence, anxious to help but not knowing what to do next. I sensed the kindness of his attitude and felt that it was up to me to somehow offer him a lead. The feeling of sickness was still there from the revolting smell of burnt flesh, but I managed to gulp out "Been a lovely summer . . . hasn't it?"

The man nodded. "Aye."

(from *Tale Of A Guinea Pig* by Wing Commander Geoffrey Page)

A Hurricane of No. 145 Squadron, operating from Westhampnett in the summer of 1940.

good company. Ten days later, Flight Lieutenant Al Deere was equally shamefaced when reporting to No. 54 Squadron's intelligence officer, Tony Allen. He had taken bursts at fully six ME 109s, but somehow his bullets had failed to connect. "We're so bloody tired," Deere shrugged it off. "We're just not getting them."

Hating this involuntary intimacy with death, men grew increasingly callous, as if to immunise themselves from caring. As Pilot Officer 'Rafty' Rafter's Spitfire spun out of control near Maidstone, Bill Read heard an angry 603 pilot break radio silence: "Bugger—he owed me a fiver!" (After hospital treatment, Rafter survived to repay it, but nobody knew that until later). It was the same when Pilot Officer David Bell-Salter was once prematurely written off by the Hurricane pilots of No. 253. A girlfriend of his who called the Kenley mess asking to "speak to David" was told curtly, "You can't—he's dead," before his pal hung up.

Since a telephone bell denoted a scramble, the fear of bells became a near primal obsession. "I even panicked at bicycle bells," remembers Ronnie Hamlyn, and Bill Read, of 603 confirms, "I was so geared up that even

on leave I'd run at the sound of an ambulance bell." Even the ground crews became infected. "For a good ten years after 1940," admitted Eric Marsden, "whenever an electric bell sounded off I jumped looking for something to do. I was conditioned like Pavlov's dogs!" With Pilot Officer Christopher Currant, of No. 605 Squadron at Croydon, the phobia extended even to running. "If you saw anyone run, you felt you'd got to, too. I hated to see airmen do it. I'd tear strips off them— 'Don't run about the place—walk properly.' You got trigger tense about it."

To pilots coming fresh to the battle, many of the older hands seemed near to the end of their tether. Even the cheerful Al Deere found his nerves at snapping-point; an unexpected shout over the radio-telephone set his heart pounding like a trip-hammer. Sergeant James 'Ginger' Lacey had to fly with his right foot tucked in the loop of the rudder bar in order to combat the twitching. Pilot Officer Charles Ambrose of No. 46 Hurricane Squadron recalls being genuinely shocked by the lethargy of No. 151 Squadron when they relieved them at Stapleford Tawney satellite on September 1. While 46 had been in reserve at Digby, Lincolnshire, 151 at North Weald had lost two C.Os and were then down to seven survivors.

The seven were lunching at 11 a.m., Ambrose remembers, when a breathless telephone orderly announced the controller's scramble order. He remembers, too, their flight commander's withering reply: "Tell him we're finishing our bloody lunch first."

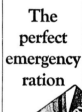

SMALL TALK

AN R.A.F. VERNACULAR
CIRCA 1940

A/C aircraft

ACE a top performer. Later, a pilot credited with shooting down five enemy aircraft

ACK ACK anti-aircraft gunfire

AFS Auxiliary Fire Service

A.I. airborne interception

AMMO ammunition

ANGELS altitude in 1,000 foot increments, i.e. angels one-five = 15,000 feet

A.M.O. Air Ministry Order

A.S.R. air-sea rescue

ATS Auxiliary Training Service

BACON, TO SAVE ONE'S to save one's life

BAGS a large quantity of something

BAG, TO to collect or secure

BAGS OF SWANK pride in a job

BALE OUT to leave an aircraft by parachute

BANDIT an enemy aircraft; raider

BAR another of the same decoration

BASE WALLAH headquarters staff

BEAT UP, TO to attack; to celebrate with vigour

BEETLE HOME, TO to go back

BINDER one who nags or bores

BINDERS brakes

BINDING TIMES a period without action

BIRD a girl

BITS AND PIECES a crash

BLACK CAT cigarette

BLACKOUT period when all but certain limited light sources must be shielded to minimise target visibility to enemy aircraft

BLACK OUT to lose consciousness briefly, when blood is drained from the brain by excessive centrifugal force encountered in certain aircraft maneuvering

BLITZ a lightning attack or offensive

BLOTTO drunk

BLOWER a supercharger; one who exaggerates

BODY SNATCHER a stretcher bearer

BODS aircraftmen/women

BOGEY an unidentified aircraft, sighted or encountered

BOOB an error

BOOST the application of extra pressure, aircraft manifold pressure

BOSCHE a German

BOUNCE a surprise attack by an aircraft on another, from a higher altitude

BOWSER a gasoline (or petrol) refuelling truck for aircraft

BRASSED fed up; irritated

BRIEFING instructions given to fighter pilots and bomber crews prior to take-off on ops

BROWNED OFF fed up; angry

BUSTER proceed as fast as possible

CAPSTAN cigarette

CART, IN THE in trouble

CAT. FOUR a write-off crash

CAT. THREE a repairable crash

CATERPILLAR one who jumps from an aircraft in flight and saves his life by the use of a parachute

CD Civil Defence

CHAT loose talk

CHEESED OFF fed up; had enough

CHIEFY a Flight Sergeant

CHOCKS AWAY let's go

CIRCUITS AND BUMPS take-offs and landings

CLAPPED OUT worn out; useless

CLOCK airspeed indicator

CLOUD 5/10TH half the sky is covered by cloud

COLLECT A GONG to receive a medal (decoration)

COLLECT, TO to shoot down an enemy aircraft; to bag

C.O. Commanding Officer

CONTAIN, TO to keep busy

CONVOY a number of ships in a formation for mutual protection

COOP perspex hood covering a pilot in a fighter aircraft

CORKER, A a mine; a woman

CORKSCREW, TO violent action taken to shake off an enemy aircraft in a dogfight

CRABBING flying close to the water; later, side-slipping an aircraft, usually on a landing approach

CRACK, TO HIT IT A to adopt a vigourous offensive; to create a major disturbance

CRATE an aircraft

CRUMPET a girl or woman

CURTAINS killed

CUSHY a comfortable job

C.W.G.C. Commonwealth War Graves Commision

DAME a girl or woman

DART cigarette

DECK the ground; sea level

DECORATIONS awards; medals; gongs

D.F.C. Distinguished Flying Cross

D.F.M. Distinguished Flying Medal

DIM one who shows a lack of common sense

DISPERSAL area on an airfield in which aircraft are dispersed as a protection against enemy air attack

DITCH to make a forced landing in the sea

Do Dornier (German) aircraft

DO any event, from an action in the air, to a social gathering in the mess

DOGFIGHT air battle or engagement sometimes involving several aircraft

DOGGO quiet; hidden

DOWN THE DRAIN in trouble

DRINK the sea

D.R.O. daily routine order

DUFF poor; bad

DUFF GEN incorrect information

du MAURIER cigarette

DUST-UP heated action

E/A enemy aircraft

ERK an Aircraftman; mechanic

E.T.A. estimated time of arrival

EVASIVE ACTION maneuvering from an attack or from flak

FAN a propeller or airscrew

F.F.I. (free from infection) body inspection

FIGHTER BOY a pilot of Fighter Command

FIX a determination of position, obtained by radio or wireless or from the observation of sun or stars

FLAP an air action; an occasion calling for action, and when such an action is under way, 'a flap is on'

FLAP UP fast

FLAT OUT as fast as possible

FLAT SPIN, IN A bewildered; at a loss to act

FLEAPIT a cinema

FLICKS searchlights; also, the cinema

FLIGHT, A normally six aircraft

FLIGHT, THE the Flight Sergeant

FLIP, A a flight

FLYBLOW, A a flying boat

FRUIT SALAD a lot of medals

FULL BORE as fast as possible

GAGGLE a formation of aircraft

GEN information

GET CRACKING get going; get a move on

GET MOBILE same as above

GET SOME IN sarcastic expression meaning, get yourself some experience

GET THE DRIFT to understand

GET UP OFF YOUR KNEES, TO to pull yourself together

GOES LIKE A BOMB very fast

GO FOR A BURTON killed; missing; destroyed; awry

GOING AND COMING two-way radio

GOLDFISH CLUB any airman downed in the sea and saved by a dinghy or life vest, is a member

GOLD FLAKE cigarette

GONE FOR SIX missing

GONG a medal or decoration

GOOD SHOW, A a meritorious performance

GRAND good; wonderful

GRAVEL CRUSHING foot drill

GREEN new; untried

HAD IT, HE'S killed; destroyed

HAND IT TO, TO credit with merit

HARE AFTER, TO to pursue

He Heinkel (German) aircraft

HEAVIES large bombs; large anti-aircraft guns

HIT THE SILK bale out

HOLD THE CAN, TO to have the responsibility

HOOVES feet

HOT new; new information

HOT UP, TO to prepare for maximum performance

H.Q. Headquarters

HUMID without personality; wet

HUN a German

HURRI a Hurricane fighter aircraft

I.F.F. Identification Friend or Foe

IN A FLAP out of control; over-active

IN THE DRINK down at sea

I.O. Intelligence Officer

JANKERS punishment; extra duty

JERRY a German

JINK to take evasive action

Ju Junkers (German) aircraft

JUICE the North Sea

K.I.A. killed in action

KILL an enemy aircraft downed in action

KIP, TO to sleep

KNOWS HIS ONIONS competent

KIPPER KITE an aircraft of Coastal Command

KITE an aircraft

LAID ON supplied

LEAD bullets

LET DOWN descend through cloud

LET UP throttle back; ease off

LINE ASTERN aircraft in trail formation, one behind another

LINE, TO SHOOT A to brag or boast

LIT UP suddenly started

L.M.F. lack of moral fibre

LOGBOOK a pilot's record of his flying activity

LOOK SEE, A a reconnaissance

LOOSE OFF, TO to fire

LOSE YOUR WOOL, TO to lose your cool or composure

LOW DOWN, THE the inside information

LUFTWAFFE the German Air Force

MAE WEST an inflatable life preserver vest worn by pilots and aircrew

MAGGIE Miles Magister training aircraft

MAIN BIT the major section of an aircraft

ME Messerschmitt (German) aircraft

MEAT DISCS pair of identity discs worn around neck by flying personnel

MEAT WAGGON ambulance

MESS dining rooms, bars and living quarters

MET meteorological weatherman

MILLING AROUND aircraft swirling about, sometimes refers to a defensive circle of aircraft protecting each others tails

MIXED DEATH various types of ammunition

MIX-UP a dogfight or air battle

M.O. Medical Officer

MOB the Royal Air Force

M.U. maintenance unit

MUSH insufficient airspeed to maintain altitude

NATTER chatter; the drone of talk

N.C.O. non-commissioned officer

N/F night fighter

N.O.K. next of kin

NOSEGAY cigarette

NUMBER aircraft serial number

NO JOY no contact with enemy aircraft

ON THE CLOCK on the airspeed indicator

ON TOP SIDE in the air

ON YOUR TOES ready for an emergency

OPS combat flying operations

OPS ROOM, THE the station operations room where information is collected and operations are planned

ORBIT, TO to circle around

OTHER HALF, THE the second drink to match the first

O.T.U. operational training unit

PACK UP cease to function; give up

PACKET, A a lot of trouble

PAN OUT, TO to happen

PANIC a more intense flap

PANIC BOWLER a steel helmet

PANCAKE to land

PANSY effeminate

PARK DRIVE cigarette

PARTY, A originally referred to a sexual experience with a female; an air battle; a difficult experience

PASS THE BUCK, TO to pass the responsibility

PASSING CLOUDS cigarette

PASSION KILLER the blackout

PASTING, A a punishment

PEEL OFF, TO to turn away from a formation, usually in a steep climbing turn

PERCH to land

PERSPEX shatter-proof, transparent material used in windscreens, cockpit hoods and gun-turrets

PICCADILLY cigarette

PICKLED drunk

PIECE OF CAKE a cinch; dead easy

PIECE OF NICE any pleasant entertainment

PIE-EYED drunk

PIN POINT, TO to locate precisely

PISSED drunk

PLAYERS cigarette

PLUMES condensation smoke trails seen in the sky during high altitude air battles

POOP OFF, TO to open fire

POOR VIEW, TO TAKE A to view with displeasure

POPSIE a girl

PRANG crash; damage; hit

PRESS ON REGARDLESS carry on, come what may

PRESS THE TIT, TO to press the button that fires the guns of a multi-gun fighter; also, to apply emergency boost

PUKKA genuine; accurate

PUSH OFF, TO to go

QUACK Medical Officer

QUAGS Quaglinos restaurant in London

QUICK SQUIRT a short burst of gunfire

RACKET a swindle; a scam

RADAR radio direction and ranging

R.D.F. radio direction finding (radar)

RANG THE BELL a good result

RASPBERRY vocal evidence of displeasure

RECCE, RECCO a reconnaissance flight

RICK VIEW, TO TAKE A to view with pleasure

RISE AND SHINE get up

R.O.C. Royal Observer Corps

ROPEY no good; decrepit, duff, doubtful

R/T radio telephone

SATURATED without personality; wet

SCRAM, TO to leave in a hurry

SCRAMBLE a very fast take-off by fighter aircraft

SCRAP, A a fight

SCREW, THE the propeller or airscrew

SENIOR SERVICE cigarette

SHAKY DO, A a bad flap

SHIP an aeroplane

SHOT DOWN IN FLAMES reprimanded

SKIPPER the pilot or boss

SKIRT a girl

SKY PILOT a Chaplain

SLAVE a servant

SLURGE a studious chap

SMASHED drunk

SMASHING super; marvelous

SNAPPERS enemy fighters

SNOGGING kissing

SOAKING GLASS OF WET, A a gin

SOBRANIE cigarette

SOGGY an aircraft is soggy when the controls react slowly

SORTIE one flight by one aircraft

SOZZLED drunk

SPARROW START very early

SPILL THE BEANS, TO to give information

SPIN, TO to lose control

SPIT Spitfire fighter aircraft

SPOT, A a drink

SPOT, TO to see

SPROG a raw recruit; someone new to a job

SQUADRON usually twelve to eighteen aircraft

SQUADRON VIC a V formation of aircraft

STAND-DOWN released from ops

STATION air base

STICK, A a line of bombs

STOOGE to idle around; to make an uneventful sortie

STRAWBERRY a rare evidence

of praise

STREAMLINED PIECE a girl with a slim, lovely figure

STRIPPED loss of rank

TAIL-END CHARLIE a pilot flying to the rear and slightly above his squadron, weaving from side to side and watching for enemy aircraft

TAKE THE DAY OFF never mind . . . its not *that* important; relax

TAKE YOUR FINGER OUT! wake up!; snap out of it! use your head!

TALLY HO! huntsman's call given over the r/t by a fighter pilot to signal that he has sighted the enemy aircraft and is starting his attack

TEAR OFF A STRIP, TO to dress down one of inferior rank

TENNER cigarette

THE CHOP killed

THROW HIS HAND IN, TO to give up

THROUGH THE GATE to get maximum power from the engine, literally by pushing the throttle through a gate on the quadrant to the emergency setting

TICKING OVER an engine running slowly and evenly

TICK OFF, TO to visit displeasure on an individual as an indication of adverse criticism

TOFFEE NOSE a snob

TRACER magnesium ammunition that traces its path to the target with a smoke trail and glow

TROC, THE Trocadero restaurant, London

TWILIGHTS summer grey knickers of the W.A.A.F.

TWIRP a simple-minded soul

TWITCHING nervous in the service; a sprog pilot running into enemy aircraft on his first operational flight might well find himself twitching

295 leave pass

TURF cigarette

UNDERCART the legs or wheels of anything

UPSTAIRS in the air

U/S unserviceable

U.X.B. unexploded bomb

VIEW to take a dim view of something or someone

V.R. the Volunteer Reserve, started in 1936 with weekend pilots in city, county and university squadrons

WAFFLE, TO to show indecision

WET without personality

WHACK, A an attempt

WHIFF, A oxygen

WIZARD! good show; well done! marvelous; great

WOODBINES cigarette

WORK OUT, TO to function

WRIST BREAKERS another term for Twilights

W/T wireless telephone

POPULAR SONGS AND FILMS IN THE SUMMER AND AUTUMN OF 1940

SOME OF THE SONGS

I'll Never Smile Again
Sierra Sue
The Breeze and I
Fools Rush In
Imagination
Where Was I?
When the Swallows Come Back to Capistrano
I'm Nobody's Baby
I'm Stepping Out With A Memory Tonight
Blueberry Hill
The Nearness of You
Practice Makes Perfect

SOME OF THE FILMS

The Lion Has Wings
Wuthering Heights
Only Angels Have Wings
The Cowboy and the Lady
The Four Feathers
Pinnochio
Charlie Chan in the City of Darkness
Andy Hardy Gets Spring Fever
Ninotchka
Jesse James
Another Thin Man
Destry Rides Again
Blondie Brings Up Baby
Courageous Dr. Christian
Secrets of Dr. Kildare
Judge Hardy and Son

EYEWITNESS

right: 'Battle of Britain', a
painting by Louis Keene.

IT WAS, ARGUABLY, World War II's smallest observation post; a promontory known as Shakespeare's Cliff, one mile west of Dover, Kent, looming 350 feet above the English Channel. From August to mid-September, this was the amphitheatre from which the free world's press viewed the Battle of Britain, squatting amid ripening red currant bushes, and beset by fluttering swarms of white chalk butterflies. Significantly, of the 150 newsmen assembled there, two-thirds were Americans, for the Battle was the stuff of which international headlines was made.

A few had been longtime observers of the Britain that stood alone: the burly red-haired Quentin Reynolds, of *Collier's* magazine, Edward R. Murrow, of C.B.S., always seen in the Savile Row houndstooth jacket that had become his trademark. Others, although connoisseurs of war in Spain and Finland, were newcomers to the English scene: the svelte blonde Virginia Cowles, a Bostonian covering for the London *Sunday Times*, the red headed Vincent Sheean of the North American Newspaper Alliance (NANA), the moon-faced young Ed Beattie, of United Press. The most colourful newsman of all this assembly was Ray Sprigle of the Pittsburgh *Post Gazette*, marked out by his corncob pipe and Stetson.

Destiny was in the air, and as they watched the thin streamers of smoke staining the sky, moving in deadly concert with the whirling, snarling ballet of planes, all of them were expectant of an historic last stand. Ben Robertson, a likeable fair-haired youngster from the New York daily, *P.M.*, thought of the settlers manning the ramparts of Daniel Boone's Kentucky stockade: the frontier then had been the west, but now England's frontier was the sky. Vincent Sheean recalled Dolores La Pasionara's exhortation at Madrid during the Spanish Civil War: "Camaradas, no podremos perder más territorio." (My friends, we can lose no more territory). Others, like Robert Bunnelle, of the Associated Press, were more impressed by the cottagers of Dover, living on in premises almost demolished by bomb blast. "It's a bit public having no windows," one householder confessed, "but the fresh air is nice."

They had brought along their typewriters and their cameras, but as they queued impatiently to file their dispatches from the phone booths in Dover's Grand Hotel, they had, almost without exception, left behind their objectivity. The London Bureau chief of *The New York Times*, Raymond Daniell, was adamant on this point. "Neutrality of thought was a luxury to which war correspondents in the first World War could afford to treat themselves," he maintained. "We, their successors, cannot."

But while their sympathies lay firmly with the Spitfire and Hurricane pilots, it was still a battle shrouded in mystery—as much for the newsmen as for the farm workers, the Home Guardsmen and the air raid wardens who watched those sky-high combats. Although young Whitelaw Reid, of the *New York Herald Tribune*, hailed an impending invasion as "the biggest story since the coming of Christ," the Germans were evasive on this score. "The censors won't let us mention the business," Murrow's Berlin correspondent,

Saturday 31 August

We did four patrols today ending up with one on which we intercepted about 30 DO17s and 20–30 ME109s. I got onto an ME109's tail, after an ineffectual attack on the bombers, and got in several long bursts at about 300 yards. However, nothing was observed in the way of damage. Another got on my tail and I had to break away. I succeeded in throwing him off in a steep turn but not before he had put an explosive bullet through my wing. Sgt Stewart was shot down, but was safe. I burst another tail wheel today.

(from the diary of Pilot Officer Denis H. Wissler No. 17 Squadron)

Ready for a raid—at the Castle Bromwich Spitfire assembly plant, 1940.

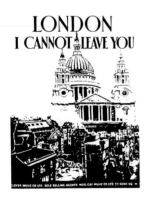

William L. Shirer, noted in his diary on August 5, three days before the Channel convoy attack, and even one month later, following the pile-driving assault on Biggin Hill, "The word 'invasion' is still taboo."

What the correspondents witnessed, on days as spectacular as Sunday September 15, was a clawing, stalling mass of fighters bent on destruction, battling within a cube 80 miles long by 30 miles broad, more than five miles high: a battle that within thirty minutes might number above 200 individual dog fights. Yet the sights as often as not, produced poetic rather than warlike images. To Hilde Marchant, of *The Daily Express*, the planes "seemed to make an aluminium ceiling to the sky." For Ben Robertson, the silver wheeling shapes were "like the white birds you see in far off parts of the Pacific Ocean, like the white birds you see off Pitcairn."

Despite their partisan stand, the American eyewitnesses still faced censorship problems. In one mid-Channel battle between Messerschmitts and Spitfires, seven German fighters retired with engines smoking and three British planes hit the water. It was, both Robertson and Quentin Reynolds agreed, "a grand story, and a fine tribute to the R.A.F.," but one censor on the Ministry of Information's staff disagreed. Robertson could mention the loss of seven Messerschmitts but the British losses were inadmissible.

Robertson, a tenacious youngster, elected to fight this. From the censor himself, he went to a higher level, and finally, three levels higher, to the Minister of Information, Alfred Duff Cooper, who had only recently announced in a radio broadcast: "We are quite ready to receive (Hitler) now and we shall really be very disappointed if he doesn't turn up." Duff Cooper thus had little option than to pass the story—but it had taken Robertson thirteen hours of impassioned argument to win his point.

Yet one incident that profoundly shocked the Americans, a broadcast by the BBC's Charles Gardner, was one to which the Ministry of Information had turned a blind eye: a highly partisan description of a dogfight above Dover's white cliffs, charged with as much adrenalin as a racetrack commentary. "Somebody's hit a German . . . and he's coming down absolutely out of control," Gardner was heard to enthuse. "The pilot's baled out by parachute . . . he's going to slap into the sea and there he goes . . . SMASH. Oh boy, I've never seen anything so good as this . . . ."

Committed though they were to the British cause, the Americans could not share this ghoulish approval to battle—and for the most part this was in keeping. Even fifty years later, the few exceptions are still traumatic memories. One eyewitness, Ernest Collier, a gardener at East Wittering, Sussex, never forgot how a Heinkel belly landed on the beach at high watermark; as the first crewman, unhurt, clambered out on to the wing, a soldier raised his rifle and shot him dead. At Coulsdon Golf Course, in Surrey, Home Guardsman Richard May, hastening towards a German who had baled out, met two soldiers who had been first on the scene. Even now, May remembers how one soldier, carrying a pilot's gauntlet glove,

162

announced tersely, "We've fixed him." Further up the course, May found a tall man wearing the Iron Cross, his head smashed to a bloody pulp.

But most who encountered the Germans recall a a lighter hearted approach—in line with one of the few chivalrous battles to stand out from World War II. Alan Henderson, a very sharp eyed ten-year-old evacuee from Charlton Park, South London, caught a glimpse of this at Hadlow Down, Sussex:

164

while the farm workers kept their pitchforks at the ready, the girls "used to doll themselves up and vie with each other to be the first on the spot . . ." In Mercery Lane, Canterbury, tobacconist George Woods remembers a puzzled Home Guard hastening into his shop with a query: was there a brand of cigarettes called State Express 555? When Woods confirmed it, the man explained: "We've bagged a German pilot and he's sent me to get them." At least one German adhered strictly to protocol. It was with flawless composure that a manservant at Buckhurst, Earl De La Warr's Sussex estate announced: "An officer of the German armed forces is waiting to see you in the drawing room my lord."

Farmer John Hacking was impressed by the Germans' sense of humour; at Cadborough Farm, one pilot who baled out landed halfway through the tiled roof of a farm worker's privy. In faultless English he hailed Hacking: "I seem to have come from the shit into the shit." And at Duxford, Squadron Leader Douglas Blackwood recalls one bomber crew begging the guard room for the loan of some boot polish; they were due for interrogation and their flying boots were a disgrace. Whether formal or frivolous, their morale measured up. Assistant Mechanic Alfred Lacy, of the Margate lifeboat, remembers with admiration, "If they could stand at all, they stood at attention."

At Biggin Hill, Flight Lieutenant Peter Brothers reminisces, the pilots of No. 32 Squadron once liberated an ME 110 pilot from the guard room, bore him off to the mess for a drink, then took him for a tour of

far top left: a pillbox on the cliffs above Folkestone; *far bottom left:* the observer post at Lympne Castle; *top left:* Lansdowne House, London WW II home of writer Quentin Reynolds. *above:* Mary Smith of Elham near Hawkinge, recorded the many local air actions in her diary which was to become the basis for the book *Harvest of Messerschmitts* by Dennis Knight.

Like a woman who has forgotten rape,/the island dozes, cosy in sunlight; no echoes shiver her still pools,/no memories play back the tramp/of jackboots/across her mossy breasts. Fortresses crumble on the cliffs/among the ghosts of guns/and concrete bunkers battened down with gorse/and jagged dentures of currents hurrying to slap against their sides.

(from *Fly Past Alderney* by Lois Clark)

165

I saw the lightning's gleaming rod//Reach forth and write upon the sky/The awful autograph of God.

(*The Ship In The Desert* by Joaquin Miller)

The vapour trails of British and German fighters twisting in actions high above Lewes, Sussex, on Monday, November 18, 1940. A rampart of Lewes Castle is partially visible at lower right. To see the image as it appeared to the photographer, Edward Reeves, please turn the book 90 degrees, putting the castle at lower left.

right: Air fighting in the summer and autumn of 1940 was commonplace over Beachy Head, where German raiders were frequently intercepted by Hurricanes and Spitfires.

their dispersal. It was not until Pilot Officer Pniak, one of the squadron's Poles, chalked "MADE IN GERMANY, FINISHED IN ENGLAND" over the squadron's trophies—a JU 88 machine gun, the fin of a Heinkel—that the atmosphere became abruptly icy. It was at Biggin Hill, too, that Squadron Leader Robert Stanford Tuck chatted so warmly with a shot-down JU 88 pilot in the sick bay that the boy, on an impulse, presented him with the Iron Cross second class he was wearing above his hospital-issue nightshirt.

He explained: "For me, the war is finished, but it would be nice for me to know that my cross is still flying—still free."

When they look back to that far-off summer, it is the calm unflinching demeanour that they remember most—almost as if, in a parody of British stoicism, it was not the done thing "to make a fuss." Professional observers noted this, even at the time. Ed Murrow, strolling in a Sussex village street, was astonished to hear a police loudspeaker announce without warning, "Clear the streets for His Majesty the King. Hold that horse's head," before King George VI's big maroon car purred sedately by. Although the country was on the brink of invasion, Murrow noted that the King's sole escort was a lone patrolman on a motor cycle.

This same phenomenon was witnessed by the *Daily Herald's* Reginald Foster at Dover's Grand Hotel. It was the lunch hour, and one guest was complaining, with marked originality of shrapnel in his soup, but the head waiter, George Garland, not only coaxed him into overlooking the slip-up but was

greeting newcomers to the dining room: "Good morning, sir! A nice table here, sir, away from the broken glass . . . ."

"We're a very stolid lot of people, after all," comments George Woods, and all along the south coast this was the prevailing mood. At Folkestone, a farmer's wife, Mrs Mary Castle, remembers queuing outside a patissier's while shrapnel and machine-gun bullets spattered the pavement. At once the airmen queuing in the shop's doorway ahead of her, stepped politely back, raising their forage caps, enabling her to pass inside. At Homefield, Kent, their ancestral home, the Smithers family recalled how William, their butler, did the rounds of the lawns after each dog-fight, sweeping up spent machine-gun bullets as deftly as he had ever brushed crumbs from a damask tablecloth. At Worthing, Sussex, the Ministry of Information's Vera Arlett found that her maid was equally matter-of-fact. "Shall we have the plums and custard for dessert—oh, and they're machine-gunning the back garden."

Later, on a bus bound for Shoreham along the coast, Miss Arlett was intrigued to see the conductor, craning from the step, was keeping toll of the battle overhead like an umpire, scribbling the score on a scrap of paper tacked by the door—but this again had become commonplace. And all along the south coast, Ben Robertson, of *P.M.*, noted that the newspaper sellers always chalked up the day's results in terms of a cricket match: "R.A.F. v GERMANS, 61 for 26—CLOSE OF PLAY TODAY 12 FOR 0."

At times this quiet sense of satisfaction

top: A JU88 shot down near Horsham, Sussex, September 9, 1940; top right: remains of a JU88 at Horsepasture Farm, August 12, 1940; right; a schoolboy plays with the partially buried engine of a downed Bf109 in Kent, 1940.

came close to cockiness. One farmer put a novel proposition—which was promptly rejected—to Kent County Council headquarters at Maidstone: he proposed to rope off a meadow, charge sixpence admission for the Spitfire Fund, and advertise it as "The Only Field in East Kent in which No German Aircraft has yet Fallen."

What so many eyewitnesses remember, in retrospect, is the noise: the fearful martial music of a bombardment that never seemed to stop. Mrs Joanna Thompson, a Folkestone confectioner's widow, recalls spending the best part of a week crouched inside her Anderson shelter with her eight-year-old son, Roger: a week in which shrapnel crashed and

170

I am purely evil;/Hear the thrum/of my evil engine;/Evilly I come. The stars are thick as flowers/In the meadows of July;/A fine night for murder/Winging through the sky.

(from *Song Of The Bomber* by Ethel Mannin)

below: An ROC observer; *top right:* Land girls at work behind Dover; *lower right:* children playing with the parachute of an R.A.F. pilot shot down over southern England on September 4, 1940; *far right:* German recon photo of Dover harbor, 1940.

bounced like thunderbolts on the shelter's tin roof, while the sky seemed to rain blazing planes, parachutes, even flying boots. Near Biggin Hill airfield, in the village of St Mary Cray, Mrs Mary Simcox has a vivid memory of darting from her mother's shelter with a dustbin lid serving as a steel helmet, but even four feet below ground, with three thick top-coats wound round her head, she could not shut out the noise.

In the darkness she felt her mother's left hand clutched in hers while her right hand told her rosary: there was no other way of communication.

The noise of the battle affected others in unpredictable ways. At Abbotsbury, Dorset, Fred Lexster, the swanherd who had had charge of the unique 1,200-strong swannery for 25 years, and had even shown off his charges to the dancer Anna Pavlova, still recalls his sense of outrage that summer. The devil's chorus of sound so distracted his birds they refused to hatch their eggs. Flight Lieutenant Geoffrey Hovenden, the medical officer at Hawkinge, tells of an entire sick parade of station defence troops complaining of wax in their ears. With the aid of an auriscope, Hovenden corrected their diagnosis: the non-stop percussion of the pom-pom guns had blocked their ears with blood clots, rendering them temporarily stone deaf.

Most eyewitnesses still insist that there was no escaping the impact of the battle. Land Girl Liz Bradburne, of the 80,000 strong Women's Land Army, remembers her alarm, in an orchard near Maidstone, as ripe red apples, lashed by shrapnel hailed down like cannonballs; she and her co-workers fell face down, shielding their heads with wicker baskets. By contrast, eighteen-year-old Brenda Hancock, picking apples to help the war effort near West Malling airfield, proved more adventurous. Every dog-fight saw her venturing still higher up the ladder—something she would never have deigned to do where mere apples were involved.

Some, almost with a sense of bravado, hark back to the pitiful coastal defences—an era when only one Home Guardsman in three had a rifle and when the Army was in little better shape. From Dover to Southampton, they recall with awe, there was only one machine-gun to defend each 1,500 yards of beach. Private Alfred Neill, of the 5th Battalion, Shropshire Light Infantry, remembers one Bren gun among 950 men to defend the port of Deal. One concrete pillbox outside Dover was defended by twenty trainee signallers, among them Private Ben Angell, with rifles they barely knew how to fire.

The weird barricade alone showed the shape of the guerilla war that many believed was still to come. At Chilham, Kent, there were tree trunks from the sawmill; at Tonbridge, tar barrels from the distillery; at Goring, in Sussex, a flimsy latticework of old iron bedsteads. A surveyor, Sidney Loweth, remembers that inland, at Sidcup crossroads, the police had dumped 100 tons of glass, as if for a medieval siege. Reginald Blunt, an agricultural contractor at Deal told of waiting each night until 11 p.m., when the last bus had finally gone, before dutifully blocking the road with his three traction engines and a

Inland, within a hollow vale, I stood;/And saw, while sea was calm and air was clear,/The coast of France—the coast of France how near!/Drawn almost into frightful neighborhood./I shrunk; for verily the barrier flood/Was like a lake, or river bright and fair,/A span of waters; yet what power is there!/What mightiness for evil and for good!/Even so doth God protect us if we be Virtuous and wise. Winds blow, and waters roll, Strength to the brave, and Power, and Deity;/Yet in themselves are nothing! One decree/Spake laws to them, and said that by the soul/Only, the Nations shall be great and free.

(from *September, 1802: Near Near Dover* by William Wordsworth)

steamroller.

For a few, the war struck mercilessly at all that they cherished. At 2 p.m. on August 18, though the air raid siren had sounded, there was nothing to warn Mrs Doris Addison, a coalman's wife and mother of Delma, aged six, and ten-year-old Frank, that danger was imminent. At their tiny cottage, 'The Warren', close by the millstream at Hurst Green, in Surrey, Doris Addison was just dishing up the Sunday joint when they heard the droning of an engine, louder and louder, until the drone gave place to a high pitched scream. Even Bob, their two-year-old liver and white spaniel, huddled uneasily beneath the table. Though the Addisons did not know it, one of thirty-one Dorniers that had raided Kenley and Biggin Hill, hotly pursued by the pilots of No. 111 Squadron, was in dire distress.

Just south of 'The Warren' the Dornier struck the ground with the screech of tortured metal, already disintegrating in a sweeping sheet of flame. Ripping through a hedge and shedding its full bomb load everywhere, it bounced partly over 'The Warren', spraying everything in its path with blazing fuel. From the Fire Service post up the lane, where he had seen everything, Auxiliary Fireman Dick Addison was racing to protect his family.

Inside the cottage, Doris Addison and the children were taken unawares; following one appalling explosion, the open kitchen door was a shaking yellow curtain of flame. The resourceful Mrs Addison bustled the children into the downstairs bathroom, then turned back for Bob. But the spaniel, panic stricken, had bolted through the open door, seemingly into the heart of the flames.

Somehow, though they never forgot that day, the Addisons managed to come through. At first, the children were inconsolable, lamenting the loss of Bob: it had been Delma's whim to dress him up in a bonnet and shawl and wheel him around in her pram. But when the dog was found a few fields away, badly burned but alive, the local vet, McConnachie Ingram, took Bob into his care and six weeks later delivered him alive and well—his black nose scorched pink, four bootees protecting his damaged pads.

After only one night spent with their neighbours, the Addisons moved back into 'The Warren' to find that the damage had been superficial after all. Opening the larder door, the first thing Doris Addison saw was the Sunday lunch blancmange, still untouched, and she told Dick triumphantly: "I think if I dust it off we can eat it after all."

*

That is how the eyewitnesses remember it now: a heightened battle, every moment fraught with excitement, as if a vast aerial circus had been staged exclusively for their diversion that summer and autumn.

Only the combatants, like Pete Brothers, recall the reality—"hours of excruciating boredom interspersed with moments of pure terror." Only outsiders like Edward R. Murrow remembered the aching tension: "Those were the days and nights and even weeks when time seemed to stand still."

THEY ALSO FOUGHT
FOR BRITAIN

below: The Polish Air
Force memorial near
R.A.F. Northholt; right:
Flight Lieutenant John A.
Kent, a Canadian, of No.
303 (Polish) Squadron, by
Sir William Rothenstein.

TOWARDS 4:35 P.M. on Friday August 30, one pilot's role-reversal, on a routine training flight, marked a turning point in the Battle of Britain. At 10,000 feet, north of the tiny cathedral city of St Albans, in Hertfordshire, the twenty-three Poles of No. 303 (Kosciuszko) Squadron, their Hurricane fuselages distinguished by small red and white checkerboards, were set to rendezvous with six Blenheims and execute dummy attacks on them. For Squadron Leader Zdzislaw Krasnodebski's pilots, all of whom had undergone two years training and clocked up 500 flying hours, it was an assignment they viewed with the profoundest contempt.

Just then Flying Officer Ludwig Paszkiewicz, a very shy and unassuming boy, saw a Hurricane much like his own plunging downwards towards a smoking cluster of rooftops. A thousand feet above the squadron, to port, he saw that German bombers, as many ME 109s and a scatter of British fighters, were caught up in a frenzied dog fight. But although Paszkiewicz alerted 303's joint commander, Squadron Leader Ronald Kellett, "Hullo, Apany Leader, bandits ten o'clock," Kellett seemed not to have heard. So, pressing the emergency control which sent his supercharger to a maximum of twelve boosts, Paszkiewicz streaked for the fray.

Kellett, a florid chunkily-built peacetime stockbroker had, in fact, heard clearly; his grunted response was no more than, "If you want to be a hero, be one." As of August 30, the squadron's status, because of well-nigh insuperable language barriers, was strictly non-operational.

But Paszkiewicz recognised no such constraints. Ahead of him, a strange plane was banking in a steep dive; as he followed in a half-roll, he glimpsed the black cross marking the wing of a slim pencil-shaped Dornier. From 100 yards dead astern Paszkiewicz fired—303's first symbolic burst in the Battle of Britain—and kept firing until the bomber's starboard engine gouted flame. Abruptly, one prescient crewman baled out before the Dornier powerdived towards the earth.

That evening, impressed despite himself, Kellett phoned Headquarters, Fighter Command, urging, "Under the circumstances, I *do* think we might call them operational." Accordingly, next day, August 31, the eve of Germany's 1939 attack on Poland, 303 was at last made part of the battle.

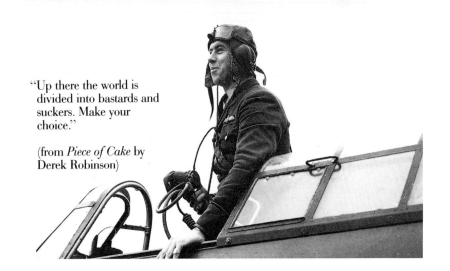

"Up there the world is divided into bastards and suckers. Make your choice."

(from *Piece of Cake* by Derek Robinson)

This was ironic, for among almost 600 Allied pilots who fought alongside the British throughout the battle, few were more seasoned in air warfare than the Poles. Yet most British commanders had known grave initial doubts as to the wisdom of all-Polish squadrons, and no one more so than Air Chief Marshal Sir Hugh Dowding. "But my doubts were laid to rest," Dowding conceded later, "because all three squadrons (besides 303, 302 *Polish* Squadron and 310 *Czech* Squadron were operational from August 20 and August 26 respectively) swung into the fight with a dash and enthusiasm which is beyond praise." For could they, many had at first wondered, preserve their fighting spirit after the disastrous campaigns in Poland and France? As Winnipeg-born Flight Lieutenant Johnny Kent summed up his reaction to an appointment as a 303 flight commander: "That really gave me the screamers! All I knew about the Polish Air Force was that it had been shot out of the sky in two days flat."

The overriding problem had been that of language. Although the Poles were fluent in French, English was an unknown quantity. Flying Officer Miroslaw Feric knew the words of *Roll Out The Barrel* and *It's A Long Way To Tipperary* through the coaching of a helpful girl on Blackpool Promenade. Squadron Leader Krasnodebski knew, "Four whiskies," though this was an order which pertained whether four Poles or eight were present. In the Battle of France, whither they had drifted through the Balkans and Italy, "as leaves driven by the wind or a ship's wreckage drifting with the tide," they had scored notable victories in such obsolete planes as Moranes and Devoitines but few had ever flown planes with retractable undercarriages. Prone to open the throttle by pulling it back instead of pushing it forward, they promptly wrote off a number of Hurricanes with undercarriages retracted.

Virtually grounded for two months following their arrival in England in June, the Poles had listened bitterly as the Station Commander of their base at Northolt Airfield, Group Captain Stanley Vincent, time and again told them forthrightly, "You can't go up until you can understand the Controller perfectly—we can't have people crashing all over the sky."

Yet as Kellett was the first to admit, from August 31 onward, 303 were "really doing the work of two squadrons," and this in a month when pilot wastage was approaching 120 men a week. In six weeks of non-stop combat, with 126 Luftwaffe planes destroyed against a loss of eight pilots, 303 would justify to the hilt the tribute of *The New York Times* war correspondent Dorothy Thompson when she wrote, "Poles are pure courage."

Understandably, Group Captain Vincent grew deeply suspicious: the Poles' claims of Luftwaffe planes written off surpassed all 11 Group's known totals. When Northolt's Intelligence Officer complained, in despair, that every pilot corroborated the other, Vincent, a World War I Royal Flying Corps veteran, determined to check for himself.

What Vincent saw, at 21,000 feet over Thameshaven, astern of the Poles and 1,000 feet below them, was a spectacle that he was

Kiwis, Aussies, Springboks, Canucks, and many others; they could/have waited, enjoyed the peace of their own lands for a little longer—but they did not. A lode-star has drawn them; Britain, standing alone/Clear in the darkness, not to be overcome,/Though the huge masses of hate are hurled against her, Wherever the spirit of freedom breathes, is Home.

(from *Airmen From Overseas* by Laurence Binyon)

below: the grave of Pilot Officer H.W. Reilley, an American, of Nos. 64 and 66 Squadrons, at Gravesend. P/O Reilley was killed in action near Crockenhill, Kent on October 17, 1940.

to recall with awe a quarter of a century later. He saw Poles crash-diving into space with near-suicidal impact, and a mighty horde of glinting Dorniers breaking formation like dolphins fleeing before a shark. Pole after Pole was holding his fire until twenty yards distant, accepting with grim equanimity the risk that the last great explosion would equally claim his own life. Planes and parachutes were fluttering like charred paper across the sky, yet even in this mass slaughter Poles were angrily nosing Vincent's Hurricane aside, grudging him so much as a shot.

"My God, they *are* doing it," the flabbergasted Vincent told Northolt's Intelligence Officer that day, "It isn't just imagination."

As Johnny Kent was to record ruefully: "The Poles were playing the game for keeps far more than we were."

Even the light-hearted ambiance of a British squadron failed to soften the Poles' implacable enmity. At Warmwell airfield, Dorset, the ranks of No. 609 Spitfire Squadron were from the first stiffened by two Poles, Flying Officers Tadeusz Nowierski and Piotr Ostaszewski. "Their hatred of the Germans was quieter and more deadly than I have ever seen before," wrote Flight Lieutenant David Crook, a flight commander, and in time every 609 survivor would bear this out. Flying Officer "Jimmie" Baraldi recalled how both men would lie for hours on their bunks at dispersal, strengthening their long-distance vision by watching flies creep up the wall. Their commander, Squadron Leader Horace Darley, who kept open house for all the pilots in a cottage by the airfield perimeter, remembered

a party when one British pilot, attempting a barrel roll over a sofa, caught his head an agonising crack.

"Nowi and Osti were pretty bloodthirsty," Darley summed up, "That was the first time they ever laughed."

At Duxford airfield, Cambridgeshire, 40 miles north of London, Squadron Leader Douglas Blackwood had faced identical problems to Kellett's. As commander of No 310 (Czech) Squadron, Blackwood, in peacetime an Edinburgh publisher, had charge of 36 Czech pilots who had travelled the same rough road, via the Balkans and France, as the Poles. Save for their interpreter, Flying Officer Cesek, no man among them was versed in either English or French. Yet from June 18 onwards, when the first contingent of Czechs emerged from a heavy bomber in southern England, they took infinite pains to demonstrate their willingness. When the contractor assembling their hutted camp at Duxford bemoaned the shortage of hands, 310, under Squadron Leader Sasha Hess, weighed in as builder's labourers—donating the £10 in wages the contractor paid to the Czechoslovak Red Cross in London.

Language, one flight commander, Flight Lieutenant Gordon Sinclair, was to recall, proved a problem so acute that "we just put them into the cockpit and said 'Fly'. Only that way could we find out whether they were navigators, bomb-aimers or—what we badly wanted—pilots."

Whatever they lacked, it was not bellyfire. On August 26, their first operational flight, 310 dispensed with the vexatious busi-

180

ness of taxiing round the airfield and took off riskily downwind—a manoeuvre that won them an extra two minutes of precious combat time. Returning to base with all their ammunition spent, they had already accounted for two Dornier 215s and one Messerschmitt 110 twin-engined fighter.

As determined as the Poles never to lose face before their R.A.F. hosts, the Czechs had a summary way with any who let down the side. On one occasion, a Czech non-com, in an abortive take-off, tipped a Hurricane clumsily on its nose. Immediately Squadron Leader Hess led the man summarily behind a hangar, prompting Blackwood to intervene. Fisticuffs between officers and men, he stressed, was strictly forbidden in the R.A.F.

"*Fists?*," echoed Hess, appalled by such a plebeian suggestion, "I shoot him!"

By chance, the Battle's top-scoring Czech pilot served not with 310 but as a lone wolf among the Poles of 303: Sergeant Josef Frantisek, a stocky impassive youngster with beetling eyebrows, who had nurtured a deadly hatred for the Germans for almost two years. A regular in the Czech Air Force, Frantisek's last act above his native soil was to strafe the German troops annexing the Republic in 1939 before flying on to Poland. Phlegmatically accepting a drop in rank from Lieutenant to Corporal, Frantisek was to serve as an air observer with the Poles until September, 1939. In that three week war, airborne in an ancient PZL fighter, he shot down three German aircraft before escaping through Rumania and Syria to France.

Few other Allied pilots—whether New Zealanders, Irishmen, Canadians, Australians or South Africans—knew any such corroding emotions. The one factor that most had in common was a burning ambition, often nourished since their teens, to fly and keep on flying. A case in point was the New Zealander, Colin Falkland Gray, born in Papanui, Christchurch, in 1914, whose whole life was changed, while still at school, by an R.A.F. recruiting talk. Told to report for a medical examination in Wellington while still groggy with flu, Gray still made the 300-mile journey in an old car, only to be turned down on grounds of nervous instability. Still convinced that flying was his life, Gray settled for a farm hand's life for almost twelve months, milking cows and mustering sheep in the open air. This single-minded determination paid off; and by 1939 he had arrived in England to join the Royal Air Force.

Francis Victor Beamish, a tough trigger-tempered Northern Irishman, had a near identical case-history. Graduating through Cranwell and serving with the peacetime R.A.F., Beamish abruptly went down with tuberculosis and was invalided from the service. As undeterred as Gray, he emigrated to Canada, went to work as a lumberjack and was cured within the year. Six months before the Battle of Britain, Beamish, back in the R.A.F. and promoted to Wing Commander, was given the command of North Weald Airfield. Although then thirty-seven and essentially an indifferent shot, Beamish would still leap clean through his open office window rather than miss a scramble—and was credited with six "kills" before the Battle petered out.

All the squadrons that had Polish pilots posted to them formed an equally high opinion of them, and the feats of the Polish Squadron, who in five days' fighting over London destroyed at least forty-four German machines, as well as probably destroying many more, must rank as one of the best shows of the whole summer. Such indomitable courage and determination cannot go unrewarded, and when this war is won we must see that Poland is again restored to her former liberty and freedom, which her sons fought so valiantly to maintain.

(—Flight-Lieutenant D. M. Crook, D.F.C.)

The grave of Czechoslovakian Sergeant Pilot Joseph Frantisek, of No. 303 (Polish) Squadron, at Northwood.

FREEDOM IS IN
PERIL/DEFEND IT
WITH ALL YOUR
MIGHT.

(—official war poster)

Much the same gung-ho spirit infused Gray's best friend and fellow New Zealander, Flight Lieutenant Al Deere. A rugged twenty-two-year-old from Wanganui, with a cheery grin and a broken nose, a legacy of his prowess as the R.A.F. middle-weight champion, Deere's appetite for danger was as legendary as his hunger for solid protein. Always the first to the breakfast table in Hornchurch mess, ready to wolf the fried eggs of any pilots feeling off-colour, Deere's ebullient cry, as the first bomber sweep approached Hornchurch, was long treasured by Squadron Leader Ronald Adam, one of the four Sector Controllers.

"Christalbloodymighty," Adam heard Deere's voice vibrate in his headphones, "Ho, tally ho! Here they come—fucking hordes of them!."

From his teens, Deere, like Gray, had envisaged no other life but flying, and following his application for an R.A.F. short-service commission, his examiners seemingly found his enthusiasm infectious; one of the first twelve accepted from 2,000 applicants he, too, was soon on his way to England. Enthusiasm was equally a marked feature of Deere's first solo flight in a Gypsy Moth. In his eagerness to take-off, land and take-off again, he three times floored his furious instructor with his slip-stream.

This was of a piece with Deere's impetuous progress throughout the Battle, although Deere still insists that there was no finite Battle of Britain period—"Dunkirk . . . the Battle of Britain . . . to me it was one thing." Already, in the third week of May, he had shot down his third ME 109 before making a pancake

landing in his Spitfire, "Kiwi," on the beaches of Dunkirk. It was only the first of a succession of "Kiwis," with good reason Deere was to entitle his best-selling 1959 memoirs *Nine Lives.* All told, Al Deere was destined to make four crash landings in ten weeks.

His first 'life' was in jeopardy as early as July 9, when Deere led a section of Spitfires in to attack two groups of Messerschmitts escorting a reconnaissance seaplane near Dover. As a 109 headed straight at him, both Deere and the German pilot were firing simultaneously, neither giving ground; with devastating impact, the aircraft collided. Unable to bale out, since the 109 had caught his propeller and hood, Deere, his engine stopped, half blinded and choked by glycol fumes, somehow headed inland, ploughed through a cat's cradle of anti-invasion poles, finally juddering to a halt in a cornfield where his plane caught fire. Next day, though sore with minor burns and abrasions, Deere was again on patrol.

On August 15, Deere was once more in dire straits—this time, as reckless as the Poles of 303, tangling with seven ME 109s over Calais-Marck airfield. "My instrument panel was shattered, my eye was bleeding from splinters, my watch had been shot clean off my wrist by an incendiary bullet," he reported later, ". . . and it seemed only a matter of minutes before the end." Miraculously his Spitfire limped back across the Channel, then, close to Folkestone and now down to 800 feet, his Merlin engine erupted in flames. Nursing the Spitfire to 1,500 feet, Deere turned the aircraft on its back and plunged from the cockpit, only to be blown alongside

I saw his round mouth's
crimson deepen as it fell,
Like a Sun, in his last
deep hour;/Watched the
magnificent recession of
farewell,/Clouding, half
gleam, half glower,/And a
last splendour burn the
heavens of his cheek.
And in his eyes/The cold
stars lighting, very old
and bleak,/In different
skies.

(from *Fragment; A
Farewell* by Wilfrid Owen)

the fuselage, fracturing his wrist on the tail-plane. With a sudden jolt, the parachute opened and Deere landed 'with a mighty thud' in a plantation of thick shrubs.

In time, a passing ambulance took him to East Grinstead Hospital, the nearest to the scene, and its chief, Archibald McIndoe, the famous plastic surgeon and a fellow-New Zealander, rang Wing Commander Bouchier, the Hornchurch station commander, to announce that Deere had arrived safely.

With a wholly-comprehensible mixture of relief and anger, Bouchier roared, "Well, keep the little bugger there—he's costing us too many Spitfires."

Along with many Commonwealth pilots, Deere was becoming increasingly conscious of the overwhelming odds they faced. On August 24, he complained bitterly of "being unable to get a decent bead because of constant attacks from behind." And in that same engagement, Colin Gray, harried by a dozen Messerschmitts, confessed "being rather outnumbered I found it difficult to get in a burst." On September 2 alone, Gray was involved in five sorties; one day earlier, he had landed at Hornchurch with his elevator control wire totally severed by a cannon shell, yet such was the pressure of combat that one hour later, with the Spitfire repaired by a ground crew working flat out, Gray was once again airborne in combat. When Churchill paid his immortal tribute to The Few, Al Deere had but one heartfelt comment: "By Christ, he can say that again. There aren't many of us left."

Thus, as the Battle wore on, more and more Allied pilots became increasingly analytical. This was in marked contrast to the devil-may-care attitudes of the aces of the Battle of France, men like the Australian Leslie Clisby, who first shot down a Heinkel 111, then landed to rugger-tackle an escaping crewman, or the New Zealander Edgar James 'Cobber' Kain, in June the R.A.F.'s top scorer, with 14 "kills" to his credit yet who, in a fit of bravado, fatally flick-rolled his Hurricane into a crash at Echmines. But from August on, the name of the game was survival. If death was an ever-present familiar, how could the pilots contrive to cheat him?

Of the twenty-three South Africans engaged in the Battle, the supreme analyst of tactics, the pastmaster of survival, was 30-year-old Flight Lieutenant Adolph Gysbert Malan, known inevitably, after service as a Third Officer with the Union Castle Steamship Line, as 'Sailor'. " 'Sailor' was incomparably the greatest," Wing Commander Bouchier was to avow later, for few but 'Sailor', commanding 74 Squadron at Hornchurch, would have taken pains to compute that a Spitfire's four Browning machine guns, blasting 1,260 rounds a minute, possessed a fire-power equivalent to a five-ton truck hitting a brick wall at 60 miles an hour. In that era, when the slow-paced and poorly-armed Blenheims fought a losing battle against the menace of the night bomber, it took a 'Sailor' Malan, airborne on the night of June 18 during a raid on Southend, to single out two Heinkels trapped by searchlight beams and put paid to both of them in ten minutes flat.

A man as modest as Al Deere—on trips

above: Flying Officer Jan Paivel Falkowski of No. 32 Squadron.

My country is the world, and my religion is to do good.

(*Rights Of Man*, Thomas Paine)

to London, both men were prone to leave their DFCs behind on the dressing table—'Sailor' once astounded the war correspondent, Quentin Reynolds, by confessing that he had never in his life read a book. "You see, I have no imagination," he admitted frankly, "If I had any imagination I'd have been dead by now." Yet after August 21, when 74 Squadron took a three-week break at Kirton-in-Lindsey, 'Sailor' surprisingly emerged as the author of one of the most cogent documents the Battle of Britain was to produce: *Ten Of My Rules For Air Fighting,* later famous as a poster pasted up in many Fighter Command dispersal huts.

Most pilots from the Western Hemisphere—87 Canadians, and nine Americans—knew a lesser emotional involvement. Squadron Leader Aeneas McDonnell, who commanded 64 Squadron at Kenley, recalled Flying Officer Art Donahue, a likeable Minnesota farmboy, who had built up his expertise barnstorming as a stunt flier in the Depression, as possessing 'almost the detachment of a war correspondent.' The way that many felt was summed up by the light-hearted aphorism of Pilot Officer Eugene 'Red' Tobin, a six-foot redhead from Los Angeles, recruited to 609 Squadron: "Ah, hell, we had a million laughs."

Even in late August, at least one squadron had seen no fighting whatsoever: No. 1 Squadron, Royal Canadian Air Force, commanded by Squadron Leader Ernest McNab, stationed alongside the seething Poles at Northolt airfield. A task force of wealthy Canadian dilettantes, they boasted a 1911 Rolls

Royce and a liveried chauffeur, Sebastian, but their vainglorious offer to furnish their own squadron of Hurricanes had misfired woefully. When Dowding learned that the planes, still on the high seas, possessed no armour plating and did not have Rotol propellers, he quietly earmarked them for an OTU.

It was the bleakest misfortune that on the afternoon of August 24, the squadron, which had fired at a moving target in the air only once, should have been ordered to intercept a force of German bombers bound to hit Tangmere Sector Station. At the same time, three slow-paced Blenheims of Coastal Command, based at R.A.F. Thorney Island were ordered up on the same mission. Few of the Canadians had ever seen a Blenheim; their sole aircraft recognition training had been an instructor's hasty shuffling through a pile of silhouettes.

Thus, when McNab first spotted the Blenheims, 6,000 feet north and east of Thorney Island, he first mistook them for Junkers 88s, although ack-ack puffs and blinding sunlight did not make for easy identification. To his section of three, McNab first ordered, "Echelon, starboard—go!," and they dived, at 300 miles an hour, faster and faster, too fast for all to hear McNab's next electrifying order, "Break, break, break! Don't attack!" For just in time McNab had seen the gun turrets which Junkers 88s lacked, and the white flash on the aircrafts' fins that marked them as British. He and his section broke to port and did not attack. But the following planes, seeing what appeared to be long yellow spears of tracer opened fire—not realising that the gunners were firing the colours of the day, yellow and red Very pistol flares, that spelt out the recognition signal.

Two of the Blenheims, though badly shot up, escaped by crash-landing on Thorney Island, but the third, its starboard engine blazing like a petrol-soaked brand, vanished beneath the waters of Bracklesham Bay, east of Thorney. It was Group Captain Stanley Vincent who gently broke the news to the appalled Squadron Leader McNab, explaining compassionately, "There's nothing you can do, these things happen in war—the one thing you must do is to fly down and see them and explain."

From this moment on, the Canadians ached to redeem themselves—and that chance at length came over Biggin Hill at 2.30 p.m. on Sunday, September 15. Swooping like angry falcons on a formation of twenty Heinkels, eleven Hurricanes between them cut them to ribbons, and one Canadian, Flying Officer Phil Lockman, of Ottawa, bellylanding his Hurricane beside one of the bombers, personally escorted the crew from the aircraft—one of the few fighter pilots ever to take a prisoner.

Long afterwards, at the Nuremberg Trials, witnesses like Field Marshal Gerd von Runstedt offered many alibis for the German defeat: the decision to delay the invasion until 1942, the sentimental bias of a Führer who had no desire to annihilate Britain. As always, Churchill had the last word.

Speaking not only for the R.A.F. but for almost 600 Allied pilots, his verdict was final: "They met better men on better planes."

185

THE BRITISH PEOPLE

AT FIRST nobody quite knew what was happening. It was such a perfect autumn day; at 2 p.m. on that sunny Saturday, September 7, it was a time to relax from the tensions of war, a time to take stock. For Londoners, it was a time for watching the ducks on the lake in St James's Park or flirting on the parched grass. Others were queuing for theatre matinees— the young Michael Redgrave in *Thunder Rock* or Dame Marie Tempest in *Dear Octopus*— and the cinemas, too, were doing booming business, with Walt Disney's *Pinocchio* rivalling Gary Cooper in *The Westerner.* At Shepperton, 18 miles down the Thames from Westminster Bridge, the writer Basil Woon, one of the spectators at that afternoon's cricket match, savoured the brisk applause from the pavilion as a batsman's stumps flew: "Oh, well bowled, sir—a beauty!"

Even over many coastal areas, random raiders were now so commonplace as to excite little comment. Thus, as the Heinkels of *Oberst* Johannes Fink's Bomber Group Two droned over the cattle market at Canterbury, Kent, the sole reaction came from a newsboy by the traffic signals, who hailed them cheekily, "Hey, wait for the lights to turn green!" At Shepperton, watching them slide at 15,000 feet towards the blue haze that marked the city boundary, Basil Woon thought complacently, but they'll never get to London.

The time was 4.30 p.m., and all over southern England, preserved until now by the valour of The Few, this was the mood of the moment. There was no hint of Armageddon.

The suspense was not long delayed. At this same hour, twenty-one Fighter Command

It so happens that this war, whether those at present in authority like it or not, has to be fought as a citizen's war. There is no way out of that because in order to defend and protect this island, not only against possible invasion but also against all the disasters of aerial bombardment, it has been found necessary to bring into existence a new network of voluntary associations such as the Home Guard, the Observer Corps, all the A.R.P. and fire-fighting services, and the like . . . They are a new type, what might be called the organized militant citizen. And the whole circumstances of their wartime life favour a sharply democratic outlook. Men and women with a gift for leadership now turn up in unexpected places. The new ordeals blast away the old shams. Britain, which in the years immediately before this war was rapidly losing such democratic virtues as it possessed, is now being bombed and burned into democracy.

(—J. B. Priestley, Out of the People)

In London's first night air raid, August 23, 1940, this Anderson shelter was buckled, but withstood a direct bomb hit.

187

Travel between 10 and 4
and don't crowd out the War Workers

top centre: Albert Obee of Gravesend holds a baby's gas mask; *top right:* staple food items of the war years; *bottom left:* from the shelter sketchbooks of Henry Moore; *bottom right:* a wartime identity card.

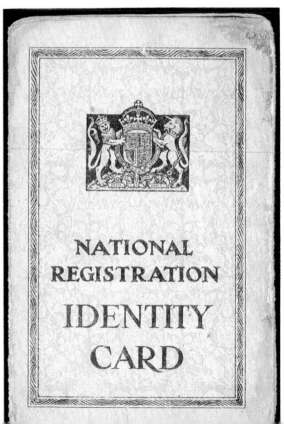

NATIONAL REGISTRATION

IDENTITY CARD

squadrons were already airborne, weaving above the battered sector stations at Biggin Hill, Northolt and Kenley. Paramount in every pilot's mind was the belief that these and aircraft factories like Vickers Armstrong, Weybridge, attacked as recently as September 4, would be the Luftwaffe's target for today. Then, due east of the Isle of Sheppey, they caught their first glimpse of a sight they would remember until they died: a formation of almost 1,000 aircraft, Heinkels, Dorniers, glinting Messerschmitt 109s, bulking over one and a half miles high, covering 800 square miles of sky. Now there could no longer be any doubt: the target was London.

What had happened? Behind this unlooked-for assault stretched a tortuous chain of argument that was as old as the Battle itself. Two men in particular had from the first urged an all-out assault on London: *Generalfeldmarschall* Albert Kesselring, commanding Air Fleet Two, and *General* Bruno Lörzer, of the 2nd Flying Corps. Stubbornly, Hitler, still hopeful for peace, had refused. And then, on the night of August 24, a few Luftwaffe bomber crews, guilty of a navigational error, had set off a chain reaction. Seeking the oil tanks at Thameshaven, on the estuary, they had drifted over central London. For the first time since the Zeppelin raid of May, 1918, bombs were scattered across the old walled City of London.

In cold anger, Churchill ordered instant reprisals, and 81 twin-engined Wellington, Hampden and Whitley bombers set out for Berlin. Although less than ten of them found their target, the British, spurred on by Chur-chill, tried again and again, four times in the next ten days.

As early as September 2, the Luftwaffe debated retaliation. At Wissant, near Calais, *Major* Adolf Galland and seven other group commanders heard from *Oberst* Theo Osterkamp: "There may be a massed attack on London on September 7." But all this was left in abeyance, pending a full-dress conference between Goering and his Air Fleet Commanders at The Hague on September 3.

It was there, in a spirited no-holds-barred exchange of views, that matters came to a head. The time had come, Goering maintained, to alter tactics, to switch all resources to a massive pile-driving attack on London. Only one problem remained a cause for concern: had Fighter Command's resources been truly depleted, or would the bombers run too great a risk?

On this score, opinions were divergent. Kesselring, the eternal optimist, maintained that Fighter Command was finished; a study of combat reports made that plain. He pointed out with truth that he had always urged a mass attack on one key objective rather than the divergent targets that had characterised Goering's approach to the battle—with ports, airfields and factories singled out in turn, then just as capriciously abandoned.

Sperrle, who liked to differ with Kesselring on principle, disagreed now. He sided with *Oberst* Werner Junck, his regional fighter commander, who maintained that a spent force could not inflict such losses—"This is a Verdun of the air." In Sperrle's estimation, the

Next morning a Pompeiian pall of dust and smoke/Loomed over all, with hosepipes snaking/Slimily in black mud across the thoroughfares./One errant spray/Trespassing into our too, too-open windows/Unkindly moistened our National bread and marge,/Our ersatz coffee, and soya-porridge/And straw-pale tea.

(from *Bomb Story* (Manchester, 1942) by Margery Lea)

"They call this spring, Mum, and they have one down here every year."

(—Evacuated child)

Hot Bovril cheers!

189

R.A.F. still had 1,000 operational fighters left. (The truth: exactly 746 were then serviceable and available.)

General Kurt Student, the commander of all airborne troops for "Operation Sealion," always nourished the intriguing theory that Goering's September 7 attack was an all-out bid to force Hitler's hand. Taking tea at Karinhall on the afternoon of September 2, Student had been shocked to hear the Reichmarschall's sudden admission, "The Fuehrer doesn't want to invade Britain." When Student pressed him for an explanation, Goering's sole answer was a massive shrug: "I don't know. There'll be nothing doing this year, at any rate."

To the relief of all, on September 4, Hitler's final angry decision had been spelt out at Berlin's Sportpalast: "If they attack our cities, we will raze *theirs* to the ground. We will stop the handiwork of these air pirates, so help us God."

The die was cast, and to every man in the Luftwaffe, the decision made impeccable sense. To the jubilant Kesselring, it was proof that his logic had carried the day: on September 7, successive waves of bombers and fighters, 1,273 in all, were scheduled to cross the coast from 4 p.m. onwards. To Goering, who had codenamed the raids operation *Loge*, after the old German god who had forged Siegfried's sword, it was a day he would commemorate by personally taking command on the Channel coast. At fighter level it was welcome news to *Major* Adolf Galland: "Only then would the English fighters leave their den and be forced to give us open battle."

Ironically, it was a decision, once known, that was welcome in the British camp too. "London was like some huge prehistoric animal, capable of enduring terrible injuries," Churchill noted with satisfaction, already scenting victory in this abrupt switch of targets. As his Hurricane, codenamed OK 1, twisted above the blazing docks at Rotherhithe, Air Vice Marshal Keith R. Park, too, breathed a sigh of relief: "Thank God for that."

As Park was to elaborate next day: "I knew that the Nazis had switched their attack from the fighter stations, thinking they were knocked out. They weren't, but they were pretty groggy."

From the sober viewpoint of military logic, it was a judgment that could not be faulted. In switching strategic priorities at this eleventh hour, Goering had been guilty of one of the battle's cardinal blunders. But for The Few in the sky, no less than the fire fighters and wardens on the ground, it was an altogether different story.

One man, at least, Pilot Officer Roger Hall, of No. 152 Squadron, Middle Wallop, was conscious of a threat looming as never before over British soil. "I saw a whole stick of bombs in a straight line advancing like a creeping barrage," he remembered, mindful of films like *Journey's End* and *All Quiet On The Western Front*, "but this time they were not over the muddy desolation of No Man's Land, but over Croydon, Surbiton and Earls Court." Another precise memory was that of Flight Lieutenant Johnny Kent of No. 303 (Polish) Squadron. "It was like a picture out of a book on air firing," was his impression of

Remnants of lives and forever lost days,/Families ended, minds that were dazed,/Clutched to the breast/Was all they had left/Of life that had gone and homes that were wrecked./Where shall we put/The shopping bag The picture of Grandma The doll of rag? Covered with dirt and with soot and with dust—/How to begin to clean them up,/To uncover the faces,/Identify people When nothing is left of human features./What shall we say/To the waiting friends?/How shall we know/Such anonymous ends?

(from *Bomb Incident* by Barbara Catherine Edwards)

A famous German photograph showing a Heinkel over London during a September 7, 1940 raid.

CHURCHMAN'S CIGARETTES

THE STIRRUP HAND PUMP

right: A commemorative ashtray made from a Rolls Royce Merlin piston; *below:* Blitz-inspired jigsaw puzzles.

The coloured nights/have
yellow and blue long
lights/splintered by air-
fire/on negative whites
backgrounding black-
snapped/scarred trees
static.
In the mornings/there are
planes on dray-biers
metal-grey moths
crumpled/signed each
with a white edged/black
grave-cross:/these days
are a diary—film drama
coloured symphony/photo-
graphic/blast and bomb
smash/death/amid flame
magnetic/passing . . .

(from *Colour Symphony*
by Catherine Brewster
Toosey)

sighting a ME 110's silhouette, " 'At this angle place your sights there and FIRE'—which is precisely what I did and his starboard engine flew to bits."

In truth, both Hall and Kent were lucky; few men were to retain such coherent impressions of September 7. "The sky became a seething cauldron of aeroplanes, swooping and swerving in and out of the vapour trails and tracer smoke," recalled Squadron Leader Sandy Johnstone, of No. 602 Squadron, "Everything became a maelstrom of jumbled impressions—a Dornier spinning wildly with part of its port mainplane missing; black streaks of tracer ahead, when I instinctively put my arm up to shield my face . . .."

Even twenty-four miles from Central London, at Gravesend, on the Thames estuary, the inexorable fury of the raid struck home. Crouched beside a haystack, on the edge of a turnip field, three seasoned American war correspondents—Edward R. Murrow of CBS, Vincent Sheean, of the North American Newspaper Alliance (NANA) and Ben Robertson of the New York daily *P.M.*—had journeyed thus far purely for professional reasons: to gain a fresh perspective on the Battle of Britain from well outside the city limits. Now they realised that the battle as they had witnessed it from Dover's Shakespeare's Cliff was drawing to a close. They had booked ringside seats for the Battle of London, a battle which was to continue for fifty-seven nights without respite.

When the sirens sounded and the ack-ack began its urgent pounding, that was no more than routine from Dover days. When the first British fighters soared overhead, intercepting the first wave of German bombers, that, too, was routine. But when more waves of German bombers, a second, a third, then a fourth passed overhead in glinting dragonfly formation, heading for the docks, and the vast columns of smoke began to rise over London, this was very far from routine.

Nor was it a routine day for Park's squadrons. Outnumbered, scrambled too late and too low, few of them had the chance to operate at full strength. In essence, it became a day for lone wolves. Pilot Officer John Bisdee from No. 609 Squadron, swam as stealthily as a shark beneath a ME 110 for seven long seconds, all the time pumping lead into its belly. Eighteen-year-old Sergeant John McAdam, of No. 41, who had never before flown at high altitude, found himself, to his intense alarm, 19,000 feet above the grey mushroom dome of St. Paul's Cathedral, hosing tracer at a line of Dorniers. The same concentrated fury possessed Flying Officer Dennis Parnall, the one member of the unlucky 249 Squadron to score. At 6,000 feet above the blazing boundary line of the estuary, he played a grim game of hide-and-seek with a homeward-bound Heinkel 111, hammering at its starboard engine each time it broke smoke-cover. He did not let up until it belly-flopped on the mudflats at Sheerness.

In that crowded sky, men recalled later, it was almost impossible to single out friend from foe. Sergeant Cyril Babbage of No. 602 Squadron saw his friend Andy McDowall, with six ME 109s on his tail and yelled, "Hang on, I'm coming;" it was weeks before

CHURCHMAN'S CIGARETTES

AIR RAID PRECAUTIONS BADGE

God is our refuge, be not afraid, He will be with you all through the raid . . .

(—from a hymn composed during the blitz)

Friday 13 September

Left home at 10:15 for Liverpool St. We left in an air raid which reached its height at the moment we arrived. We had to go down the hotel shelter, and missed the train. Eventually caught the 2:20. I went out to the pictures in the evening with Birdy, now D.F.C., and Steve. Bed at 10:30 thinking very hard of Mummy and Pop as I could see a hell of a barrage over town. God damn and blast Hitler.

(from the diary of Pilot Officer Denis H. Wissler No. 17 Squadron)

SHELTERERS' BEDDING

The practice of shaking bedding over the platforms, tracks and in the subways is strictly forbidden

⊖

below: a Home Guardsman practising concealment; *centre:* shelters were often over-crowded; *right:* heavy raid damage at St. Paul's.

McDowall forgave him for that quixotic gesture. The rallying cry brought down another dozen 109s on top of them both. Flying Officer Keith Ogilvie, a Canadian from No. 609, found the 109s, "zooming and dancing round us like masses of ping pong balls," equally disconcerting. Taking careful aim at the first of the swarm, he was mortified to find that he had hit the second.

These men were at least professionals, who were learning little by little, the skills of survival. But for the gunners of General Sir Frederick Pile's Anti-Aircraft Command, unblooded until now, the day was followed by a night of sheer futility. Untrained to deal with the twisting jinking flight path of a bomber under fire, they failed to wing even one plane. For London's 9,000 air raid wardens and their part-time unpaid volunteers, the picture was no brighter. In Finsbury, bordering on the city, one of them, Barbara Nixon, recalled that when the sirens sounded around 5 p.m., she was armed with little more than a whistle, a tin hat, the knowledge that Lewisite was a poison gas smelling of geraniums and that bomb blast travelled in all directions. Thus equipped, she, like all the others, set out to face her first Blitz.

The true onus, as Assistant Divisional Geoffrey Blackstone of the London Fire Brigade knew to his disquiet, lay squarely on his own firemen.

Blackstone had valid reasons. Among the Brigade, 30,000 strong, 28,000 were wartime auxiliaries, some of them conscripts, more of them volunteers, but all with one factor in common: at least 90 per cent of them had

never tackled a fire of any kind. And while a very serious peacetime fire called for thirty pumps, as fire engines were known, midnight on September 7 would see the Brigade battling to control nine 100-pump fires, across dockland, Woolwich Arsenal and Bishopsgate Goods Yard.

At Surrey Commercial Docks, on the Thames at Rotherhithe, the 30-year-old Blackstone, a six foot-plus ex-public schoolboy, had hastened from a friend's tennis party in Dulwich, South London, to take command. From his control car he watched in fascination as 250 acres of resinous timber, stacked twenty feet high, burned with a dry and terrible crackling. Even the wooden blocks that formed the dockland roadway were blazing like a Guy Fawkes night bonfire. From Paget's Wharf fire station in the true heart of the conflagration, the hard pressed Station Officer Plimlett was urging Fire Brigade headquarters at Lambeth: "Send every pump you've got. The whole bloody world's on fire."

By now the heat was so intense that the paint was blistering on fireboats slipping past 300 yards away on the opposite shore. Solid embers were tossed like cabers into far-off streets to start fresh fires. Telegraph poles took light, along with fences, and rum fires, their barrels exploding like liquid oxygen cylinders, mingled with the white hot flare of paint fires and the black choking noxious fumes from rubber fires. The whining shuddering roar of high explosive bombs drowned out the sizzling of cannisters of incendiaries, and armies of rats, driven from the warehouses, were scurrying in terror through the streets. Auxiliary

194

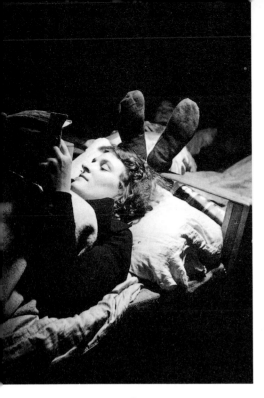

Issued by the Ministry *of Home Security.*

WHAT TO DO ABOUT GAS

OTHER COUNTRIES LOST THEIR FREEDOM in this war because they allowed the enemy to create confusion and panic among their civilian population so that the movement of defending armies was impeded.

We are not going to allow that to happen here. It won't happen if we are all on our guard, prepared to meet anything the enemy may do.

He may use gas. THE DANGER IS NOT SERIOUS if you do the right thing, both NOW and when the time comes. If you do, this weapon will have failed and you will have helped to beat it.

Here are the things to know and do. Read them carefully and remember them well in case the day comes. Keep this leaflet and look at it again.

HOW NOT TO GET GASSED.

NOW

1. In your gas mask you have the best possible protection against gases that affect your lungs or your eyes. It is a sure defence if you use it properly and in time. Make sure your own and your children's gas masks fit and are in working order: your warden or A.R.P. post can tell you. Practise putting them on and get used to wearing them with confidence. Your life may depend on whether you can put your mask on quickly. Remember to take off your spectacles before putting on your gas mask.

2. CARRY YOUR GAS MASK ALWAYS, and have it handy at night.

3. To prevent the face-piece misting over, smear a little soap lightly on the inside once a week.

4. If your chemist has " No. 2 Anti-gas ointment " (price 6d.) in stock, buy a jar. Read the instructions on the jar and carry it always. This ointment is for use as a protection against the effects of liquid blister gas.

IF THE GAS RATTLES SOUND.

1. PUT ON YOUR GAS MASK AT ONCE, wherever you are, even in bed.
2. TAKE COVER. Get into any nearby building as soon as you hear the rattle. Go upstairs if the building is a tall one. Close all windows in your house.

Don't come out or take your gas mask off till you hear the handbells ringing the " Gas clear ".

NEVER LOOK UPWARDS—you may get a drop of liquid gas in your eyes.

COVER YOUR SKIN UP so long as you are out of doors—hands in pockets, collar turned up. Or if you have an umbrella, put it up.

IF YOU DO GET GASSED.

GAS OR VAPOUR. If you breathe any gas or vapour—

1. PUT ON YOUR GAS MASK AT ONCE.

2. KEEP YOUR MASK ON, even though you may still feel some discomfort.

Fireman Bill Ward voiced what most of them felt: "I don't think any fireman has ever seen anything like it before."

To the German bombers which had powered those fires, the run up to the target had been child's play, as trouble-free as a peacetime run-in over a bombing range. In Bomber Group Two, as *Oberleutnant* Karl Kessel recalled it, the mood was so light-hearted that every time shrapnel beat a tattoo on his Dornier's fuselage, his gunner *Oberfeldwebel* Felix Hipp, cheerily called *"Herein!"* (Come in), as if to a room service waiter. For some, the dangers were more in the mind than in the reality. Ahead of *Oberst* Johannes Fink, an excitable rear-gunner, convinced he was under heavy attack, was heedlessly riddling his own tailplane with bullets. It was the fatherly Fink who eventually broke it to him: "You yourself were your own worst enemy, my dear boy."

Back in Northern France, Goering's fighter pilots were already rendering succinct reports on the day's sortie. At Guines, near Calais, *Major* Hannes Trautloft, commanding Fighter Group 54, spoke for most: "Only single British fighters, which could do nothing . . . there were thick black clouds drifting with the wind all the way across the Channel." *Major* Max Ibel, of Fighter Group 27, added a rider: although the fighters had stuck close to the bombers it had been a close run thing. Every warning bulb was glowing red—signalling ten litres of petrol, twenty minutes flying time at most—as they reached the Channel, and on the return journey, with the defenders alerted, the going had been that much tougher.

One vigilant defender was 20-year-old Sergeant John Burgess, a Spitfire pilot who had been operational with No. 222 Squadron, Hornchurch, for exactly ten days. Late on that chaotic Saturday Burgess first found himself roughly three miles behind a formation of Heinkels heading back towards France. Dogging them some two miles to the rear were what he took to be a pair of Hurricanes and he had joined up with them, planning on a concerted attack, when he spotted the yellow noses which marked a German fighter. And as if by reflex, Burgess "pulled in behind the leader and opened up on him . . . he immediately rolled on to his back and went down and a stream of white smoke came out." Now, at almost 500 miles an hour, "absolutely vertical and full throttle." Burgess was diving in pursuit and "at this point I suppose I was down to about 2,000 feet, but he kept straight on, straight into the ground." His first emotion was one of extreme contrition. "I was very shaken . . . I was shaking because I'd obviously killed a man and . . . I had never killed anyone before."

What followed was a dismal anti-climax. His vision reduced to "a white opaque view" following the dive, Burgess was making for Hornchurch's satellite drome, Rochford, when his tanks ran dry; he side-slipped steeply to land in a ploughed field, bending his propeller blades. Among the reception committee of villagers was a teenage girl, who asked abruptly, "Is this a Spitfire?" When Burgess admitted it, she confided, "We're saving for a Spitfire in our village. We're saving £5,000." Then the triumphant air ace of September 7 was

I feel quite exhausted after seeing & hearing so much sadness, sorrow, heroism and magnificent spirit. The destruction is so awful, and the people so wonderful—they deserve a better world.

(—Queen Elizabeth, in a letter to Queen Mary, October 19, 1940)

I burn for England with a living flame/In the uncandled darkness of the night./I share with her the fault, who share her name,/And to her light I add my lesser light./She has my arm—who had my father's arm,/Who shall not have my unborn children's arms.
I burn for England, even as she burns/In living flame, that when her peace is come/Flame shall destroy whoever seeks to turn/her sacrifice to profit—and the homes/Of those who fought—to wreckage,/In a war for freedom—who were never free.

(from *Poem* by Gervase Stewart)

197

I was pushing the glass across the counter for a refill when we heard it coming. The girl in the corner was still laughing and for the first time I heard her soldier speak. "Shut up!" he said, and the laugh was cut off like the sound track in a movie. Then everyone was diving for the floor.

The barmaid (she was of considerable bulk) sank from view with a desperate slowness behind the counter and I flung myself tight up against the other side, my taxi-driver beside me. He still had

abruptly cut down to size, "I don't think *that* thing's worth £5,000."

For Londoners living far from dockland, the first intimation of disaster came from an apparent freak of nature: tonight the sun was not setting in the west, over Richmond and Chiswick, but in the east above Stepney, its entire skyline a shifting orange glow. Many were already conscious of a night of apocalypse. "One day this will be history," a London girl explained, recording her impressions for Mass Observation, "and I shall be one of those who actually saw it." On the colonnade of St. Paul's Cathedral, the Dean, the Very

Reverend William Matthews, heard someone mutter close at hand, "It's like the end of the world." Another voice responded quietly, "It's the end of *a* world."

At Gravesend, after seeking shelter in a pub for a pie and a pint, Ed Murrow and his companions had once again returned to the hay stack. Yet out of that long and awful night they afterwards retained only fleeting impressions. Robertson recalled it as "a night like the Revelation of St. John," he had no memory of repeating over and over the childish jingle, "London is burning, London is burning." Sheean remembered prophesying that "The

fire they set this night would consume them, too, before it was quenched," but, though fluent in five languages, he did not remember cursing in all of them. Murrow remembered most, for on the Sunday his CBS broadcast from Studio B4 in the basement of Broadcasting House would be followed by 30 million American listeners, tuned to his sepulchral lead-in "This . . . is London." In Murrow's recollection, "The fire up the river had turned the moon blood-red . . . huge pear-shaped bursts of flame would rise up into the smoke and disappear . . . the world was upside down."

But even a retrospective account as vivid as Murrow's paled beside the actuality of living through September 7. In King Street, Poplar, 18-year-old Len Jones recalled how "the suction and the compression from the high explosive blasts just pulled and pushed you . . . you could actually feel your eyeballs being sucked out. I was holding my eyes to try and stop them going." In the nearby street shelter, which he shared with several Chinese families, that same awful suction was still a presence— "It was lifting and moving, rolling almost as if it was a ship in a rough sea . . . the suction and the blasts coming in and out of the steel door . . . was smashing backwards and forwards and bashed us all around against the walls."

Later, surveying the mangled remains of the family home and the corpses of Chinese neighbours, Len Jones was "just convulsed . . . I thought well, I must be dead . . . so I struck a match and tried to burn my finger. I kept doing this to see if I was still alive."

For the R.A.F., from first to last, it had been a bitter and frustrating day. At Middle Wallop, despite all the cajoling of Mess Steward Joseph Lauderdale, Flight Lieutenant James MacArthur of No. 609 Squadron could not be tempted to eat, even though the cold buffet boasted a prime Scotch salmon. "I couldn't face a bite of it, Mr Lauderdale" he protested, "We've been up there all afternoon and done nothing—there wasn't a British plane in the sky."

Although this was scarcely an accurate situation report, MacArthur had come uncomfortably close. The Luftwaffe's losses had totalled forty-one planes, the bulk of them bombers, and for this toll the R.A.F. had paid dearly, with a loss of twenty-eight fighters. Nineteen of Dowding's pilots were dead and only one German plane in thirty had been harmed in any way.

Yet almost as if in mockery, it was the Luftwaffe, not the R.A.F., who faced an inquest. At Cap Blanc Nez, near Wissant, *Reichmarschall* Herman Goering had arrived in his private train, code-named "Asia," with its ornate mahogany-panelled saloons, determined to infuse his fighter arm with the valour he was convinced they lacked. Although a meeting with four of Galland's pilots—Gerhard Schöpfel, Joachim Müncheberg, "Micky" Sprick and Hans Ebeling—all claiming seventeen victories apiece, momentarily cheered him, he was less gratified by the sight of *Hauptmann* Heinz Bär, a dour Saxonian, shot down by a Spitfire, within sight of France. When he enquired as to the pilot's thoughts over the Channel, Bär harked back grumpily

his glass in his hand and the beer shot across the floor, making a dark stain and setting the sawdust afloat. The soldier too had made for the bar counter and wedged the girl on his inside. One of her shoes had nearly come off. It was an inch from my nose: she had a ladder in her stocking.

My hands were tight-pressed over my ears but the detonation deafened me. The floor rose up and smashed against my face, the swing-door tore off its hinges and crashed over a table, glass splinters flew across the room, and behind the bar every bottle in the place seemed to be breaking. The lights went out, but there was no darkness. An orange glow from across the street shone through the wall and threw everything into a strong relief.

I scrambled unsteadily to my feet and was leaning over the bar to see what had happened to the unfortunate barmaid when a voice said, "Anyone hurt?" and there was an AFS man shining a torch. At that everyone began to move, but slowly and reluctantly as though coming out of a dream. The girl stood white and shaken in a corner, her arm about her companion, but she was unhurt and had stopped talking. Only the barmaid failed to get up.

(from *The Last Enemy* by Richard Hillary)

The bombed shell of
Coventry cathedral;
right: British 3.7 in. anti-
aircraft gun, the type that
greeted German raiders
throughout the Blitz; *top
right:* from Henry Moore's
shelter sketchbooks.

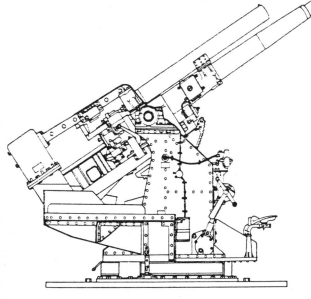

201

In Coventry . . . there were more open signs of hysteria, terror, neurosis observed than during the whole of the previous two months together in all areas. Women were seen to cry, to scream, to tremble all over, to faint in the street, to attack a fireman, and so on. The overwhelmingly dominant feeling on Friday was the feeling of utter helplessness. The tremendous impact of the previous night had left people practically speechless in many cases. And it made them feel impotent. There was no role for the civilian. Ordinary people had no idea what they should do.

Mass Observation report on Coventry after the major attack in November, 1940.

When people's ill, they
come to I,/I Physics,
bleeds, and sweats 'em;
Sometimes they live,
sometimes they die.
What's that to I? I lets 'em

(On Himself by
Dr. J. C. Lettsom)

top left: Evacuees leaving
London; *top right:* a
crashed Heinkel burns at
its French base; *lower
right:* young raid victims
at a London hospital
during the Blitz, a Cecil
Beaton photograph.

to a Goering pronouncement of August 16: "Your speech, Herr *Reichsmarschall*—that England isn't an island any more."

As the teleprinter clattered out its first reports, Goering grew progressively more angry. The loss of almost forty bombers, out of 247 despatched in the first wave, was imsupportable. The commanders of each fighter group and wing were ordered to report to his private train without delay. What the *Reichsmarschall* failed to see—or refused to admit—was that a fighter escort 600 strong had created the havoc in the sky over London to which the R.A.F. had borne witness. The fighters had been too busy dodging one another to prevent the Spitfires and Hurricanes singling out the bombers.

But Goering, as every commander saw plainly, was insensible to reason. "Your job is to protect the bombers" he castigated them roundly, "and every time you fall down on it." To every question of R.A.F. tenacity he turned a deaf ear: "Don't tell *me* the sky is full of enemies—I know they haven't more than seventy fighters left." In vain, commanders like Galland, resurrected their earliest contentions: the ME 109 was a plane built for attack, not protection, and thus, on escort flights, was forever throttling back.

If Goering could have witnessed the devastation that was London's East End on the morning of Sunday, September 8, he might have taken heart. The sights that Ed Murrow and his companions witnessed, as their car inched its way through rubble-blocked streets, were at first beyond belief: the truckloads of shattered glass, the cars "with stretchers

racked on the roofs like skis," the ruptured gas mains, searing and flaring, the red buses lined up to evacuate the homeless. Nine miles of waterfront were still burning unchecked, despite all the endeavours of Blackstone's men. Already the flight of bombed-out East Enders was on—to Epping Forest, to Reading and Windsor, Oxford and Kent—from a carnage that had claimed 448 civilian lives and 1,600 injured. "Moving, ever moving," noted Vincent Sheean, "like the poor in all wars, taking to the roads."

Within five days, almost 150,000 of them were to seek shelter in the London Underground Railway, 80 feet below street level, a *fait accompli* which the government was powerless to avert. Yet one factor, amorphous in itself, might have escaped Goering: more than half of them were children, evacuated in September 1939, who had returned to the city, feeling that at such a time London was the place to be. "That they were prepared to do so," wrote the historian, Laurence Thompson, "is as essential a part of the Battle of Britain as the numbers and dispositions of Park's fighters or of Pile's anti-aircraft guns."

Ed Murrow saw it in much the same way, and he made that plain to his CBS listeners. He had looked out over the city from a rooftop on a late September afternoon, he recounted, and the dominant impression was of "many flags flying from staffs." Essentially it was a spontaneous act—"No one told these people to put out the flag. They simply feel like flying the Union Jack above their roof."

It was a gesture that to Murrow pointed its own moral. "No flag up there was white."

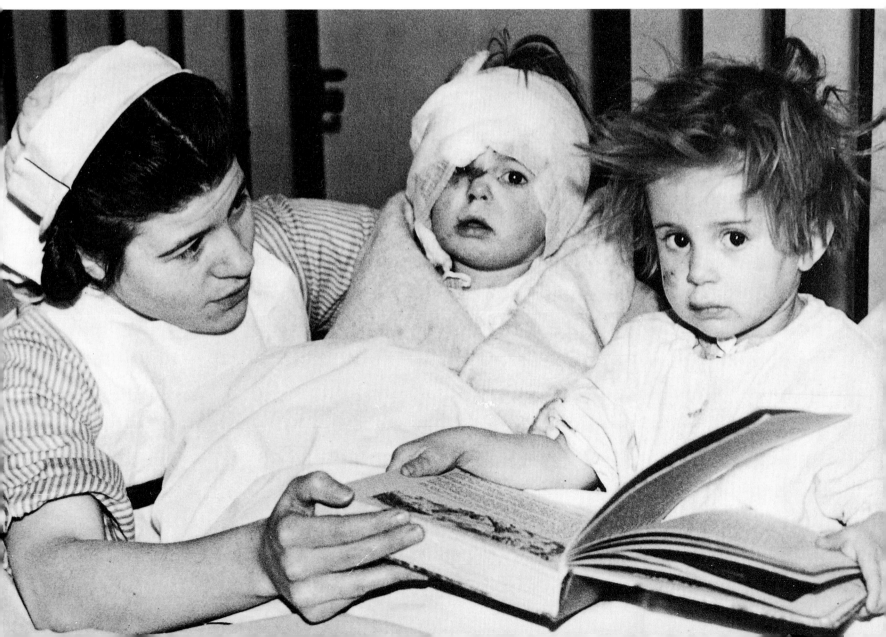

IT JUST STOPPED

ON SUNDAY, September 15, the final all-clear sounded at HQ, 11 Group, Uxbridge, at 3.50 p.m. The battle that Winston Churchill had watched with trepidation for almost five hours in the underground Ops Room was over. For the Premier it had been a tense yet static battle, its crisis points marked by the red bulbs glowing ominously on every squadron panel, beside the legend "Enemy Intercepted." By contrast for the twenty-one squadrons airborne it had been a wheeling snarling non-stop saraband of planes in the overcast skies above London—in the words of No. 242's Squadron Leader Douglas Bader, "the finest shambles I'd ever been in."

It was a day when even a veteran like Squadron Leader Bryan Lane, of No. 19 Squadron, could exclaim with awe; "Why, it's the whole Luftwaffe"—seeing their planes advance towards the city like a dense black swarm of insects, trailing ever lengthening ribbons of white exhaust smoke above the huddled rooftops. It was a day when combat was joined so fiercely, and so many parachutes blossomed white above the south coast, that one cheerful Pole yelled a warning, "They'll take us for a bloody parachute division." Everyone knew it as the day when The Few claimed 183 German aircraft shot down for a loss of under forty—a claim later ruefully amended to fifty-six.

In short, it was a day instantly recognised for everything save what it actually was: the last classic intercept of the Luftwaffe by Dowding's fighters, the moment when the Battle, like a spent rocket, hesitated, then sputtered into extinction.

Monday, September 16 saw the growing recognition of this in the Luftwaffe camp: the first of many bitter inquests in the Pas de Ca-

ADOLF: "I thought you had a winning system, Hermann" —By *Illingworth*

lais and at Karinhall, punctuated by Goering's increasingly irrational outbursts. From August through September, Luftwaffe losses had totalled some 1,140 planes of all types—and at this rate of bomber losses, as Mölders and Galland had warned all along, the force would surely bleed to death. Attacks by single fighters rendered clumsy by 500-kilo bomb loads, in the tradition of Test Group 210, would persist until December—but their losses, too, would spiral as the surprise element *Hauptmann* Rubensdörffer had pioneered against the radar stations was lost altogether.

Unknown to any group commander, "Operation Sea-Lion" had not been geared to air supremacy since July 29—ten days before the historic Channel convoy attack of August 8. On that day, at Bad Reichenhall, Bavaria, *Oberst* Walter Warlimont and the officers of Hitler's Operations Department (Section L) were astounded to hear from *General* Alfred Jodl that a major attack on Russia—later code named "Operation Barbarossa"—was scheduled for May, 1941. The Fuehrer had decided "once for all" to rid the world of the "disease of Bolshevism."

When one of Warlimont's officers protested that England was surely the first priority, Jodl's reply was revealing: "The Fuehrer is afraid that the mood of the people after a victory over England would hardly permit him to embark on a new war against Russia."

Thus, on August 15, the day when all three Air Fleets made the greatest effort of the battle, the War Diary of the German Navy recorded: "Independent of the eventual decision, the Fuehrer wishes the *threat* of invasion to be maintained against England in every way. The preparations must therefore proceed, however the decision may fall." It was thus logical that on September 17, *Grosadmiral* Erich Raeder dictated for the War Diary: "The enemy air force is by no means defeated. On the contrary, it shows increasing activity. The Fuehrer therefore decides to postpone "Sea-Lion" indefinitely."

Some felt that this decision rankled. To *Oberst* Karl Koller, Sperrle's chief of staff, Hitler announced angrily: "The world would have been very much better off if the aircraft had never been invented." *Oberst* Martin Harlinghausen, the 10th Flying Corps chief of staff, found the Fuehrer's decision more rational, rooted in the fertile lands of the Ukraine: "I want colonies I can walk to without getting my feet wet." At the Reich Chancellery, on September 23, *Major* Werner Mölders, awarded the Oak Leaves to the Knights Cross, sensed that Hitler, inexplicably, had sickened of the whole campaign.

"The way across the Channel will soon be clear," Mölders had predicted cheerfully, but at once the Fuehrer's face had clouded. Totally disregarding Mölder's remark he turned irritably away. An uneasy thought crossed Mölder's mind: If "Sea-Lion" was no longer reality, then why were lives still being put at risk?

Goering, too, veered wildly in his attitudes. And when Kesselring suggested that it was time to concentrate on the Blitz—which throughout the autumn was extended to Bristol, Cardiff, Newcastle, Plymouth, Glasgow,

Tuesday 24 September

I had just one and one blitz only (8:30). We were attacked by ME109s and having made one attack on a 109 I was making a second at four who were well above, when I realised that I should stall so I levelled off. Suddenly, there was a blinding flash on my port wing and I felt a hell of a blow on my left arm, and then blood running down. I went into a hell of a dive and came back to Debden. A cannon shell had hit my wing and a bit of it had hit me just above the elbow and behind. The shell had blown away most of the port flap so I tried to land without flaps. I could not stop and crashed into a pile of stores just off the field, hitting my face and cutting it in two places. I was taken to Saffron Walden General Hospital. They operated but had to leave small pieces in as it had penetrated the muscle.

(from the diary of Pilot Officer Denis H. Wissler No. 17 Squadron)

"There'll Always Be An England"

(—song by Ross Parker)

Belfast and Hull—Goering was at first disdainful: "Night raids? What insanity! I can finish the air war without that." But within days, following the devastating London raid of September 7, he had hailed this as the way to cripple British morale: "After all, man isn't a nocturnal animal." He rallied *Oberst* Johannes Fink, whose misjudged assault on Eastchurch had begun it all: "You must give the German people air superiority as a Christmas present to hang on their trees."

In time, the historians, surveying the battle, would debate its place in the annals of war, and their verdicts, too, were mixed. Certainly it marked the first setback the Luftwaffe had suffered in World War II, and thus had dented their hitherto invincible myth. It had shown a demoralised Europe that the all-conquering Wehrmacht could itself, given time, be overthrown. *Major* the Baron Günther von Maltzhahn, commanding the 54th Fighter Group, had voiced that certainty as early as September 16: "We're not going to win this war; we can't."

The threat of British intervention from the west would pin down more than thirty-five German divisions in Europe—forces which could ill be spared from "Operation Barbarossa." And Hitler's tireless search for alternate routes to victory would founder time and again in costly ventures in the Balkans, the Mediterranean and the Middle East.

For the historians, Dowding would always rank high among the immortal commanders; the victory that he and his pilots achieved drew comparisons with Nelson at Trafalgar and Wellington at Waterloo. Yet perhaps the historian Christopher Dowling came closest in viewing Dowding's achievement as akin to Lord Howard of Effingham's worsting of the Spanish Armada of 1588—"not a set-piece encounter but a string of engagements of varying size and intensity. Both were successful defensive battles . . . more akin to the combat between Hector and Achilles than to that between David and Goliath.

The shrewdest arbiter, Dowling suggests, was the laconic 65-year-old *Feldmarschall* Gerd von Rundstedt, commanding Army Group A. Throughout the early summer of 1940, von Rundstedt, sceptical of what the War Diary described as "the fiction of an invasion," had steadfastly refused to attend the invasion manoeuvres staged as a propaganda exercise at Le Touquet's exclusive Paris Plage. His attitude towards the entire charade was summed up in one explosive comment, "Sea-Lion, rubbish!"

In the postwar period, when teams of Allied academics picked the brains of the German generals on "the other side of the hill," a delegation of Russian historians called on von Rundstedt in captivity. What, they asked him, had been in his view the decisive battle of the war? Their notebooks open, they were poised to set down one word: Stalingrad.

Von Rundstedt was to disappoint them. Had the Luftwaffe won the Battle of Britain, he told them, Germany would have defeated Russia in 1941. *That* had been the decisive battle.

His verdict left the Russians dumbfounded. They closed their notebooks and went quietly away.

THE FEW

top left: Pilot Officer E.D. Glaser, No. 65 Squadron, in 1986; *top and far right:* memorial windows in the Biggin Hill chapel, centre: a kneeling pillow from Tangmere church; *right:* the White Hart at Brasted, Kent; *top centre:* the medals of a Battle of Britain pilot; *centre:* a handsewn statement from the war years.

WHEN THEY GO BACK to the stations—to Biggin Hill, or to Tangmere, or Hornchurch—they know mostly conflicting emotions. Returning to North Weald for a TV documentary in 1984, Wing Commander Geoffrey Page was conscious, primarily, of "sadness and regret," a sense of "grass growing up through the runway and the concrete." And at Hornchurch, the Officers' Mess, where Old Sam, the chef, coaxed his bone-weary pilots to eat against a background of flickering candlelight—"Try a shaving of rare roast beef—must keep up your strength, young sir"—is an Officers' Mess no longer, merely a sprawling block of anonymous flats. The site of No. 54 Squadron's dispersal, where Al Deere, who retired a few years back as Air Commodore, once skidded upside down along the drome at 100 miles an hour, is now the Mitchell School, named after the designer of the Spitfire. "They've got four houses in the school," Deere notes wryly, "and one of them is named after me and I go over occasionally and do my stuff."

Much more than memories live on at Biggin Hill, now an R.A.F. crew-selection centre. In the Chapel, rebuilt in 1951 to replace the burned-out shell of the 1943 original, the oaken reredos still bears witness to the station's great engagements: the 30 squadrons who fought there, the 11 nations whose pilots were part of it. The Officers' Mess, where the pilots of No. 32 Squadron once treated a captured Luftwaffe pilot to a binge of Westerham Ale, has in no way changed. "I walk with ghosts when I re-visit my old station," admits Group Captain Brian Kingcome, now a furniture manufacturer, "but they are friendly ones."

Often it takes little enough to evoke those 'friendly ghosts'. One glimpse of the Tangmere airfield and Group Captain Peter Townsend, now a writer in France, is back in a world that vanished for ever in September, 1939: the long-obsolete Hawker Furies, looping and rolling against a clear blue sky, the leisurely day that ended sharp at 1 p.m., the lotus eating life of a flying club that called for no more than 20 hours airborne a month. At Manston, too, the ghosts materialise, in the shape of a new Spitfire Museum, though the peacetime swimming pool, where the 'erks' washed and shaved at the height of the Battle, once the water mains were ruptured, has long since gone. "It hasn't changed much," Al Deere relates. "It's never been developed, except for a big emergency runway, the biggest in the country and it's used for civil and military diversions. The actual airfield itself is still grass as it used to be."

All of The Few share memories of what Brian Kingcome calls "the strange double life, each one curiously detached from the other. One moment high above the earth, watching a sunrise not yet visible below, killing and avoiding being killed; and the next chatting with the locals over a pint of beer in a cosy country pub." Sometimes, Kingcome recollects, a local would comment critically "on the aerial activity he had witnessed that day as though he were discussing his football team. This sort of thing could only happen to a fighter pilot."

Looking back fifty years, it was indeed the strangest of 'double lives'. "A longish day,

The cap was a fighter pilot's badge of rank New boys had clean, circular caps with neat, smooth peaks. Old sweats like Pip had battered caps that had been sat on, stuffed into cockpits, twisted a thousand ways, soaked by rain, baked by sun. All fighter pilots went around with the top tunic button undone, but that was just tribal swank. Men like Pip had earned the right to wear a really beat-up cap.

(from *Piece of Cake* by Derek Robinson)

below: Flight Lieutenant C.B.F. Kingcome of No. 92 Squadron at Biggin Hill.

of course—from half an hour before dawn to half an hour after dusk . . . we averaged three, sometimes four, sorties a day, but a sortie seldom lasted more than an hour." That was one facet of Kingcome's life with No. 92 Squadron at Biggin Hill; the other was a frenzied blur of "scooting up to London, when ten shillings (the bulk of our day's pay of fourteen shillings) would cover an evening at Shepherd's or The Bag O'Nails (the Four Hundred if we could raise a quid)." In leaner times, Biggin pilots flocked to Teddy Preston's pub, *The White Hart*, at Brasted, "Where five shillings would keep us in beer until the local bobby moved us on at closing time."

At North Weald, this same unreal dichotomy was known to Geoffrey Page and all those of No. 56 Squadron: the breakfasts of lukewarm baked beans and tepid tea, the dawn 'scramble', the lunches, begun at noon, yet so interrupted by 'scrambles' that dessert was not served until 3 p.m. Much later, "we'd go off to a night club, and then come back in the early hours of the morning and get about an hour's sleep . . . a pretty crazy sort of life." Most often, Page too, made for Shepherd's in Shepherd's Market, Mayfair, "the unofficial headquarters of R.A.F., Fighter Command," where Oscar, the Swiss manager, "knew where every fighter Pilot was . . . who was dead and who was alive and who was shacked up and everything like that."

But those based on the coastal airfields tell a different tale even now. As Al Deere calls to mind, No. 54 Squadron, fighting from the Manston satellite by day, returning to Hornchurch to eat and sleep, lived an anchorite life

for weeks on end. Often Hornchurch reeled under the weight of five 'daylights', as Luftwaffe sweeps were known, seven days a week. "There were no girlfriends or pubs or things," Deere insists. "We just didn't get off the airfield. How could you? . . . We were so short of pilots, that was our big thing."

On September 3, 1940, when 54 Squadron flew north to Catterick, No. 41 Squadron, who relieved them, were appalled by the same punishing routine. "It wasn't long," says Group Captain Norman Ryder, Secretary of the Royal Aero Club, then a No. 41 flight commander, "before we founded the Honourable Order of Fog Worshippers. We all bowed down, touching the ground with our forehead three times, praying for the fog that would give us a break."

But these were small disparities, when matched against the articles of faith that The Few held in common. "Surprising how fierce one's protective instincts became at the sight of an enemy violating one's homeland," Brian Kingcome reflects, yet hatred played little part in the make-up of The Few. "The enemy was just another aeroplane that happened to be the wrong type with the wrong markings," was how Flight Lieutenant 'Ginger' Lacey, then a seargeant pilot with No. 501 Squadron, summed up. "I didn't have any strong anti-German feelings." Wing Commander Douglas Blackwood, the publisher, who commanded No. 310 (Czech) Squadron, is more impersonal still: "The aircraft was the object. I never pictured a man in there." Few could match the experience of Wing Commander Robert Doe, then a pilot with No. 234 Squadron, now proprietor of a Kentish filling station. "We were very close," he records, of one of the 14½ 'kills' with which he was ultimately credited, "and looking at one another. He was a huge blond man wearing pale blue overalls. But he showed no fear—he knew I wouldn't fire on him further when it was obvious the plane was about to crash."

Doubt was another element that never seemed to trouble them. "Never once did I ever hear a discussion . . . that there was any possibility of ever losing the fight," Geoffrey Page maintains. "And we didn't see it as 'The Battle of Britain'. The media and history have since named it that . . . and the thought never crossed our minds that we were being beaten." Al Deere supports that contention to the hilt. "We knew that invasion was on and we knew that we had to somehow, not so much beat them in the air, as at least make it bloody difficult for them." And he stresses, "Up until the last moment we expected to have to fight an air-supported invasion."

At the annual Battle of Britain dinner, catering for diminishing numbers each year, at sporadic reunions of 'The Guinea-Pig Club', one common emotion is freely admitted: naked, paralysing fear. This was a state of mind that Station M.Os, like Flight Lieutenant John Buckmaster, at Northolt, knew well, as squadrons returned from combat: "First of all, they were terribly excited. They leapt about on the tarmac, made as much noise as possible, shouted, never stopped talking . . . In less than an hour, this exuberance was replaced by exhaustion—a complete flopout."

Geoffrey Page, perhaps, treats it more lightly than most: "Butterflies in your stomach, rather like a swimming race or tennis match . . . it was just a great big game, a dangerous game . . . but then so is Russian roulette." Though Wing Commander Innes Westmacott of the R.A.F. Benevolent Fund, another 'guinea-pig' from No. 56 Squadron, has never forgotten a more disturbing aspect. "The fear made sociable chaps become morose—introverts went on the grog. You got young pilot officers turning on the Station Adjutant, an R.F.C. type, and snarling, "You wear wings—why the hell don't *you* fly?""

Clinically, as if they were speaking of other men, The Few analyse that fear. "By far the worst part was the waiting at readiness," says Wing Commander Ralph Havercroft, then a sergeant pilot under Kingcome at Biggin Hill. "It felt like ten years till the telephone rang." And Kingcome, too, confirms "The inevitable stomach-churning telephone ring, and the voice from Ops: '92 Squadron, scramble!'." "I've never believed in the theory that some people don't know fear," Al Deere affirms. "I just don't believe that. You sure got frightened every time you went off. You felt quite sick and some chaps used to be sick, like that, physically sick."

Yet, speaking on the twenty-fifth anniversary, James 'Ginger' Lacey saw that fear as a positive 'plus'. "I knew some people who weren't frightened," he explained gently, "and they have been dead for 25 years."

A healthy contempt for non-combatants is never far from the surface, even now. Wing Commander Gordon Sinclair, a former air attaché, then with 310 (Czech) Squadron, re-

Sunday 27 October

We went over to North Weald this morning and did three patrols, two of which were at 28,000 feet. I did 5½ hours and am I tired tonight. Or am I? I am going to bed early tonight, but I shall be just as tired tomorrow morning. We saw some ME109s and chased them but failed to get close enough. There was a flap as soon as we landed back at Martlesham (which was bombed by ME109s today, no bad damage) and we all took off to make a dusk landing.

(from the diary of Pilot Officer Denis H. Wissler No. 17 Squadron)

Pilot Officer Wissler survived the Battle of Britain but was killed in action on 11 November (Armistice Day) 1940.

He is with me still./The years have cast up and drifted out again;/And the memories, dried on the shore,/Have been bundled and stored/For this time,/For this quiet while I am alone.

(from *War Widow* by J. B. Warr)

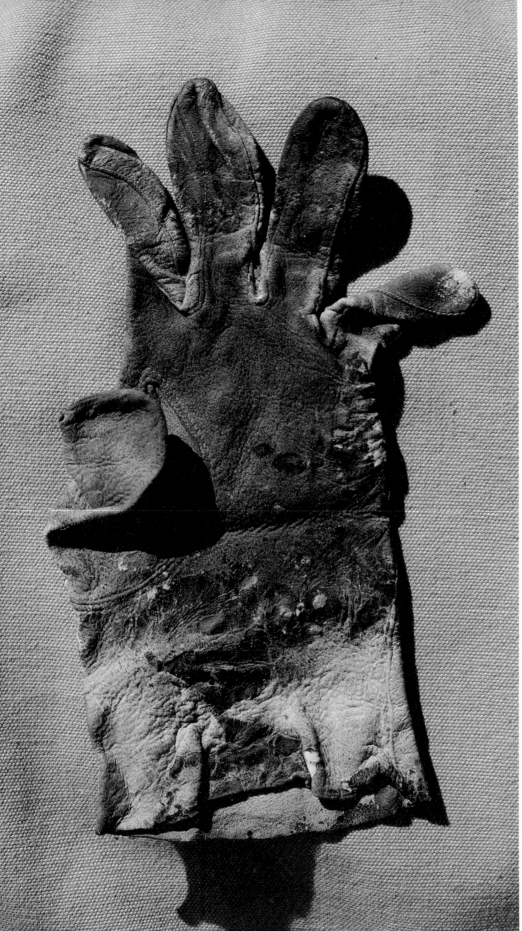

members baling out near an Army camp in Kent, unshaven, carrying his flying helmet and wearing all-too-visible pyjamas beneath his service trousers. "I'm afraid we can't admit you here looking like *that*," huffed a Colonel who did things by the book. And only with difficulty did Sinclair wheedle a railway warrant to facilitate his train journey back to Duxford. And Geoffrey Goodman recalled the time, in September, 1940, when his Hurricane, attacked successively by two ME 109s, arrived back at Croydon "shot to ribbons." With no spare planes available, Goodman was ordered to fly "this battered wreck" to Henlow Maintenance Unit, Bedfordshire, to get another machine off the line.

One of the first souls he encountered at Henlow was a corporal in the Service Police, truly enraged that Goodman was not carrying his gas mask. "Do you realise, Sergeant," he asked the speechless Goodman, "that there is a war on?"

One conundrum puzzles all who remain of The Few: how did they manage to survive? Were they good pilots? Lucky pilots? Pilots who conformed to the Medical Board's yardstick, their reactions one-fifth of a second quicker than the next man's? Geoffrey Page, for one, is none too sure: "There was and probably still is a theory going round that if you're too good a pilot you were a bad fighter pilot, because if you're doing the correct type of nicely balanced turn you're far more likely to be shot down than someone who is hamfisted and kicking on too much rudder." Keen eyesight, he thinks, had much to do with it, and "to be very lucky besides."

212

To an extent, Al Deere concurs, though he sees endurance as equally a 'must'—"a certain determination to keep going . . . too easy to turn away and too easy to give up." Yet both men see teamwork between a pilot and his No. 2 as perhaps the most determinant factor of all. "We used to advise them (the No. 2s) to drop back to about thirty yards," notes Deere, "so you could see what was going on . . . I can remember saying to them, 'What you've got to do is just stick with your leader. Don't lose him at all cost'."

So how do they view themselves now, after fifty years, The Few who survived? As a special breed of men, whose like will not be seen on this earth again? On behalf of them all, Brian Kingcome gives the lie to that:

"I mourn them, but they had counted the cost and they died with regret but without surprise. They were typical of all others. The young of all generations are the same. They may dress differently and have different rites and rituals, but give them a crisis and they are all the same."

far left: The burned flying glove of Pilot Officer D.R. 'Dickie' Turley-George, No. 54 Squadron, which he was wearing when shot down on August 12, 1940; *above:* the grave of Sgt. Geoffrey Goodman (ret. Wing Commander), No. 85 Sq; *left:* Ward 3, Queen Victoria Cottage Hospital, East Grinstead, where Sir Archibald McIndoe treated his "Guinea Pig" pilots who were burned in the Battle.

Now, he will spend a few sick years in Institutes. And do what things the rules consider wise,/And take whatever pity they may dole./To-night he noticed how the women's eyes/Passed from him to the strong men that were whole./How cold and late it is! Why don't they come/And put him into bed? Why don't they come?

(from *Disabled* by Wilfrid Owen)

I felt strangely tired and lazy, not realizing that this was my initiation to a strange feeling of exhaustion with which I was to get better acquainted in the following days. I didn't want to sleep, but I didn't want to move, or talk, or fly, or anything else either, just relax. It's a feeling that's always pervaded me after a fight or a nerve-racking patrol. As nearly as I can describe it, it is a sensation of being drained completely, in every part of your body, though I don't know what of. But you seem to want to just surrender to relaxation, sitting or lying inert and absorbing whatever it is back into your system. I've heard many other pilots say they get the same feeling.

(from *Tally Ho!* by Pilot Officer A.G. Donahue)

CONCEPT DEVELOPMENT, EDITING, RESEARCH, PRINCIPAL COLOUR PHOTOGRAPHY, AND DESIGN BY PHILIP KAPLAN

TEXT BY RICHARD COLLIER
ADDITIONAL RESEARCH BY PAT AND RICHARD COLLIER

PICTURE CREDITS

Photographs by Philip Kaplan are credited: PK. Photographs from the author's collections are credited: AC.

Jacket front: PK. Jacket back: Courtesy of Frank Wootton. P3: AC, P7: R.A.F. Museum.

ORIGINS: THE UNEASE P9: AC, P10–11: R.A.F. Museum, P13: all-Imperial War Museum, P14: AC, P15: AC-David Low.

A STATE OF WAR EXISTS P16–17: AC, P18: both-PK, P20: top-Imperial War Museum, bottom-AC, P21: top-Imperial War Museum, bottom-Michael O'Leary, P22–23: PK, P23: PK courtesy of Andy Saunders Collection, P24: by courtesy The News Portsmouth, P25: Imperial War Museum, P26: courtesy Tangmere Military Aviation Museum, P27: PK, P28: by courtesy The News Portsmouth.

THE FALL OF FRANCE P30: PK, P32: Bundesarchiv-Koblenz, P33: Bundesarchiv-Koblenz, P34: AC, P35: courtesy of Frank Wootton, P36: courtesy of Andy Saunders Collection, P37: AC, P38: AC, top-PK, P40: Bundesarchiv-Koblenz, P41: Bundesarchiv-Koblenz, P43: Bundesarchiv-Koblenz, P44: Bundesarchiv-Koblenz, P45: AC, P46: Bundesarchiv-Koblenz, P47: AC, P49: AC, P50: Bundesarchiv-Koblenz, P51: AC.

HITTING THE RADAR CHAIN P52: courtesy of Andy Saunders Collection, P54: AC, P55: PK, P56: AC, P58: courtesy Margaret Mayhew, P59: AC-Jim Rush, P61: Imperial War Museum, P62: PK, P63: courtesy of Andy Saunders Collection, inset: PK, P65: Bundesarchiv-Kiblenz, P66: PK, P67: PK, P68: courtesy of Margaret Mayhew and Edith Kup.

THE HUNT MOVES TO ENGLAND P69: courtesy of Andy Saunders Collection, P70: PK, P71: R.A.F. Museum, P72: R.A.F. Museum, P73: R.A.F. Museum, P74: all-PK, P75: all-PK, P76: courtesy of Monique Agazarian, P77: R.A.F. Museum, P78: all-PK, P79: both-PK, P80: AC, P81: Bundesarchiv-Koblenz, P82: PK, P83: AC, P84–85: PK, P86–87: courtesy of Andy Saunders Collection.

DEFENCE VERSUS OFFENCE P88–89: courtesy of Frank Wootton, P90: courtesy of Vickers, P91: courtesy of Vickers, P93: PK-courtesy of Stephen Grey, P95: Imperial War Museum, P96: AC-Jim Rush, P97: courtesy of Andy Saunders Collection, P98–99: courtesy of Ian Shoobridge, P100: R.A.F. Museum, P102: PK-courtesy the Lindsay Collection and Tony Bianchi, P104: The BBC Hulton Picture Library, P105: Michael O'Leary, P106: AC, bottom: PK, P107: AC, P108: Bundesarchiv-Koblenz, P109: Bundesarchiv-Koblenz, P110–111 & 112–113: Bundesarchiv-Koblenz.

EAGLES P114: AC, P115: PK-courtesy of Andy Saunders Collection, P116: AC, P117: R.A.F. Museum, P118–119: PK, P120–121: courtesy of Andy Saunders Collection, P122: Bundesarchiv-Koblenz, P123: PK, P124: top-all AC, bottom: Bundesarchiv-Koblenz, P125: top-Bundesarchiv-Koblenz, top right: courtesy of Kathy Horniblow, bottom-both AC, P126: courtesy of R.F.T. Doe, inset: PK, P127: PK-courtesy of the Lindsay Collection and Tony Bianchi, P128: Imperial War Museum, P129: courtesy of Andy Saunders Collection, P130: courtesy of Andy Saunders Collection, P131: courtesy of D.R. Turley-George, P132: both-PK, P133: top-PK-courtesy of Andy Saunders, bottom-Bundesarchiv-Koblenz, P134: AC, P135: left-AC, right-courtesy of Margaret Mayhew, P136: R.A.F. Museum, P137: all-PK, P138: top-PK, bottom-courtesy of Andy Saunders Collection, centre: AC.

SCRAMBLE P140: courtesy of Eric Marsden, P141: PK, P142: Imperial War Museum, P143: the BBC Hulton Picture Library, P144: PK-courtesy of the Lindsay Collection and Tony Bianchi, P145: courtesy of Andy Saunders Collection, P146: PK, P147: AC, P148–149: AC, P150: both-PK, P151: both-PK, P152: Imperial War Museum P153: R.A.F. Museum, P154: top-PK, bottom-courtesy of Frank Wootton, P155: AC, P156–157: courtesy of Eric Marsden.

EYEWITNESS P161: 'Battle of Britain' by Louis Keene-Access number 14118-Canadian War Museum, P163: courtesy of Vickers, P164: both-PK, P165: PK, centre: AC, P166–167: courtesy of Edward Reeves, P169: PK, P170–171: all-courtesy of Andy Saunders Collection, P172: top left-by courtesy The News Portsmouth, top-Imperial War Museum, bottom-courtesy of Andy Saunders Collection, P173: AC.

THEY ALSO FOUGHT FOR BRITAIN P175: William Vandivert-Life Magazine © copyright 1941 Time Inc., P176: PK, P177: Sir William Rothenstein, P178: top left-AC, top right-courtesy of Andy Saunders Collection, bottom-courtesy of A.C. Deere, P180: PK, P181: PK, P182: AC Cuthbert Orde, P183 & P184: R.A.F. Museum, P185: 'S/L G.R. McGregor by Eric Kennington-Canadian War Museum.

PUNISHING THE BRITISH PEOPLE P186: The BBC Hulton Picture Library, P188: PK, bottom left-Henry Moore, P190: AC, P192: all-PK, P193: AC, P194: courtesy of Michael O'Leary, P195: both-Imperial War Museum, bottom left-AC, P197: top-AC, bottom left-Imperial War Museum, bottom right-Bundesarchiv-Koblenz, top right-AC, P198: Imperial War Museum, P200: PK, P201: Henry Moore, P202: AC, P203: top left-Imperial War Museum, top right-Bundesarchiv-Koblenz, bottom-Imperial War Museum.

IT JUST STOPPED P204: courtesy of Margaret Mayhew.

THE FEW P207: R.A.F. Museum, P208: all-PK-medals courtesy of Andy Saunders, P209: PK, P210: courtesy of Brian Kingcome, P212: courtesy of D.R. Turley-George, P213: both-PK, P214: courtesy of Andy Saunders Collection, P215: top left-courtesy of Andy Saunders Collection, top right-courtesy of D.R. Turley-George, bottom-courtesy of Andy Saunders Collection,

Front endsheet: courtesy of Andy Saunders Collection. Back endsheet: AC.

ACKNOWLEDGMENTS

We thank Margaret Mayhew, whose kind and generous help and suggestions, ideas, and assistance in countless ways have been invaluable during our work on this book.

Special thanks to Andy Saunders, who so kindly made his wonderful photo collection available to the authors during their research. We thank Andy too, for his advice and suggestions throughout the development of the book.

We thank the many Battle of Britain participants whose enthusiastic assistance has proven invaluable in developing and preparing this book for publication. We are grateful to the pilots, their wives, families and widows, to the Royal Air Force and those among its personnel whose generosity of time and effort we will long remember. We thank the dozens of eyewitnesses of England whose willingness to share the memories of 1940, the Blitz and the war years, is gratefully acknowledged here and is appreciated more than we can say.

We are particularly indebted to the following people whose contributions and assistance in providing additional photographs, book and article reference materials, the loans and gifts of personal memorabilia, interviews, research information, and other forms of assistance, have aided greatly in the preparation and presentation of this work. A special thank you to Monique Agazarian, Squadron Leader Tad Andersz, Lieutenant Commander J.A. Baker, RN, Malcolm Bates, R.A.F. Bentley Priory, Tony Bianchi of Personal Plane Services Ltd. and the Lindsay Collection, Air Vice Marshal Harold Bird-Wilson, C.J. Bunney, Sergeant John Burgess, Richard Bye, Geoffrey Charters, Pat Collier, Air Commodore Alan C. Deere, Wing Commander R.F.T. Doe, Gary Eastman, Richard Erven, Gilly Fielder, Bob Fisher, Flight Lieutenant Brian Forbes-R.A.F. Northolt, Air Chief Marshal Sir Christopher Foxley-Norris, Pilot Officer Dave Glaser, Joan Goodman, Barry Gregory, Stephen Grey, Jonathan Grimwood, Anthony Iacono, Lynn Johnson, Claire and Joe Kaplan, Neal Kaplan, Group Captain Brian Kingcome, Bud Knapp, Tadeusz Krzystek, Edith Kup, Reg Mack, Eric Marsden, Mike Mathews, Ella Mayhew, Tilly Mayhew, Lynn Newmark, John Newth, Michael O'Leary, Wing Commander Geoffrey Page, Pauline Page, Alan and Sandra Reeves, Edward Reeves, R.A. Reiss, Mark Ritchie, Mary Smith, Tangmere Military Aviation Museum, Group Captain Peter Townsend, Mary and Keith Vanstone, Chris Von Glahn, Ray Wagner, Frank Wootton.

POETRY / MARGIN TEXT CREDITS

Tangmere M.A. Museum, Jack Ashford, *A Filter's Lament*; Dodd, Mead, Don Blanding, *Air & Leopards*; The Bodley Head, David Bourne, *Parachute Descent*; R. Yeoman-Clark, Lois Clark, *Fly-Past Alderney*; Faber & Faber, D.M. Crook, *Spitfire Pilot*; Jonathan Cape, Ernest Hemingway, *Death in the Afternoon*; Macmillan, Richard Hillary, *The Last Enemy*; Harcourt, Brace Jovanovich, Amelia Earhart, *Courage*; Virago, Margery Lea, *Bomb Story*; Jean Faulks, Ethel Mannin, *Song of the Bomber*; Methuen & Co, Alice Duer Miller, *The White Cliffs*; Virago, May Morton, *To A Barrage Balloon*; the estate of the author, editor

and Chatto & Windus. for poems by Wilfred Owen: Granada. J. B. Priestley. *Out of the People / The People's War*: The Bodley Head. John Pudney. *For Johnny*: Alfred Knopf. Derek Robinson. *Piece of Cake*: Muller. Sheila Shannon. *A Child Asleep in a Tube*: The Bodley Head. Gervase Stewart. *I Burn for England*: Fortune Press/Charles Skilton Ltd. Gervase Stewart. Poem: Virago. Catherine Brewster Toosey. *Colour Symphony*: Selma Press. Barry Winchester. *Boy At War / 54 Days*: Methuen & Co. Noel Coward. *Don't Lets Be Beastly To The Germans*.

Every attempt has been made to clear copyright. The Publisher apologises if any credits have been missed.

BIBLIOGRAPHY

Arct, Bohdan. *Polish Wings in the West*. Warsaw: Interpress, 1971.

Bader, Group Captain Douglas. *Fight For The Sky*. Doubleday, 1973.

Barker, A.J. *Dunkirk: The Great Escape*. New York: David McKay Co., 1977.

Battle of Britain Then and Now, The. After The Battle Magazine, 1980.

Benes, B. *Wings in Exile*. London, 1942.

Bickers, Richard Townshend. *Ginger Lacy Fighter Pilot*. New York: Beagle Books, 1962.

Bishop, Edward. *The Battle of Britain*. Geo. Allen and Unwin Ltd., 1960.

'Blake'. *Readiness at Dawn*. Victor Gollancz Ltd., 1941.

'Blake'. *We Rendezvous at Ten*. Victor Gollancz Ltd., 1942.

Blitz Then and Now, The. Battle of Britain Prints Int'l. Ltd., 1987.

Bolitho, Hector. *Combat Report*. B.T. Batsford Ltd., 1943.

Bowyer, Chaz. *Fighter Command*. London: J.M. Dent Sons, 1980.

Bowyer, Michael J.F. *Action Stations: Military Airfields of East Anglia*. Cambridge: Patrick Stephens, 1979.

Brickhill, Paul. *Reach For The Sky*. London: William Collins, 1954.

Calder, Angus. *The People's War*. Granada, 1969.

Carne, Daphne (Griffiths). *The Eyes of The Few*. London: P.R. Macmillan, 1960.

Churchill, Sir Winston. *The Gathering Storm*. Boston: Houghton Mifflin, 1949.

Churchill, Sir Winston. *Their Finest Hour*. Boston: Houghton Mifflin, 1949.

Clark, Ronald W. *Tizard*. Methuen, 1965.

Collier, Basil. *Leader of The Few*. London: Jarrolds, 1957.

Collier, Richard. *Eagle Day*. New York: E.P. Dutton, 1966.

Collier, Richard. *1940: The World in Flames*. London: Hamish Hamilton, 1979.

Collyer, David G. *Battle of Britain Diary*. Kent Aviation Historical Society, 1980.

Constable, Trevor J. and Toliver, Raymond F. *Horrido! Fighter Aces of the Luftwaffe*. Macmillan, 1968.

Crook, D.M. *Spitfire Pilot*. London: Faber and Faber,

Deere, Group Captain Alan C. *Nine Lives*. Hodder and Stoughton, 1959.

Deighton, Len. *Battle of Britain*. Jonathan Cape, 1980.

A LETTER FROM SIR KEITH PARK TO RICHARD COLLIER 5/7/65

Dear Collier,
In reply to your letter of April 20, I apologise for some delay but my work as a City Councillor, Civil Defense, several charities, apart from business in the city, has left me no time to delve into the past.
My daily task in 1940 was to outwit and out-live a greatly more numerous enemy Air Force flushed by many victories in Europe. In achieving that aim I was ordered to prevent the bombing of many Vital Targets spread over the South of England and upon which our War Effort depended.
The German Air Force being stronger and the attacker had unfettered choice of *Time*, *Place*, *Height* and *Weather* for three months of the Battle. As the GAF operated on a 200-mile front it meant that I had, on an average to twice daily have to judge which was his main attacking force and concentrate the maximum Fighter Squadrons I had available at short notice onto attack on the Bombers *before* they reached a Vital Target. The head-on attack from below by a squadron of Fighters was more devastating to massed Bombers than the 1st World War tactics of Fighters attacking from rear in full view of escorting German Fighters. We varied our Fighter Tactics as also did the GAF, but we kept one

step ahead.

From 8am to 5pm daily I was at my H.Q. No. 11 Group so as to be ready to take charge of Fighter Operations for the usual morning (and) the mid-afternoon German Bomber attacks.

Then as the squadrons were landing from 1st combat I flew round visiting the most badly bombed aerodromes also to visit squadrons nearing their time for withdrawal from the Front line for rest and re-training of new pilots.

Some squadrons stayed fighting fit for over a month like the Scottish and Polish Squadrons. Others, who had lost their best leaders, began to crack up in less than two weeks. This was a daily concern of mine as we were to short of trained replacement Squadrons, in rear areas of Nos. 12 and 13 Fighter Groups. Thanks to Beaverbrook, who telephoned me nightly, I was never dangerously short of Hurricanes or Spitfires. The pity was that he was not also given the supply of trained Fighter pilots instead of Air Staff or Air Ministry! Not till the Battle was nearly over in September 1940 did D.C.A.S. Air Minister Sholto-Douglas appear to realise the grave-no the critical-shortage of trained pilots in my squadrons in the Front line also in Groups in rear areas of Fighter Command.

For many weeks I had been desparately short of pilots and kept reporting

Deighton, Len. *Fighter*. New York: Ballantine, 1977.

Dickson, Lovat. *Richard Hillary*. London: Macmillan, 1951.

Dowding, H.C.T. Air Chief Marshal. *The Battle of Britain*. Despatch of 20 August 1941 to the Secretary of State for Air.

Duval, G.R. *Presentation Aircraft*. D. Bradford Barton Ltd., 1976.

Eden, Guy. Portrait of Churchill. Hutchinson and Co. Ltd.

Everett, Susanne. *London The Glamour Years 1919–39*. Bison Books, 1985.

Falkowski, W/Cdr. J.P. *With The Wind In My Face*.

Farrar, David. *G For God Almighty*. London: Weidenfield and Nicholson, 1969.

Farrar, David. *The Sky's The Limit*. London: Hutchinson, 1943.

Farson, Negley. *Bomber's Moon*. Victor Gollancz Ltd., 1941.

Fedden, Robin. *Churchill and Chartwell*. The National Trust, 1984.

Fiedler, Arkady. *Squadron 303*. New York: Roy Publishers, 1943.

Fitzgibbon, Constantine. *London's Burning*. New York: Ballantine Books, 1970.

Fitzgibbon, Constantine. *The Blitz*. London: Allan Wingate, 1957.

Fitzgibbon, Constantine. *The Winter of the Bombs*. New York: WW Norton, 1957.

Fleming, Peter, *Invasion 1940*. London:Ruper Hart-Davis, 1957.

Flying Officer 'X'. *How Sleep The Brave*. Jonathan Cape, 1943.

Forbes, W/Cdr. A. and Allen, S/L H. *Ten Fighter Boys*. London: Collins, 1942.

Forbes-Robertson, Diana, and Straus Jr., R.W. *War Letters From Britain*. Jarrolds,

Forrester, Larry. *Fly For Your Life*. Bantam Books, 1956.

Franks, Norman. *Battle of Britain*. Bison Books, 1981.

Galland, Adolf. *The First and The Last*. New York: Ballantine Books, 1954.

Gallico, Paul. *The Hurricane Story*. Doubleday, 1959.

Gleed, W/Cdr. Ian. *Arise To Conquer*. Victor Gollancz, 1942.

Grant, Ian and Madden, Nicholas. *The Countryside At War*. Jupiter Books Ltd., 1975.

Grant, Ian and Madden, Nicholas. *The City At War*. Jupiter Books Ltd., 1975.

Graves, Charles. *London Transport at War*. London Transport, 1978.

Graves, Charles. *The Home Guard of Britain*. Hutchinson Co. Ltd.,

Green, William. *Aircraft of the Battle of Britain*. Janes, 1969.

Greer, L. and Harold, A. *Flying Clothing: The Story of Its Development*. Airlife Publishing, 1979.

Hall, Roger. *Clouds of Fear*. Coronet Books, 1975.

Halliday, Hugh. *242 Squadron The Canadian Years*. Midland Counties publications, 1981.

Halpenny, Bruce Barrymore. *Action Stations: Military Airfields of Greater London*. Cambridge: Patrick Stephens, 1984.

Hamann, Fred. *Air Words*. Superior Publishing Co., 1945.

Hart, Liddell. *The Defence of Britain*. London: Faber and Faber Ltd., 1939.

Hastings, Max. *Military Anecdotes*. Oxford University Press, 1985.

Heinnemann, William Ltd. *Destiny Can Wait*. Polish Air Force Association, 1949.

Henshaw, Alex. *Sigh For A Merlin*. John Murray Publishers Ltd., 1979.

Hering, S/L P.G. *Customs and Traditions of the RAF*. Aldershot: Gale and Polden Ltd., 1961.

Hewes, J.V. *The High Courts of Heaven*. London: Peter Davies, 1942.

Hewison, Robert. *Under Seige: Literary Life in London 1939–45*. Oxford University Press.

Hillary, Richard. *Falling Through Space*. New York: Reynal and Hitchcock, 1942.

Holmes, S/L J.D.V. *Fighter Controllers*. London: Bernards Ltd.,

Humphreys, Roy S. *Hawkinge 1912–1961*. Meresborough Books, 1981.

Ingersoll, Ralph. *Report On England*. New York: Simon and Schuster, 1940.

Ishoven, Armand van. *The Luftwaffe in the Battle of Britain*. Charles Scribner's Sons, 1980.

Ismay, *The Memoirs of General Lord*. New York: Viking Press, 1960.

Jackson, Carlton. *Who Will Take Our Children?* Methuen, 1985.

Jenkins, Paul. *Battle Over Portsmouth*. Middleton Press, 1986.

Johnson, B.S. *The Evacuees*. London: Victor Gollancz, 1968.

Johnson, David. *The City Ablaze*. London: William Kimber, 1980.

Johnson, Group Captain J.E. *Full Circle*. New York: Ballantine Books, 1964.

Johnson, Group Captain J.E. *Wing Leader*. New York: Ballantine Books, 1957.

Joseph, Shirley. *If Their Mothers Only Knew*. Faber and Faber, 1944.

Julian, Marcel. *The Battle of Britain*. New York: Orion Press, 1965.

Kaplan, Philip and Smith, Rex Allen. *One Last Look*. New York: Abbeville Press, 1983.

Kennington, Eric. *Drawing The RAF*. Oxford University Press, 1942.

Kent, Group Captain J.A. *One Of The Few*. London: William Kimber, 1971.

Kinsey, Gordon. *Bawdsey—Birth of the Beam*. Terence Dalton Ltd., 1983.

Knight, Dennis. *Harvest of Messerschmitts*. Frederick Warne, 1981.

Knoke, Heinz. *I Flew For The Fuhrer*. London: Evans Brothers Ltd., 1953.

Landau, Rom. *The Wing*. Faber and Faber, 1940.

Lee, Asher. *Goering: Air Leader*. New York: Hippocrene Books, 1972.

Leske, Gottfried. *I Was A Nazi Flier*. New York: Dial Press, 1941.

Longmire, Norman. *Air Raid: The Bombing of Coventry, 1940*. David McKay Co., 1976.

Lucas, Laddie. *Flying Colours*. Panther Granada Books, 1981.

Lynn, Vera. *Vocal Refrain*. London: Star Books, 1975.

Mack, Joanna and Humphries, Steve. *London At War*. Sidgewick and Jackson, 1985.

Mann, Thomas. *The Coming Victory of Democracy*. New

York: Alfred A. Knopf, 1938.

Mason, Francis K. *Battle Over Britain*. New York: Doubleday, 1969.

Mason, Francis K. *The Hawker Hurricane*. Astor Publications, 1987.

Mathews, W.R. *St. Paul's Cathedral in Wartime 1939–1945*. Hutchinson and Co. Ltd., 1946.

McKee, Alexander. *Strike From The Sky*. New York: Lancer Books, 1960.

Michie, Allan A. and Graebner, W. *Their Finest Hour*. New York: Harcourt Brace, 1941.

Middleton, Drew. *The Sky Suspended*. Longmans, Green and Co., 1960.

Minns, Raynes. *Bombers and Mash*. Virago Ltd., 1980.

Mitchell, Alan W. *New Zealanders In The Air War*. George G. Harrap and Co., Ltd., 1945.

Monk, Noel. *Squadrons Up!* Victor Gollancz Ltd., 1943.

Moore, Henry. *Shelter Sketch Book*. London: Editions Poetry,

Moran, Lord. *Churchill Taken From The Diaries of Lord Moran*. Boston: Houghton Mifflin, 1966.

Mosley, Leonard. *Backs To The Wall*.

Mosley, Leonard. *Faces From The Fire*. Quality Book Club, 1962.

Murrow, Edward R. *This Is London*. New York: Simon and Schuster, 1941.

Nancarrow, F.G. *Glasgow's Fighter Squadron*. London and Glasgow: Collins, 1942.

Nixon, Barbara. *Raiders Overhead*. Scholar/Gulliver, 1980.

Odhams Press Ltd. *Ourselves In Wartime*.

Orange, Vincent. *Sir Keith Park*. London: Methuen, 1984.

Page, Geoffrey. *Tale Of A Guinea Pig*. Corgi Books, 1981.

Panter-Downes, Mollie. *London War Notes 1939–1945*. Farrar, Straus and Giroux.

Partridge, Eric. *A Dictionary of RAF Slang*. Michael Joseph Ltd., 1945.

Price, Alfred. *Blitz On Britain*. London: Ian Allen Ltd., 1977.

Price, Alfred. *Spitfire: A Documentary History*. London: Macdonald and Janes, 1977.

Price, Alfred. *Spitfire At War*. London: Ian Allen Ltd., 1974.

Price, Alfred. *The Spitfire Story*. Janes, 1982.

Price, Alfred. *The Hardest Day*. New York: Charles Scribner's Sons, 1979.

Price, Bernard. *Chichester: The Valiant Years*. Phillmore, 1978.

Priestly, J.B. *Britain At War*. New York: Harper and Brothers, 1942.

Priestly, J.B. *Britain Speaks*. New York: Harper and Brothers, 1940.

Priestly, J.B. *British Women Go To War*. London: Collins,

Quill, Jeffrey. *Birth Of A Legend The Spitfire*. London: Quiller Press Ltd., 1986.

Quill, Jeffrey. *Spitfire: A Test Pilot's Story*. University of Washington Press. 1983.

Raff. *Behind The Spitfires*. London: Methuen, 1941.

RCAF Overseas, The First Four Years. Oxford University Press, 1944.

Reynolds, Quentin. *A London Diary*. New York: Random House, 1941.

Richards, Denis. *The Fight At Odds (Royal Air Force 1939–1945)*. Crown Copyright, 1953.

Robertson, Ben. *I Saw England*. London: Jarrolds, 1941.

Robertson, Bruce. *Spitfire: The Story of a Famous Fighter*. (Harleyford) Arco,

Robinson, Derek. *Piece of Cake*. New York: Alfred A. Knopf, 1983.

Rootes, Andrew. *Front Line County*. Robert Hale Ltd., 1980.

Rothenstein, Sir William and Cecil, Lord David. *Men of the R.A.F.* Oxford University Press, 1942.

Saunders, Hilary St. George. *Ford At War*.

Shachtman, Tom. *The Phoney War 1939–1940*. New York: Harper and Row, 1982.

Sheean, Vincent. *Between The Thunder and The Sun*. London: Macmillan. 1943.

Shores, Christopher. *Duel For The Sky*. 1985.

Sperber, A.M. *Murrow: His Life and Times*. New York: Freundlich, 1986.

Strachey, John. *Digging For Mrs. Miller*. New York: Random House, 1941.

Sundquist, James L. *British Cities At War*. A Report of the American Municipal Association. 1941.

Sutton, Barry. *The Way Of A Pilot*. London: Macmillan, 1942.

Taylor, A.J.P. *Beaverbrook*. London: Hamish Hamilton, 1972.

Taylor, A.J.P. *English History 1914–1945*. Oxford University Press, 1965.

Taylor, Telford. *The Breaking Wave*. Simon and Schuster, 1970.

Terkel, Studs. *The Good War*. New York: Ballantine Books, 1984.

Thompson, Laurence. *1940*. New York: William Morrow and Co., 1980.

Townsend, Peter. *Duel Of Eagles*. New York: Simon and Schuster, 1970.

Trevor, Elleston. *Squadron Airborne*. New York: Ballantine Books, 1962.

Turner, John Frayn. *The Bader Tapes*. The Kensal Press, 1986.

Turner, E.S. *The Phoney War*. New York: St. Martin's Press, 1961.

Watson-Watt, Sir Robert. *Three Steps to Victory*. Oldhams, 1958.

Weld, Jim. *Flying Headgear of the World 1934–1945*. Jim Weld, 1980.

Westall, Robert. *Children Of The Blitz*. Viking Penguin, 1985.

Whiting, Charles. *Britain Under Fire/The Bombing of Britain's Cities, 1940–1945*. Century, 1986.

Whitnell, Lewis. *Engines Over London*. Carroll and Nicholson, 1949.

Williams, P. and Harrison, T. *McIndoe's Army*. London: Pelham Books, 1979.

Wood, Derek and Dempster, Derek. *The Narrow Margin*. McGraw Hill, 1961.

Woon, Basil. *Hell Came to London*. London: Peter Davies, 1941.

Wright, Esther Terry. *Pilot's Wife's Tale*. John Lane The Bodley Head, 1942.

Wright, Robert. *Dowding And The Battle of Britain*. Macdonald, 1969.

Wright, Robert. *The Man Who Won The Battle of Britain*. New York: Charles Scribner's Sons, 1969.

Wykeham, Peter. *Fighter Command*. London: Putnam, 1960.

this daily to Lord Dowding who daily reported to Air Staff, Air Ministry. This shortage very nearly cost us the critical Battle of Britain. The very Air Staff responsible for this failure arranged: after the Battle has been won: for the Commander of Fighter Command and myself to appear late October before the full Air Council—not to be thanked, but to be questioned as to why we did not try out certain minor tactics favoured by the Commander of a Fighter Group in a back area that had little fighting experience in 1940.

If I had time I could relate several other spheres in which D.C.A.S. and Air Ministry failed to meet the urgent needs of Fighter Command in 1940. When I was posted in Dec. 1940 for a "rest" in Flying Training Command they were amazed to hear for the first time of a shortage of pilots in Fighter Command in 1940. The C-in-C Patterson swore he had never been told by Air Ministry. Moreover when I took Command of No. 23 Training Group I found the Advanced Flying Schools were working only 2/3 capacity on a peace-time routine complete with long week-ends Friday to Monday. Air Ministry records will show 23 Group's increase in Pilot Output in *1941* long after the Battle of Britain after Dowding had been displaced by Sholto-Douglas.

Yours sincerely
Keith R. Park

ADDITIONAL REMARKS OF SIR KEITH PARK ON THE BATTLE OF BRITAIN

Because Air Chief Marshal Joubert, R.A.F. (Retired) has criticized my tactical handling of Fighter Squadrons in the Battle of Britain, I am entitled to describe how the Fighters were handled during these fateful four months.

In July 1940 Fighter Command had a total of 50 Fighter Squadrons for the defence of Great Britain against the Luftwaffe, which had concentrated about 4000 Bombers and Fighters in N.W. Europe. Twenty-five of the R.A.F. Fighter Squadrons were in my Command, No. 11 Fighter Group, covering the S.E. of England. The remaining twenty-five Squadrons were divided between three smaller Fighter Groups: No. 10 Fighter Group on my right covered the S.W. of England, No. 12 Fighter Group in my rear covered the Midlands and North of England, and No. 13 Fighter Group covered Scotland.

As the bulk of the fighting was in No. 11 Group area, their Squadrons became battle-weary and were regularly exchanged with Squadrons in Fighter Groups in rear. Owing to the shortage of fresh Squadrons, my orders from Lord Dowding were not to call on the Fighter Groups on my flank or rear for reinforcements unless absolutely essential. However I was sometimes

SELECTED INFORMATIONAL SUMMARY FOR THE BATTLE OF BRITAIN PERIOD

PRINCIPAL ROYAL AIR FORCE COMMANDERS IN THE BATTLE OF BRITAIN

AIR OFFICER COMMANDING-IN-CHIEF, FIGHTER COMMAND AIR CHIEF MARSHAL SIR HUGH CASWALL TREMENHEERE DOWDING, G.C.B., G.C.V.O., C.M.G., A.D.C.

AIR OFFICER COMMANDING, NO. 10 GROUP AIR VICE MARSHAL SIR CHRISTOPHER JOSEPH QUINTIN BRAND, K.B.E., D.S.O., M.C., D.F.C.

AIR OFFICER COMMANDING, NO. 11 GROUP AIR VICE MARSHAL KEITH RODNEY PARK, M.C., D.F.C.

AIR OFFICER COMMANDING, NO. 12 GROUP AIR VICE MARSHAL TRAFFORD LEIGH-MALLORY, C.B., D.S.O.

AIR OFFICER COMMANDING, NO. 13 GROUP AIR VICE MARSHAL RICHARD ERNEST SAUL, D.F.C.

PRINCIPAL GERMAN AIR FORCE COMMANDERS IN THE BATTLE OF BRITAIN

REICHSMARSCHALL HERMANN GOERING

COMMANDER, LUFTFLOTTE 2 GENERALFELDMARSCHALL ALBERT KESSELRING

COMMANDER, LUFTFLOTTE 3 GENERALFELDMARSCHALL HUGO SPERRLE

COMMANDER, LUFTFLOTTE 5 GENERALOBERST HANS-JÜRGEN STUMPFF

PRINCIPAL AIRCRAFT OPERATING IN THE BATTLE OF BRITAIN

ROYAL AIR FORCE

HAWKER HURRICANE I
WING SPAN: 40 ft. 0 in.,/LENGTH: 31 ft. 4 in.,/HEIGHT: 13 ft. 1 in.,/WING AREA: 258 sq. ft., POWERPLANT: one 1,030 hp Rolls-Royce Merlin III twelve-cylinder liquid-cooled engine. ARMAMENT: Eight .303 in. Browning machine guns mounted in the wings. MAXIMUM SPEED: 328 mph at 20,000 ft. MAXIMUM RANGE: 505 miles. SERVICE CEILING: 34,200 feet. ROLE: fighter.

SUPERMARINE SPITFIRE IA
WING SPAN: 36 ft. 11 in.,/LENGTH: 29 ft. 11 in.,/HEIGHT: 12 ft. 3 in.,/WING AREA: 242 sq. ft., POWERPLANT: one 1,030 hp Rolls-Royce Merlin III twelve-cylinder liquid-cooled engine. ARMAMENT: Eight .303 in. Browning machine guns mounted in the wings . . . 300 rounds per gun. MAXIMUM SPEED: 362 mph at 19,000 ft. RANGE: 395 miles. SERVICE CEILING: 31,900 feet. ROLE: fighter.

BRISTOL BLENHEIM IF
WING SPAN: 56 ft. 4 in.,/LENGTH: 39 ft. 9 in.,/HEIGHT: 9 ft. 10 in.,/WING AREA: 469 sq. ft. POWERPLANT: two 840 hp Bristol Mercury VIII nine-cylinder air-cooled engines. ARMAMENT: one .303 in. Browning machine gun in the port wing, four .303 in. Browning machine guns in the ventral fairing, one .303 in. Vickers K machine gun in hydraulically-operated semi-retractable dorsal turret. MAXIMUM SPEED: 285 mph at 15,000 ft. MAXIMUM RANGE: 1,125 miles. SERVICE CEILING: 27,280 feet. ROLE: fighter.

BOULTON PAUL DEFIANT I
WING SPAN: 39 ft. 4 in.,/LENGTH: 35 ft. 4 in.,/HEIGHT: 12 ft. 2 in.,/WING AREA: 250 sq. ft., POWERPLANT: one 1,030 hp Rolls-Royce Merlin III twelve-cylinder liquid-cooled engine. ARMAMENT: four .303 in. Browning machine guns mounted in electrically-operated B.P. "A" Mk IID turret . . . 600 rounds per gun. MAXIMUM SPEED: 304 mph at 17,000 ft. RANGE: 465 miles. SERVICE CEILING: 30,350 feet. ROLE: fighter.

GLOSTER GLADIATOR II
WING SPAN: 32 ft. 3 in.,/LENGTH: 27 ft. 5 in.,/HEIGHT: 11 ft. 7 in.,/WING AREA: 323 sq. ft., POWERPLANT: one 840 hp Bristol Mercury VIII.AS nine-cylinder air-cooled engine. ARMAMENT: four .303 in. Browning machine guns, two mounted in the

nose . . . 600 rounds per gun, two mounted under the lower wing . . . 400 rounds per gun. MAXIMUM SPEED: 257 mph at 14,600 ft. NORMAL RANGE: 444 miles. SERVICE CEILING: 33,500 feet. ROLE: fighter.

GERMAN AIR FORCE

MESSERSCHMITT Bf 109E-4
WING SPAN: 32 ft. 4½ in./LENGTH: 28 ft. 8 in./ HEIGHT: 11 ft. 2 in./WING AREA: 174 sq. ft., POWERPLANT: one 1,150 hp Daimler-Benz DB601A twelve-cylinder liquid-cooled engine. ARMAMENT: two 7.9 mm MG17 machine guns on the engine crank-case firing through the upper nose decking . . . 1,000 rounds per gun, two 20 mm MG FF cannon in the wings . . . 60 rounds per gun. MAXIMUM SPEED: 357 mph at 12,300 ft. RANGE: 412 miles. SERVICE CEILING: 36,000 feet. ROLE: fighter.

MESSERSCHMITT Bf 110C-4
WING SPAN: 53 ft 4¾ in./LENGTH: 39 ft. 8½ in./HEIGHT: 11 ft. 6 in./WING AREA: 413 sq. ft., POWERPLANT: two 1,150 hp Daimler-Benz DB601A twelve-cylinder liquid-cooled engines. ARMAMENT: four 7.9 mm MG17 machine guns . . . 1,000 rounds per gun, and two 20 mm MG FF cannon . . . 180 rounds per gun in the nose; one rear-firing 7.9 mm MG15 machine gun . . . 750 rounds in the cockpit. MAXIMUM SPEED: 349 mph at 22,960 ft. NORMAL RANGE: 530 miles. SERVICE CEILING: 32,000 feet. ROLE: fighter.

HEINKEL He IIIP-2
WING SPAN: 74 ft. 1¾ in./LENGTH: 53 ft. 9½ in./HEIGHT: 13 ft. 1½ in./WING AREA: 942 sq. ft., POWERPLANT: two 1,100 hp Daimler-Benz DB601A-I twelve-cylinder liquid-cooled engines. ARMAMENT: three 7.9 mm MG15 machine guns in nose, dorsal and ventral positions. BOMB CAPACITY: 4,410 lbs. MAXIMUM SPEED: 247 mph at 16,400 ft. MAXIMUM RANGE: 1,224 miles. SERVICE CEILING: 26,250 feet. ROLE: bomber.

DORNIER Do 17z-2
WING SPAN: 59 ft. ¾ in./LENGTH: 52 ft./ HEIGHT: 14 ft. 11½ in./WING AREA: 592 sq. ft., POWERPLANT: two 1,000 hp Bramo 323P nine-cylinder air-cooled engines. ARMAMENT: four to eight 7.9 mm MG15 machine guns in the front, rear and beam cockpit mountings and ventral position. BOMB CAPACITY: 2,200 lbs. MAXIMUM SPEED: 265 mph at 16,400 ft. NORMAL RANGE: 745 miles. SERVICE CEILING: 26,400 feet. ROLE: bomber.

JUNKERS Ju 87B-2
WING SPAN: 45 ft. 3¼ in./LENGTH: 36 ft. 1 in./ HEIGHT: 13 ft. 10½ in./WING AREA: 343 sq. ft., POWERPLANT: one 1,100 hp Junkers Jumo 211A-I twelve-cylinder liquid-cooled engine. ARMAMENT: two 7.9 mm MG17 machine guns in the wings, one 7.9 MG15 machine gun in a rear cockpit mounting. BOMB CAPACITY: one 1,100 lb. bomb carried on a crutch mounting under the fuselage, four 110 lb. bombs carried under the wings. MAXIMUM SPEED: 232 mph at 13,500 ft. RANGE: (with 1,100 lb. bombload) 370 miles. SERVICE CEILING: 26,500 feet. ROLE: dive-bomber.

JUNKERS Ju 88A-I
WING SPAN: 59 ft. 10¾ in./LENGTH: 47 ft. 1 in./ HEIGHT: 15 ft. 5 in./WING AREA: 540 sq. ft., POWERPLANT: two 1,200 hp Junkers Jumo 211B-1 twelve-cylinder liquid-cooled engines. ARMAMENT: three 7.9 mm MG15 machine guns in front and rear cockpit mountings and ventral gondola. BOMB CAPACITY: normal load 3,968 lbs. carried on four underwing pylons, plus a small internal capacity. MAXIMUM SPEED: 286 mph at 16,000 ft. RANGE: 1,553 miles. SERVICE CEILING: 26,500 feet. ROLE: dive-bomber, level bomber and various.

DORNIER Do 215B-1
WING SPAN: 59 ft. ¾ in./LENGTH: 52 ft./ HEIGHT: 14 ft. 11½ in./WING AREA: 592 sq. ft., POWERPLANT: two 1,075 hp Daimler-Benz DB601A twelve-cylinder liquid-cooled engines. ARMAMENT: three to five 7.9 mm MG15 machine guns mounted singly in front, rear and beam cockpit positions and rear of the ventral gondola. BOMB CAPACITY: 2,200 lbs. MAXIMUM SPEED: 292 mph at 16,400 ft. NORMAL RANGE: 965 miles. SERVICE CEILING: 31,170 feet. ROLE: reconnaissance bomber.

GERMAN AIRCRAFT LOSSES DURING THE BATTLE OF BRITAIN CLAIMED AND DEFINITE

PERIOD	RAF CLAIMS DESTROYED	GERMAN DESTROYED	STATISTICS DAMAGED
JULY 10 TO AUG 7	188	192	77
AUG 8 TO AUG 23	755	403	127
AUG 4 TO SEPT 6	643	378	115
SEPT 7 TO SEPT 30	846	435	161
OCT 1 TO OCT 31	260	325	163
TOTAL	2692	1733	643

forced to call for small reinforcements when all my Squadrons had been sent forward to engage the main enemy raids before they could bomb a target. Many were the occasions I had nothing left to defend vital targets like Portsmouth or Southampton and Fighter aerodromes. On scores of days I called on No. 10 Fighter Group on my right for a few Squadrons to protect some vital target. Never on any occasion can I remember this Group failing to send its Squadrons promptly to the place requested, thus saving thousands of lives of civilians, also saving the Naval Dockyards at Portsmouth, also the port of Southampton and Aircraft factories.

In view of Joubert's published criticism of No. 11 Group, I have no option but to record the very unsatisfactory state of affairs in my left rear occupied by No. 12 Fighter Group throughout the Battle of Britain.

On a few dozen occasions when I had sent every available Squadron of No. 11 Group to engage the main enemy attack as far forward as possible, I called on No. 12 Group to send a couple of Squadrons to defend a Fighter airfield or other vital targets which were threatened by out-flanking and smaller bomber raids. Instead of sending two Squadrons quickly to protect the vital target, No. 12 Group delayed while they despatched a large Wing of four or five Squadrons, who wasted valuable time taxiing and taking off, then climbing and assembling into mass formation in a back area before advancing South into the area of fighting. Consequently, they invariably arrived too late to prevent (the) enemy bombing his target.

On one occasion I asked for two Squadrons to protect North Weald Fighter aerodrome from an approaching raid, but no reinforcing Squadrons arrived from No. 12 Group before this vital station was heavily bombed with loss of life and destruction of hangars, workshops, Operations room etc.

On another occasion No. 12 Group was asked to send a couple of Squadrons to protect the Fighter Station at Hornchurch, but again no reinforcements arrived in time to prevent heavy bombing of this aerodrome. To continue the battle it was vitally important to defend the Fighter bases.

No. 12 Group's mass formations were nick-named "BALBOs" because they were so slow, cumbersome and unreliable. Having failed to carry out the task requested these "Balbos" went off on roving missions in No. 12 Group's area and on occasions intercepted enemy bomber formations when retreating after having bombed London and having been engaged by No. 11 Group Squadrons who had drawn off their escort and reduced the

PRODUCTION/WASTAGE OF RAF FIGHTER AIRCRAFT

PRODUCTION

WEEK ENDING	HURRICANE	SPITFIRE	DEFIANT	TOTAL
JUNE 29	68	26	13	107
JULY 6	65	32	12	109
JULY 13	57	30	12	99
JULY 20	67	41	11	119
JULY 27	65	37	14	116
AUG 3	58	41	13	112
AUG 10	54	37	10	101
AUG 17	43	31	11	85
AUG 24	64	44	8	116
AUG 31	54	37	3	94
SEPT 7	54	36	11	101
SEPT 14	56	38	10	104
SEPT 21	57	40	6	103
SEPT 28	58	34	10	102
OCT 5	60	32	12	104
OCT 12	55	31	11	97
OCT 19	55	25	8	88
OCT 26	69	42	16	127
NOV 2	56	41	10	107

CATEGORY 1 = READY FOR IMMEDIATE ISSUE
CATEGORY 2 = ESTIMATED READY FOR ISSUE WITHIN FOUR DAYS
CATEGORY 3 = UNDER PREPARATION FOR ISSUE
CATEGORY 4 = AIRCRAFT AWAITING MODIFICATION OR SPARES

WASTAGE

WEEK ENDING	HURRICANE		SPITFIRE		DEFIANT	
CATEGORY	2	3	2	3	2	3
JULY 6	3	4	1	5	—	—
JULY 13	6	22	6	15	2	—
JULY 20	5	13	5	6	1	6
JULY 27	3	12	8	14	—	—
AUG 3	4	7	7	11	—	—
AUG 10	4	16	4	12	1	1
AUG 17	21	82	11	40	—	—
AUG 24	9	53	3	21	1	5
AUG 31	4	70	7	50	1	7
SEPT 7	8	84	8	53	3	1
SEPT 14	6	47	10	26	1	—
SEPT 21	8	34	11	21	—	—

WASTAGE

WEEK ENDING	HURRICANE		SPITFIRE		DEFIANT	
CATEGORY	2	3	2	3	2	3
SEPT 28	11	40	5	35	—	2
OCT 5	16	29	5	10	—	—
OCT 12	3	28	4	22	—	2
OCT 19	10	28	2	9	—	—
OCT 26	7	34	2	9	1	—
NOV 2	9	16	2	14	—	—

FIGHTER AIRCRAFT OF THE SQUADRONS WHICH TOOK PART IN THE BATTLE OF BRITAIN

Squadron	Aircraft	Squadron	Aircraft
No. 1	Hurricane	No. 253	Hurricane
No. 1 (Canadian)	Hurricane	No. 257	Hurricane
No. 3	Hurricane	No. 263	Hurricane
No. 17	Hurricane	No. 264	Defiant
No. 19	Spitfire	No. 266	Spitfire
No. 23	Blenheim	No. 302 (Polish)	Hurricane
No. 25	Blenheim and Beaufighter	No. 303 (Polish)	Hurricane
		No. 310 (Czech)	Hurricane
No. 29	Blenheim	No. 312 (Czech)	Hurricane
No. 32	Hurricane	No. 501	Hurricane
No. 41	Spitfire	No. 504	Hurricane
No. 43	Hurricane	No. 600	Blenheim and Beaufighter
No. 46	Hurricane		
No. 54	Spitfire	No. 601	Hurricane
No. 56	Hurricane	No. 602	Spitfire
No. 64	Spitfire	No. 603	Spitfire
No. 65	Spitfire	No. 604	Blenheim and Beaufighter
No. 66	Spitfire		
No. 72	Spitfire	No. 605	Hurricane
No. 73	Hurricane	No. 607	Hurricane
No. 74	Spitfire	No. 609	Spitfire
No. 79	Hurricane	No. 610	Spitfire
No. 85	Hurricane	No. 611	Spitfire
No. 87	Hurricane	No. 615	Hurricane
No. 92	Spitfire	No. 616	Spitfire
No. 111	Hurricane		
No. 141	Defiant		
No. 145	Hurricane		
No. 151	Hurricane	*Fleet Air Arm*	
No. 152	Spitfire	*Squadron*	*Aircraft*
No. 213	Hurricane		

No. 219	Blenheim and Beaufighter	No. 804	Sea Gladiators and Martlett
No. 222	Spitfire	No. 808	Fulmar (Flown Solo)
No. 229	Hurricane		
No. 232	Hurricane		
No. 234	Spitfire		
No. 235	Blenheim (Coastal Command)	*Royal Air Force Flights*	
No. 236	Blenheim (Coastal Command)	No. 421	Hurricane and Spitfire
No. 238	Hurricane	No. 422	Hurricane
No. 242	Hurricane		
No. 245	Hurricane		
No. 247	Gladiator		
No. 248	Blenheim (Coastal Command)	*Fighter Interception Unit*	Hurricane, Blenheim and Beaufighter
No. 249	Hurricane		

CONFIRMED CLAIMS BY RAF FIGHTER SQUADRONS JULY THROUGH NOVEMBER 1940

H = HURRICANE, S = SPITFIRE, D = DEFIANT, B = BLENHEIM, G = GLADIATOR, (C) = COASTAL COMMAND SQ., (N) = NIGHT FIGHTER SQ.

303 SQUADRON H	126½
602 SQUADRON S	102
603 SQUADRON S	98
92 SQUADRON S	94⅖
501 SQUADRON H	93
41 SQUADRON S	92⅖
609 SQUADRON S	90⅓
74 SQUADRON S	86
213 SQUADRON H	81
249 SQUADRON H	75
601 SQUADRON H	73½
234 SQUADRON S	73
32 SQUADRON H	71
610 SQUADRON S	71
43 SQUADRON H	70
238 SQUADRON H	69½
242 SQUADRON H	68½
19 SQUADRON S	68
17 SQUADRON H	67½
72 SQUADRON S	61½
54 SQUADRON S	60
56 SQUADRON H	59½
85 SQUADRON H	59
152 SQUADRON S	59
605 SQUADRON H	56½
87 SQUADRON H	54
145 SQUADRON H	54
66 SQUADRON S	50
222 SQUADRON S	49⅖
111 SQUADRON H	47½
64 SQUADRON S	43
310 SQUADRON H	40
615 SQUADRON H	36½
65 SQUADRON S	34½
253 SQUADRON H	33
1 SQUADRON H	32
616 SQUADRON S	31
151 SQUADRON H	30
1 (CANADIAN) SQUADRON H	28½
257 SQUADRON H	28
46 SQUADRON H	27½
79 SQUADRON H	27
302 SQUADRON H	26½
504 SQUADRON H	21
607 SQUADRON H	21
229 SQUADRON H	20½
73 SQUADRON H	19½
264 SQUADRON D	16
611 SQUADRON S	15
235 SQUADRON (C) B	13
266 SQUADRON S	10
141 SQUADRON D	6
25 SQUADRON B	4
236 SQUADRON (C) B	3
29 SQUADRON (N) B	2
219 SQUADRON (N) B	2
3 SQUADRON H	1
232 SQUADRON H	1
254 SQUADRON (C) B	1
312 SQUADRON H	1
600 SQUADRON (N) B	1
604 SQUADRON (N) B	1

AIR ATTACKS ON BRITISH TARGETS JULY TO DECEMBER 1940

BOMB TONNAGE DELIVERED

TARGET	HIGH EXPLOSIVE AND LAND MINES (BOMB TONNAGE)	INCENDIARY BOMBS TONS	BOMBS
LONDON	23716	2918	2951000
LIVERPOOL	2114	274	278300
BIRMINGHAM	1780	141	143000
COVENTRY	965	231	234700
MANCHESTER	933	105	107000

enemy's ammunition and fuel supply. Sir Philip Joubert claims that No. 12 Group's tactics were correct and economised in the lives of pilots, but I believe that if No. 11 Group had adopted similar "With-holding" tactics, tens of thousands of Londoners and all our Fighter bases in the South of England would have been destroyed by September 1940.

In support of my contention, the Official Air Ministry account published in 1943 says—"No. 12 Group was very successful in attacking the RETREATING enemy bomber formations, which had often been separated from their escort or broken up by Anti-Aircraft Defence." (and Fighters of No. 11 Group).

When the Battle of Britain had been safely won, the Commander of No. 12 Group aided and abetted by one or two armchair critics at the Air Ministry, including Sir Philip Joubert, claimed that No. 11 Group had used the wrong tactics in winning the Battle of Britain and that No. 12 Group could have done the job much better. But I can say after further experience as Commander of the Air Forces in Malta, then in the Middle East, and lastly on the Burma Front, that we could have lost the Battle of Britain if I had adopted the "With-holding" tactics of No. 12 Group as advocated by Sir Philip Joubert.

The Air Ministry in 1942 selected me to take Command of Malta when it was being bombed three or four times daily by the Luftwaffe. In Malta I introduced the same "Forward Interception" policy that I used in the Battle of Britain, and without receiving one single reinforcement we put a stop to the Luftwaffe bombing within two weeks. During the second Blitz of Malta in 1942, I again used these tactics and my Squadrons inflicted a decisive defeat on a more numerous German Air Force in Sicily.

I wonder how General Freyberg would have advanced along the North coast of Africa in 1942 if the 2nd N.Z. Division continually had to contend with a British Division on its left flank which failed to advance and capture its objective when ordered? I had to endure this grave handicap for four months and repeatedly reported the facts verbally and in writing to higher authority, but without result, because the Commander of No. 12 Group had the ear of the then Chief of Air Staff, Lord Newall, who early in the war retired from the Royal Air Force and was appointed a Governor General.
No. 10 Group was commanded by a famous South African pilot named Air Vice Marshal Sir Christopher Brand, the first man to fly from England to Johannesburg. His Group did four times as much fighting as No. 12 Group, but never complained about my tactical handling of our Fighter Squadrons.

BRISTOL	360	112	113500
SOUTHAMPTON	421	106	108000
PLYMOUTH	362	95	96000
AIRFIELDS	1710	28	28100
OTHER RAIDS	4303	211	205000
TOTAL	36664	4221	4264600

CIVILIAN AIR RAID CASUALTIES (MEN, WOMEN AND CHILDREN)

MONTH	KILLED	INJURED
JULY	258	321
AUGUST	1075	1261
SEPTEMBER	6954	10615
OCTOBER	6334	8695
NOVEMBER	4588	6202
DECEMBER	3793	5044
TOTAL	23002	32138

RAF FIGHTER COMMAND PILOT CASUALTIES JULY THROUGH OCTOBER 1940

MONTH	KILLED, MISSING OR PRISONER	WOUNDED OR INJURED
JULY	74	49
AUGUST	148	156
SEPTEMBER	159	152
OCTOBER	100	65
TOTAL	481	422

BATTLE OF BRITAIN PILOTS AND AIRCREW

Nationalities of Pilots and Aircrew

United Kingdom, including Commonwealth Pilots who cannot be identified separately, but serving in the Royal Air Force

Pilots	(Killed)	Aircrew	(Killed)	Total	(Killed)
1783	(329)	548	(58)	2331	(387)

United Kingdom, serving in the Fleet Air Arm, including those F.A.A. Pilots seconded to R.A.F. squadrons

Pilots	(Killed)	Aircrew	(Killed)	Total	(Killed)
56	(9)	—	—	56	(9)

Americans

Pilots	(Killed)	Aircrew	(Killed)	Total	(Killed)
9	(2)	—	—	9	(2)

Australians

Pilots	(Killed)	Aircrew	(Killed)	Total	(Killed)
21	(14)	—	—	21	(14)

Belgians

Pilots	(Killed)	Aircrew	(Killed)	Total	(Killed)
24	(6)	3	—	27	(6)

Canadians

Pilots	(Killed)	Aircrew	(Killed)	Total	(Killed)
90	(19)	1	—	91	(19)

Czechoslovakians

Pilots	(Killed)	Aircrew	(Killed)	Total	(Killed)
87	(7)	—	—	87	(7)

Free French

Pilots	(Killed)	Aircrew	(Killed)	Total	(Killed)
13	—	—	—	13	—

Irish

Pilots	(Killed)	Aircrew	(Killed)	Total	(Killed)
9	—	1	—	10	—

Jamaicans

Pilots	(Killed)	Aircrew	(Killed)	Total	(Killed)
—	—	1	—	1	—

Israeli

Pilots	(Killed)	Aircrew	(Killed)	Total	(Killed)
1	—	—	—	1	—

Poles

Pilots	(Killed)	Aircrew	(Killed)	Total	(Killed)
143	(29)	1	1	144	(30)

Newfoundlander

Pilots	(Killed)	Aircrew	(Killed)	Total	(Killed)
1	(1)	—	—	1	(1)

New Zealanders

Pilots	(Killed)	Aircrew	(Killed)	Total	(Killed)
94	(11)	35	(3)	129	(14)

South Africans

Pilots	(Killed)	Aircrew	(Killed)	Total	(Killed)
23	(9)	—	—	23	(9)

Southern Rhodesians

Pilots	(Killed)	Aircrew	(Killed)	Total	(Killed)
2	—	—	—	2	—

Total

Pilots	(Killed)	Aircrew	(Killed)	Total	(Killed)
2354	(435)	590	(62)	2944	(497)

BATTLE OF BRITAIN DISTINCTION

To distinguish all aircrew of fighter aircraft who took part in the Battle of Britain between 10 July and 31 October, 1940, a bar to the 1939–1945 Star was awarded, and is embellished with a gilt rose emblem on the ribbon when it alone is worn. A bar which is inscribed BATTLE OF BRITAIN is affixed to the full ribbon when the medal is worn. The distinction of qualifying for this award requires that the applicant must have been a Battle of Britain pilot or aircrew member and must have flown at least one operational sortie in an accredited Battle of Britain squadron, flight or unit during the Battle of Britain period.

INDEX